WHAT IS THE STATUS OF WOMEN AND CHILD

IN DEVELOPING COUNTRIES?

MARIAM ABBAS SOHARWARDI

Dedication

TO

MY HUSBAND MUHAMMAD AZHAR

AND

MY SONS

ABDULLAH AZHAR AND ABDUL REHMAN AZHAR

TABLE OF CONTENTS

LIST OF TABLES

LIST OF FIGURES

List of Equations

List of Abbreviations

CEDAW	Convention Elimination All Forms of Discrimination Against Women
CIAF	Composite Index of Anthropometric Failure
DHS	Demographic and Health Survey
GDI	Gender-Related Hunger Index
GEEE	Gender Empowerment Enabling Environment
GEM	Gender Empowerment Measure
GGGR	Gender Global Gap Report
GGI	Gender Inequality Index
GHI	Global Hunger Index
GII	Gender Inequality Index
GPI	Gender Party Index
MDGs	Millennium Development Goals
SDG	Sustainable Development Goals
UNDP	United Nation Development Program
WE	Women Empowerment
WEAI	Women's Empowerment in Agriculture Index

ABSTRACT

Context: Development entails security regarding the fulfilment of its three core values, viz. sustenance, self-esteem, and freedom of choice. In the developing world, the adversities concerning human development have women's and children's faces predominantly.

Objective: Hence, the prime aims of the study were first, to probe the status (quantitative, qualitative) of women empowerment and child health in developing economies and investigate the role of women empowerment in child health for the developing world.

Limitations: Data-wise, the study is confined to the micro-data from Demographic and Health Surveys (DHS) datasets of 33 developing economies from the regions of South & Southeast Asia, Central Asia, West Asia, Latin America & Caribbean, and Sub-Saharan Africa.

Methodology: Initially, from the respective DHS datasets, 19 indicators depicting women empowerment were identified and condensed through principal component analysis into 5 sets named work status, awareness status, and participation in decision making, self-esteem, and self-confidence. A composite of women empowerment encapsulating the 5 dimensions of women empowerment was also constructed. The study also constructed its own composite index for child health outcomes for a child's anthropometric failure (CIAF) by incorporating child stunting, child wasting, and child under-weight. The ordinary least squares method had been used in the models where women's empowerment status regarding a particular dimension (in continuous form) had been regressed on the determinants of empowerment. Binary logistic regression was used in the models where child anthropometric status (binary: favorable, non-favorable) was regressed on women empowerment and other child health correlations. Ordinal logistic regression had been applied to the models in which women's composite empowerment status (ordered: less-, moderately-, highly-empowered) was regressed on its explanatory variables.

Findings:

Regarding women employment/work status—amongst the 33 developing economies—Uganda, Burkina Faso, and Nepal are ranked 1st, 2nd, and 3rd (at the top, showing higher empowerment regarding work status). Regarding composite women empowerment index (CWEI) score (constructed as a multidimensional and quantitative measure of women empowerment), Tonga, Peru, and Honduras are respectively ranked 1st, 2nd, and 3rd (top scorers; showing higher empowerment status of women).

Across the regions, Central Asia stands first, showing the highest empowerment status of women, while Sub-Saharan Africa stands 5th, offering the lowest empowerment status of women.

Woman's higher educational status, woman's age greater than husband, woman's age at the time of her first birth (> 19 years), woman's body mass index (> 18 mKg^{-2}), number of children ever born (< 4), and relative wealth status of the household were positively associated with all the five dimensions of women empowerment and with composite women empowerment index. The husband's education level above secondary was positively associated with awareness status and self-esteem, while negatively associated with work status, participation in decision-making, and self-confidence.

At the time of her first birth (except for West Asia and Sub-Saharan Africa), women's age was negatively associated with women empowerment in South & Southeast Asia, Central Asia, and Latin America & Caribbean. Similarly, except for South & Southeast Asia and

Sub-Saharan, male headedness of household was negatively associated with women empowerment in West Asia, Central Asia, and Latin America & Caribbean. The total number of children ever born was negatively associated, whereas the residential status of woman as urban was positively associated with women empowerment in all the regions (except in West Asia). Except in South & Southeast Asia and Latin America & Caribbean, family size was negatively related to women empowerment in the regions.

Regarding the incidence of child stunting, Timor Leste and Congo Democratic are among the most prevalent economies. Regarding the prevalence of child wasting, Timor Leste, Chad, and Nepal are amongst the topmost. Across the regions, South and Southeast Asia portray the worst statistics, while the region of West Asia (except for under-weight) depicts the least adversities on all child health measures.

Work status (except for child underweight) and self-confidence were positively associated while awareness status, participation in decision making, and self-esteem (excluding for child underweight) were negatively related with the four measures of child health, viz., child stunting, child wasting, child underweight, and child composite anthropometric failure. Mother's education, mother's age between 20-35 years, mother's body mass index, mother's age at the time of birth (> 19), the total number of children ever born (≤ 4), father's age (> 25), father's educational level, father's work status as employed, household's wealth status, and residential place of child's family as urban were improving the child health by lowering the probabilities of child anthropometric failures. As compared to the region of Sub-Saharan Africa (reference category), the regions of West Asia, Central Asia, and Latin America & Caribbean were showing less probabilities, whereas the region of

South & Southeast Asia showed a higher likelihood for the children to be anthropometrically poor. Countries with higher net imports were associated with the low anthropometric status of the children. The religiously secular status of the country was positively related to child anthropometry.

Policy Proposal: For the developing economies, financial resource reallocation coupled with the programs with integrated interventions and multi-level implementations would require coming out of these concerns.

Keywords: Work status, Self-confidence, Child anthropometry, South & Southeast Asia, Sub-Saharan Africa

CHAPTER 1: INTRODUCTION

1.1 Women Empowerment: Significance, Context, and Correlates

Women empowerment and their relationship with society intertwined with equity and fairness for women and men in access to resources, participation in decision-making and control over the circulation of resources and benefits. Women's empowerment has gained a higher status in today's global development plan, and it is strongly linked with multiple development outcomes (Hanmer and Klugman , 2016). The post-2015 development agenda incorporates gender equality & women empowerment as the 5th Sustainable Development Goals (SDG 5) to be accomplished up until 2030 (Assembly, 2015; United Nations, 2015). Women's empowerment has gained a higher status in today's global development plan, and it is strongly linked with multiple development outcomes. Even though extensive literature has been created and theorizing women's empowerment and its dimensions. And operationalizing those concepts to frame the measures of women empowerment. However, there is no universal definition and measures of women's empowerment. The formation of agency or achievements may indicate empowerment in some contexts but not in others (Mahmud, Shah, & Becker, 2012).

The Gender Empowerment Measure (GEM) and the Gender-related Development Index (GDI) developed by the UNDP is the internationally known index was measured by using the country level (aggregated) data (UNDP, 2015). To measure women's empowerment in the agricultural sector across five domains (production, resources, income, leadership, and time) of empowerment at the individual and household levels, the Women's Empowerment in Agriculture Index (WEAI) is a recently developed tool(Alkire et al., 2013) . Empowerment is constructed as a multi-dimensional index, regardless of diverse views and congruence.

Shreds of evidence are there on what determines changes in the empowerment status of women. Across developing countries, previous literature has observed many correlates of empowerment, amongst those are: age Alkire et al. (2013) for Bangladesh and Guatemala; Allendorf (2012) for India; Anderson and Eswaran, 2009 for Bangladesh; Goldman and Little (2015)for Tanzania; Gupta and Yesudian (2006) for India; Trommlerová, Klasen, and Leßmann (2015) for the Gambia, Alkire et al. (2013) for Uganda; Allendorf (2012) for India; Garikipati (2008) for India; Goldman and Little (2015) for Tanzania; Gupta and Yesudian (2006) for India; Hanmer and Klugman (2016) for 58 countries; Mahmud et al. (2012) for Bangladesh, Samarakoon and Parinduri (2015) for Indonesia, Trommlerová et al. (2015) for the Gambia,   Alkire et al. (2013) for Bangladesh and Uganda; Anderson and Eswaran (2009) for Bangladesh; Garikipati (2008) for India; Gupta and Yesudian (2006) for India; Hanmer and Klugman (2016) for 58 countries; Mahmud et al. (2012) for Bangladesh , family structure Allendorf (2012) for India ; Jejeebhoy (2000)for India.

1.2   Child Health: Significance, Context, and Correlates

Child health and child survival are ultimately related to mothers' health, diet, and care (WHO, 2016). In less than 18 years, a malnourished girl cannot give birth to a healthy baby (WHO, 2011, 2016). Malnutrition is a common problem in developing countries. During pregnancy women cannot get proper food, which is necessary during pregnancy; either they overeat or suffer from nutrition, vitamins, minerals, and iron deficiencies (Endris,

Asefa, & Dube, 2017; WHO, 2016, 2018). The main reason for malnutrition is lack of care, unavailability of food, unawareness about proper diet, expensive food prices that are not affordable by their husbands. The ultimate malnutrition outcomes are the stunting, wasting, and underweight problems in their children (Dasgupta, Parthasarathi, Biswas, & Geethanjali, 2014).

In most developing countries, pregnant women do not get the proper health care and diet according to their choice and need. The most crucial reason for malnutrition is the lack of awareness about nutritional food (Tsiboe, Zereyesus, Popp, & Osei, 2018). But media, society, doctors, and different national and international organizations guide about nutrition. In these cases, developing regions do not have financial resources to buy nutritional food (Bhandari & Chhetri, 2013; Chipili, Msuya, Pacific, & Majili, 2018; WHO, 2016, 2018). Children having a low height for age are considered to be stunted that is caused by malnutrition. Stunting is associated with households, social, and economic conditions. Unfortunately, stunting is starting during the pregnancy because the mother is not treating well, and their health and food got ignored (UNICEF, 2019; Vonaesch et al., 2017). In pregnancy, women need more nourishing food full of vitamins, minerals, and irons to give healthy birth. Malnutrition may also cause wasting, which is a severe problem regarding weight for height in children. Studies have proposed that women should care about their health during pregnancy and child health from their birth to five years (Endris et al., 2017; Khan & Raza, 2014; Smith & Haddad, 2000; UNICEF, 2018). In case of a mismatch between a child's weight and height, there is a need to take precautionary measures and medicines to reduce death's risk in wasting children (Scantlan & Previdelli, 2013; WHO, 2016,

2018). Underweight is less weight of a child according to its age. It is prevalent in developing countries because women do not get proper food to maintain their health and their babies' health. Underweight is a child's severe health condition because a thin child may prone to stunting and wasting (WHO, 2018). In 2014, approximately 462 million adults worldwide were underweight (WHO, 2018). In 2016, an estimated 155 million children under five years were suffering from stunting (WHO, 2018). Around 45% of deaths among children under five years occur due to undernutrition. These deaths mostly occur in low-income and middle-income countries (WHO, 2018).

Mother health and age is too much important for marriage and for their child health. The girls who got married in their early age they face different practical problems like adjustment in their homes, maturity in their behavior, food problem, health and care problem, and pregnancy problems during their childbirth (Mullany, Hinde, & Becker, 2005; Mumtaz & Salway, 2007). Mothers age and their health got too much importance, awareness and motivated in advanced countries. In contrary, in developing countries, the fundamental right of health and wedding age has ignored. The approximately one hundred million girls got married in less than 18 years old (Murshid, 2016a; Sujarwoto & Tampubolon, 2013; WHO, 2011). Its extraordinary fact that 14 million girls become pregnant in their young age, unfortunately, 90% belong from developing countries (WHO, 2011) .

Women Empowerment (WE) is a social network that focuses on providing events and communication to improve child health with the power of collaboration, engagement, and growth,_women education, health, the right to vote freely, may take part in economic activities, may take part in every walk of life as independent citizens of the country, decision making, should be religiously free, etc. (Deutsch & Silber, 2017).

1.3   Gap Identification

In terms of the measure of women empowerment, in literature, women's empowerment has been defined as a process (Bates, Schuler, Islam, & Islam, 2004; Batliwala, 1993; Batliwala, 1994; Batliwala, 1995; Batliwala et al., 1995; Kabeer, 1999, 2001, 2002, 2011; Lee-Rife, 2010; Mosedale, 2005), while others realize it as a goal (Kishor, 2000; Tengland, 2008; Zimmerman & Rappaport, 1988). Additionally, the understanding of women's empowerment has been complicated by the interchangeable uses of carefully related terms like women's status, women's autonomy, and gender as research phenomena Tengland (2008). In previous literature, women empowerment has been measured through seasonality of occupation, violent attitudes (Pambe, Gnoumou, & Kaboré, 2014). Women's status and the skilled birth attendant has been discussed as women empowerment in previous literature (Shimamoto & Gipson, 2015).

Based on Kabeer (1999) resource-agency-achievement framework, the present study measures women empowerment in terms of five interrelated dimensions: work status, awareness status, decision making, self-esteem, and self-confidence. Work status and awareness status are considered as the preconditions (resources) to exercise decision making (agency) and then finally to have consequences (achievement) in the forms of self-esteem and self-confidence. This comprehensive framework's rationale is that people who can make choices in their daily lives may be more potent in one domain, but they may not be empowered in other fields (Kabeer, 2011, 2012).

This study has documented five domains of women empowerment to cover the resources required for self-transformation, agency for self-determination, and achievement in the form of self-esteem and self-confidence. Besides the previous literature, this study has expressed empowerment as the process of change through work status, awareness, participation in decision making, self-esteem, and self-confidence following the Kabeer's resource-agency-achievement approach.

Regarding women empowerment determinants, in light of previous literature, women empowerment has been determined through socioeconomic characteristics like age, education, occupation, wealth, marital status, and microcredit. Previous studies have focused on household wealth, ownership of assets, and knowledge exposure in Ethiopia to determine women's empowerment (Tadesse, Teklie, Yazew, & Gebreselassie, 2013). Women empowerment has a relationship with achieving desired fertility has been concentrated in Sub Saharan Africa (Upadhyay & Karasek, 2010). In the previous literature, women empowerment is related to education and their maternal health, which showed that if women are empowered, then their maternal health is good (Ahmed, Creanga, Gillespie, & Tsui, 2010; Allendorf, 2012; Asaolu et al., 2018).

In this study, an attempt has been made to determine the contextual factors (Batool 2018, Toufique 2016), women characteristics, husband characteristics, and household characteristics to determine women empowerment in developing countries in a single model. This study incorporated the five regions to determine the women empowerment in separate models to capture the effect of each region on women empowerment.

Child health is a very crucial factor for family, society, and country. Child health is related to parental investment was empirically tested in previous literature (Habibov, Barrett, & Chernyak, 2017). The relationship between child health, fertility, and women's schooling has correlated in Uganda (Keats, 2018). The link between women empowerment and child stunting observed in India and Bangladesh, which has found an association in previous literature (Siddhanta & Chattopadhyay, 2017). The malnutrition and its effects were found through CIAF in Ethiopia (Endris et al., 2017). Besides, the determinant of malnutrition (measured through CIAF) has also been studied in Indian children (Khan & Raza, 2016a). The effects of malnutrition on child health (under five years old) were found in rural India and Bangladesh (Roy et al., 2018). Women's decision making is the most important factor for child health from the social and family perspective, which has also been concentrated in the earlier literature.

In-depth literature about women empowerment and child health has been reviewed. In the end, the researcher found that there is a literature gap about determinant and indicators that have not been fully considered. Most studies have examined only one or two indicators/dimensions for women empowerment and child health. A comprehensive framework for women empowerment and child health is missing in the literature. Women's empowerment and child health both are essential. So, it would be unjust to measure women empowerment and child health with only one or two indicators.

Furthermore, most studies considered only one or two countries, and these studies are regional. There is a need to test women empowerment and child health in cross regions. In this study, both women's empowerment and child health phenomena are explored. Based on a comprehensive framework, women empowerment has been measured through its five dimensions and nineteen indicators. Likewise, in this study, child health has been measured through stunting, wasting, underweight, and CIAF (composite index of anthropometric failure) in 33 developing countries. So, by filling the existing gap, after empirical investigation, the findings of this study could be generalized for developing regions and economies to initiate child health and women empowerment related interventions.

Women who have more participation in employment, access to media, and control over decision-making have a more significant contribution to women empowerment and positively impact child health. This study's prime purpose is to find out the link between women's empowerment and child health in developing countries.

According to the World Bank classification, developing countries are referred to as, low-income (GNI per Capita $1,035 or less), middle-income(GNI per capita between $1,036 and $4,045), and upper-middle-income(GNI per capita between$4,046 and $12,535) countries. Developing Countries are the economies with the low gross domestic product per capita, heavily dependent on the agriculture sector, less developed industrial sector, and low Human Development Index than other countries(WorldBank, 2019a).

1.4 Problem Statement

Women empowerment is a complete process for psychological, family, interpersonal, social, and economic benefits and creating a balance in the society (Arnof, 2011). Child health is always correlated with the mother's health (Baig et al., 2018; Jin, 1995; Wiklander, 2010). Women empowerment, which is defined as a process of transfers of power from the powerful *to the powerless* (Anand & Sen, 1994), is also imperative to better child health (Akram, 2018; Akter et al., 2017). In developing countries, women are not able to make decisions about their own and children's life. Moreover, women's disempowerment is more rural than an urban phenomenon. Women living in rural areas face poor health status because they take insufficient food, have less knowledge of healthcare facilities, and lack enough money to attain basic health necessities (Jali & Islam, 2017; Sanghamitra, 2016). This study explores the significance of women's women empowerment to achieve child health outcomes.

1.5 Research Questions

In the present scenario, research questions are as follow:

- What is the empowerment status of women in developing economies?
- How does women's personal, family-related, and household-specific characteristics translate into women's empowerment status?
- Are regional disparities there in the developing world regarding the empowerment status of women?

- What is the situation of child health (health status of children) in the developing economies?

- What is the role of women empowerment status in determining child health?

- How women empowerment effect varies on child health in developing economies?

- Are regional disparities there in the developing world regarding the health status of children?

1.6 Objectives

Main Objective

The main objective of the study is to investigate the influence of women empowerment on child health in developing economies

Specific Objectives

The specific objectives of this study are as follows:

- To gauge the extent and nature of women empowerment in the developing economies

- To find the socioeconomic factors affecting women empowerment in the developing economies

- To highlight the child health status in the developing economies

- To examine the socioeconomic factors of child health in the developing economies

- To suggest policy recommendations regarding women empowerment and child health

1.7   Hypotheses

- H_1: There is an association between women empowerment and child health in the developing economies.
- H_2: Differences are there among the developing regions regarding the association between women empowerment and child health

1.8   Thesis Structure

This study is divided into ten chapters. After presenting the study's introduction in the first chapter, the second chapter portrays the contextual realities of the developing economies. Chapter three provides the literature reviewed. The theoretical framework of the study has been established in chapter four. In chapter five, details on the data and methodology of the study have been given. In chapter six and chapter seven, the findings on women empowerment status and its correlates have been discussed. The findings on child health status, determinants of child health, and the role of women empowerment in child health outcomes are discussed in chapter eight and chapter nine. The last chapter presents the conclusion and policy suggestions from the study.

CHAPTER 2: CONTEXTUAL REALITIES OF THE DEVELOPING ECONOMIES UNDERSTUDY

Developing economies are not homogeneous regarding their macroeconomic, demographic, health, and social environment. This chapter compares macroeconomic indicators, demographic indicators, gender inequality index, and global hunger index of thirty-three economies. All the economies in the understudy regions are considered highly populated, and, in these economies, sustained development depends on the growth and development of human resources. The movement toward continued progress is necessary to improve their peoples' economic, social, and health status without any gender-based discrimination. Classification of developing countries, according to the World Bank, is described in Table No. 2.1

It tries to explain the facts and figures of gender inequality and global hunger index, to check whether both are present simultaneously in developing economies or have a different situation. Because in the economies where gender inequality is high, women faced deprivation in their fundamental rights, or they are not empowered. Besides, all of these a higher score of the global hunger index is a sign of poor health.

Table 2.1: World Bank Analytical Classification (presented in World Development Indicators) GNI per capita in US$ (Atlas methodology)

	Bank's fiscal year:	FY12	FY13	FY14	FY15	FY16	FY17	FY18	FY19	FY20	FY21
	Sr#	2010	2011	2012	2013	2014	2015	2016	2017	2018	2019
	Low income (L)	<= 1,005	<= 1,025	<= 1,035	<= 1,045	<= 1,045	<= 1,025	<= 1,005	<= 995	<= 1,025	<= 1,035
	Lower middle income (LM)	1,006-3,975	1,026-4,035	1,036-4,085	1,046-4,125	1,046-4,125	1,026-4,035	1,006-3,955	996-3,895	1,026-3,995	1,036 - 4,045
	Upper middle income (UM)	3,976-12,275	4,036-12,475	4,086-12,615	4,126-12,745	4,126-12,735	4,036-12,475	3,956-12,235	3,896-12,055	3,996-12,375	4,046 - 12,535
	High income (H)	> 12,275	> 12,475	> 12,615	> 12,745	> 12,735	> 12,475	> 12,235	> 12,055	> 12,375	> 12,535
1	Armenia	LM	LM	LM	LM	LM	LM	LM	UM	UM	UM
1	Azerbaijan	UM	UM	UM	UM	UM	UM	UM	UM	UM	UM
1	Jordan	UM	UM	UM	UM	UM	UM	LM	UM	UM	UM
2	Pakistan	LM	LM	LM	LM	LM	LM	LM	LM	LM	LM
2	Nepal	L	L	L	L	L	L	L	L	L	LM
2	India	LM	LM	LM	LM	LM	LM	LM	LM	LM	LM
2	Cambodia	L	L	L	L	L	LM	LM	LM	LM	LM
2	Timor-Leste	LM	LM	LM	LM	LM	LM	LM	LM	LM	LM
3	Tajikistan	L	L	L	L	LM	LM	LM	L	L	L
3	Kyrgyz Republic	L	L	L	LM	LM	LM	LM	LM	LM	LM
4	Haiti	L	L	L	L	L	L	L	L	L	L
4	Honduras	LM	LM	LM	LM	LM	LM	LM	LM	LM	LM
4	Peru	UM	UM	UM	UM	UM	UM	UM	UM	UM	UM
4	Guatemala	LM	LM	LM	LM	LM	LM	LM	UM	UM	UM
5	Burkina Faso	L	L	L	L	L	L	L	L	L	L
5	Cameroon	LM	LM	LM	LM	LM	LM	LM	LM	LM	LM

Chad	L	L	L	L	L	L	L	L	L	L
Comoros	L	L	L	L	L	L	L	L	LM	LM
Congo, Dem. Rep.	L	L	L	L	L	L	L	L	L	L
Côte d'Ivoire	LM	LM	LM	LM	LM	LM	LM	LM	LM	LM
Ethiopia	L	L	L	L	L	L	L	L	L	L
Gabon	UM	UM	UM	UM	UM	UM	UM	UM	UM	UM
Gambia, The	L	L	L	L	L	L	L	L	L	L
Malawi	L	L	L	L	L	L	L	L	L	L
Mali	L	L	L	L	L	L	L	L	L	L
Mozambique	L	L	L	L	L	L	L	L	L	L
Namibia	UM	UM	UM	UM	UM	UM	UM	UM	UM	UM
Nepal	L	L	L	L	L	L	L	L	L	LM
Nigeria	LM	LM	LM	LM	LM	LM	LM	LM	LM	LM
Tanzania	L	L	L	L	L	L	L	L	L	LM
Tonga	LM	LM	UM	UM	UM	LM	UM	UM	UM	UM
Uganda	L	L	L	L	L	L	L	L	L	L
Zambia	LM	LM	LM	LM	LM	LM	LM	LM	LM	LM
Zimbabwe	L	L	L	L	L	L	L	L	LM	LM

Source: (WorldBank, 2019a)

14

After finding the coexistence of a high score of gender inequality and global hunger index in Table 2.3 and 2.2 simultaneously, it is necessary to view the macroeconomic and demographic background of these economies in Table 2.4 for a comprehensive overview analysis.

Prevalence of global hunger and gender inequalities, along with macroeconomic and demographic characteristics, are explained as follows:

2.1 Women Status and Situation of Child Health in Developing Countries

Gender Inequality index explains the status[1] of women across the countries. It sheds light on the gender gaps in different areas of human development. Dimensions of this index are health[2], empowerment, [3] and labor market participation[4](UNDP, 2015).

The global hunger index is a comprehensive measure to figure out the hunger at global and national levels. This index is handy to compare malnutrition levels between countries and highlights the countries struggling against hunger. For each country, the index score has been calculated by the percentage of undernourishment, child stunting, child wasting, and child mortality(Otekunrina, Otekunrinb, Momoh, & Ayindea, 2019).

---

[1] With respect of labor force participation, Political Participation, Education and Health
[2] Maternal mortality ratio and Adolescent birth rate
[3] Share of male-female seats in parliament and male-female population with at least some secondary education) and labor market
[4] male -female labor force participation rate

Global Hunger Index and Gender Inequality index explain the status of women empowerment and health outcomes through the facts present in Table 2.1& 2.2. Stunting, wasting, and underweight is a global issue that no country has saved, but the prevalence of malnutrition is unacceptable in developing economies, especially in South Asia & South East Asia and Sub-Saharan Africa (2018 Global Nutrition Report). Developing countries reduced the global rate of stunting under five years children from 32.3% in 2000 to 22.2% in 2017. The same decline has been seen in underweight, wasting, and in the rate of child mortality. However, this progress's speed is slow, and the countries under study economies are very far away to achieve zero malnutrition.

Table 2.2: Child Health Profile of the Developing Economies

Regions		Stunting (% of children under 5)	Wasting (% of children under 5)	Underweight (% of children under 5)	Child Mortality Under Five (Per 1000)	Countries where hunger is low from 0-9.9, moderate 10.0 to 19.9, serious 20.0–34.9, alarming 35.0-49.9 & extremely alarming above than 50.0				
	Developing Economies					2000	2005	2010	2018	Rank
West Asia	Azerbaijan (2013)	18	3.2	4.9	23	27.4	17.4	12.3	9.5	040
	Jordan (2012)	7.8	2.4	3	17	12.2	8.5	8.3	11.2	048
	Armenia (2016)	9.4.	1.5	2.6	12.6	18.4	12.8	11.3	7.6	025
	Average	**12.7**	**4.8**	**4.4**	**18.7**	18.6	13.25	12.05	10.7	43.5
————	Pakistan (2012)	45	10.5	31.6	74.9	38.3	37.0	36.0	32.6	106
	Timor-Leste (2013)	50.2	11	37.7	47.6	-	41.8	42.4	34.2	110
	Cambodia (2014)	32.4	9.6	23.9	29.2	43.5	29.6	27.8	23.7	78
	India (2014)	39.5	21	35.7	39.4	38.8	38.8	32.2	31.1	103
	Nepal (2016)	35.8	9.7	27	33.7	36.8	31.4	24.5	21.2	72
South and Southeast Asia	**Average**	**40.3**	**12.3**	**31.1**	**44.9**	31.48	35.72	32.58	30.9	93.8
	Tajikistan	26.8	9.9	13.3	33.6	…	…	..	…	..
	Kyrgyz Republic (2016)	12.9	2.8	2.8	20	18.8	14.0	12.4	9.3	038
	Average	**19.8**	**6.35**	**8.05**	**26.8**	18.8	14.0	12.4	9.3	038
Latin America and Caribbean	Haiti	21.9	5.2	11.6	71.7	42.7	45.2	48.5	35.4	113
	Honduras	22.7	1.4	7.1	18.2	20.6	17.7	14.7	14.4	059
	Peru	13.1	1.0	3.1	15	20.9	18.4	12.5	8.8	035
	Guatemala	46.5	0.7	12.6	27.6	27.5	23.8	22.0	20.8	70
	Average	**22.2**	**2.14**	**7.68**	**32.5**	26.0	24.5	22.1	17.9	64
Sub-Saharan Africa	Ethiopia	38.4	9.9	23.6	58.5	55.9	45.9	37.3	29.1	93
	Gabon	17.5	3.4	6.5	48.3	21.1	19.0	16.7	15.4	063
	Gambia	25	11.1	16.2	63.6	27.3	26.2	22.3	22.3	75
	Comoros	32.1	11.1	16.9	69	38.0	33.6	30.4	30.8	101

Congo Democratic	42.6	8.2	23.4	91.1	37.8	37.2	32.2	30.4	99
Cote d'Ivoire	21.6	6.0	12.8	88.8	33.7	34.7	31.0	25.9	085
Cameroon	31.7	5.2	14.8	84	41.2	33.7	26.1	21.1	71
Chad	39.9	13	28.8	123.2	51.4	52.0	48.9	45.4	118
Kenya	26	4.0	11	45.6	36.5	33.5	28.0	23.2	77
Malawi	37.1	2.7	11.7	55.4	44.7	37.8	31.4	26.5	87
Mozambique	43.1	6.1	15.4	72.4	49.1	42.4	35.8	30.9	102
Namibia	37.1	7.1	13.2	44.2	30.6	28.4	30.9	24.3	80
Nigeria	43.5	10.8	31.2	100.2	40.9	34.8	29.2	31.1	103
Sierra Leon	37.9	9.5	18.1	110.5	54.4	51.7	40.4	35.7	114
Tanzania	34.4	4.5	13.7	54	42.4	35.8	34.1	29.5	95
Tonga	8.1	5.2	1.9	16	39.1	36.4	27.1	24.3	80
Uganda	28.9	3.6	10.5	49	41.2	34.2	31.3	31.2	105
Zimbabwe	40	3.2	8.4	50.3	38.7	39.7	36.0	32.9	107
Burkina Faso	27.3	7.6	19.2	81.2	47.4	48.8	36.8	27.7	89
Average	**31.8**	**7.16**	**16.01**	**70.3**	41.6	37.9	32.4	29.4	93.5

Source: (WorldBank, 2019b)

15

In Table 2.1, the Global Hunger Index of thirty-three developing countries has presented along with GHI indicators. According to table thirty-three, economies of five different regions struggle against hunger, but the situation is challenging to handle in South & South East Asia and Sub Saharan Africa (GHI score 30.9 and 29.4, respectively). The scores of West Asia, Central Asia and Latin America, and the Caribbean countries range from 10.7, 9.3, and 17.9. The range of hunger scores in Haiti, and Sierra Leone (35.0-49.9) is very alarming. According to the Table, 2.3 stunting rate is 40.3%,30.8%,22.2%,19.3%, and 12.7 % in the South & South East Asia, Sub Saharan Africa, Latin America & Caribbean Countries, Central Asia, and West Asia.

Table 2.2, it is shown that South Asia and South East Asia, Latin America and the Caribbean, and Sub-Saharan Africa face higher value of gender inequality index 0.51, 0.49, and 0.55 while Central Asia and West Asia having the 0.27 and 0.37. It has been observed that regions with higher gender inequality are facing the problem of hunger. In South & South Asia, Sub- Saharan Africa and Latin America, and Caribbean's are the regions where the gender inequality index and global hunger index are higher.

Table 2.3: Women Empowerment Profile of the Developing Economies

Regions		Gender Inequality Index	SDG3.1	SDG3.7	SDG5.5	Population with at least some secondary education		Labor force participation rate	
			Maternal mortality ratio	Adolescent birth rate	Share of seats in parliament Political Empowerment	(% ages 25 and older) Social Empowerment		(% ages 15 and older) Economic Empowerment	
			(deaths per 100,000 live births)	(births per 1,000 women ages 15–19)	(% held by women)	Female	Male	Female	Male
	Developing Economies	2017	2015	2015	2017	2010–	2010–2017	2017	2017
West Asia	Azerbaijan	0.318	25	53.5	16.8	93.8	97.5	62.9	69.5
	Jordan	0.460	58	22.4	15.4	81.4	85.8	14.0	63.7
	Armenia	0.262	25	23.2	18.1	96.9	97.6	51.4	**70.6**
	Egypt	0.449	33	50.0	14.9	58.2	70.7	22.2	73.7
	Average	**0.37**	**35.25**	**37.28**	**16.3**	**82.58**	**87.9**	**37.63**	**69.38**
South and Southeast Asia	Pakistan	0.480	258	60.5	29.6	27.3	43.1	82.7	85.9
	Timor-Leste	....	100	13.9	0.0	...	...	....	......
	Cambodia	0.517	224	82.8	18.0	39.2	52.4	70.1	79.7
	India	0.524	174	23.1	11.6	39.0	63.5	27.2	78.8
	Nepal	0.456	178	28.7	10.2	28.7	22.3	51.3	79.9
	Average	**0.51**	**186.8**	**41.8**	**13.88**	**33.55**	**45.32**	**57.82**	**81.18**
Central Asia	Tajikistan	0.317	32	36.4	20.0	98.9	87.0	45.5	73.3
	Kyrgyz Republic	0.197	76	38.1	19.2	98.6	98.3	48.2	75.7
	Average	**0.25**	**54**	**37.25**	**19.6**	**98.75**	**92.65**	**46.85**	**74.5**
Latin America and Caribbean	Haiti	0.653	396	64.5	27.4	11.4	36.9	19.5	86.7
	Honduras	....	215	44.0	32.3	...	...	24.9	52.3
	Peru	0.368	68	47.5	27.7	57.1	67.5	.... 69.0	84.5
	Guatemala	0.493	...	....	...	...	...		

		0.451	92	95.0	24.3	58.6	54.4	54.4	79.5
	Dominican Republic								
	Average	**0.49**	**192.7**	**62.75**	**27.92**	**31.77**	**39.7**	**24.7**	**75.75**
Sub-Saharan Af-rica	Ethiopia	....	229	18.8	10.8	...	...	49.5	68.5
	Gabon	0.534	291	95.3	17.4	65.6	49.8	42.9	59.4
	Gambia	0.502	353	62.5	37.3	11.2	21.4	77.2	87.8
	Comoros	0.515	...	...	...	...	....	....	....
	Congo Democratic	0.542	679	135.3	21.9	...	....	63.0	65.4
	Cote d'Ivoire	0.601	359	37.5	2.7	26.9	39.9	63.8	72.6
	Cameroon	0.541	178	36.9	20.0	27.0	47.3	24.9	82.7
	Chad	0.471	712	26.8	37.8	7.5	10.5	80.2	77.5
	Kenya	.....	342	155.6	19.7			55.7	61.8
	Liberia	0.552	489	135.2	39.6	16.1	27.3	82.5	74.6
	Mali	0.656	725	127.5	9.9	18.5	39.6	53.9	57.4
	Malawi	0.663	645	132.7	9.2	17.8	34.1	48.1	66.2
	Mozambique	.....	501	51.6	22.0	.....	.....	75.4	87.4
	Namibia	0.472	265	73.8	36.3	39.9	41.0	58.5	65.2
	Nigeria	0.534	443	104.1	36.2	55.9	66.3	78.5	89.1
	Sierra Leone	0.610	371	104.3	11.0	6.0	11.7	58.2	75.2
	Tanzania	0.537	398	115.1	37.2	11.9	16.9	79.5	87.4
	Tonga	0.416	335	65.4	6.1	....	....	36.0	50.2
	Uganda	0.523	343	106.5	34.3	26.7	32.4	66.6	74.9
	Zimbabwe	0.547	68	38.6	13.2	37.1	42.6	11.9	70.2
	Zambia	0.569	389	77.0	14.7	30.0	32.7	42.7	67.2
	Burkina Faso	0.678	587	169.1	8.8	7.3	16.4	60.8	82.5
	Average	**0.55**	**414.4**	**89.02**	**21.24**	**22.52**	**29.43**	**57.60**	**72.53**

Source: (UNDP, 2015; WorldBank, 2019b)

Reduction in gender inequality or improving women's empowerment is most important to strengthen them by refining their political, social, economic, and health conditions. Besides it, there is a need to get sustainable development by reducing gender inequality and focusing on women's empowerment. Equal participation for women and men is essential for productive and reproductive life, including joint responsibility for childcare and family maintenance (Benebo, Schumann, & Vaezghasemi, 2018). Women and men have shared responsibilities for their children's care, but women are always close to their children due to their caring and loving nature. Unfortunately, women face poor health conditions throughout the world due to the overburden of domestic and professional responsibilities and lack of power in decision-making about their health. In most parts of the world, women are getting less education than men. Unfortunately, their knowledge, skills, and surviving mechanisms are not recognized (Sultana, 2010)

In 1990, when the goal of expanding the primary education all over the World was dedicated to implementing, then it was realized that approximately 960 million illiterate adults were in the world, of whom two-thirds were women. After that, countries were declared to take necessary steps to eliminate this inequality at all levels—political, health, public, and equalize their rights related to reproductive and sexual health (Chabbott, 1998).

In the millennium development goals, 3rd   , 4th   , and 5th   goals were focused on women's equal rights and promote women empowerment to reduce poverty, hunger, and disease for the sustainable development in the real sense(Motala et al., 2015). While from the 1990' many countries are continually struggling against gender inequality and trying to empower their women, but still, most developing countries are far from equality in health, politics, education, and employment. Moreover, in the sustainable development goals, the fifth goal is to "Achieve gender equality and empower all women and girls" at the end of 2030. To achieve this goal, every country needs to be given special attention to reducing gender inequality and empowering their women(Abrar-ul-Haq, Jali, & Islam, 2017). Because all over the mothers are the primary answerable for their child's health, they should be authorized to choose or decide(Anselma, Chinapaw, & Altenburg, 2018). However, lacking the decision powers, how a mother can take care of herself and her child (Fawole & Adeoye, 2015). Improving the health and education of children is essential for sustainable development. Children's health and education depend on the participation in decision-making by the parents (Hedges, Mulder, James, & Lawson, 2016).

Compared to men, women think and make decisions differently and have different preferences(Winter, 1994). The health of a household depends on the nutritional choices made by women. Moreover, she has the knowledge and independence to make decisions; she can choose a proper diet for her children (Madjdian & Bras, 2016). According to a Global Nutrition Report 2016, more women are empowering through education and skills. More women can improve their spouse, children, and other family members' social and health status.

The health and diet of a child indeed depend on the nutrition and health of the mother(Chipili et al., 2018). Therefore, mothers' nutritional status and knowledge about the nutritious diet got immediate attention at the international forums. Because children are suffering from stunting, wasting, underweight, obesity, and non-communicable diseases(Beal, Tumilowicz, Sutrisna, Izwardy, & Neufeld, 2018). In early years, children are at the mercy of their mother's diet during gestation and breastfeeding(Hadju, 2017). Therefore, the nutritional status of mothers and adolescent girls should be focused on higher priorities. According to Hawkes and Fanzo (2017), fifty out of all the pregnant women are anemic, and approximately 120 million women are underweight in developing countries. These women (and adolescent girls) give birth to the stunted and underweight children, continuing the malnutrition cycle.

2.2 Women Empowerment and Child Health in Developing Economies (Macroeconomic Scenario)

Economic and demographic status has a strong association with health status and gender equality among the developing economies. Women's empowerment and health outcomes of any country depend on the presence of gender inequalities and hunger, along with their macroeconomic and demographic characteristics(Torlesse, Kiess, & Bloem, 2003). An overview of few important macroeconomic indicators like a share of all sectors to GDP, GDP per Capita, Inflation rate, unemployment rate, poverty headcount ratio, and demographic indicators like the percentage of rural population and fertility rate is presented in Table 2.3. All these indicators determined the living standard, purchasing power, and social status of their people, and ultimately, these factors influence health or gender-based discrimination.

Table 2.4: Socioeconomic Realities of Developing Economies

Regions		Value-added % of GDP			GDP per capita US Dollar	Inflation (CPI)	Unemployment Rate (% of the total labor force)	Fertility Rates	Poverty Head Count Ratio	Rural Pop. %
		Agriculture	Industry	Services						
	Developing Economies									
West Asia	Armenia	15	26	51	3936.8	0.97	17.83	1.6	1.4	37
	Azerbaijan	6	50	37	4135.1	12.90	5.00	1.9	2.7	45
	Egypt	11	34	53	2412.7	29.50	11.77	3.2	1.3	57
	Jordan	4	28	64	4129.8	3.32	14.88	3.3	0.1	9
	Average	9	35	51	3653.6	11.6	12.4	2.5	1.375	37
South and	Cambodia	23	34	40	1384.4	2.89	1.06	2.53	40.9	77
Southeast Asia	India	16	26	49	1979.4	2.49	2.56	2.304	21.2	66
	Nepal	26	13	52	849.0	3.63	1.25	2.083	15	81
	Pakistan	23	18	53	1547.9	4.09	3.18	3.414	3.9	64
	Timor-Leste	11	45	43	2279.3	0.56	2.96	5.391	30.7	70
	Average	20	27	47	1608	2.732	2.20	3.1	22.34	71.6
Central Asia	Kyrgyz Republic	12	27	50	1219.8	3.18	6.89	3	1.5	64
	Tajikistan	20	27	42	800.97	6.00	10.74	3.3	4.8	73
	Average	16	27	49	1010.35	4.59	8.8	2.1	3.15	68
Latin America	Dominican Republic	6	27	60	7052.3	3.28	5.83	2.392	1.6	20
and Caribbean	Guatemala	10	25	62	4471.0	4.42	2.68	2.92	17.2	49
Countries	Honduras	13	26	57	2480.1	3.93	4.05	2.423	17.2	44
	Haiti	18	55	23	765.7	14.67	13.40	2.868	25	46
	Peru	7	31	54	6571.9	2.80	3.46	2.37	3.4	22
	Average	11	33	51	4268.2	5.82	5.9	2.6	12.88	32
Sub Saharan	Burkina Faso	29	18	55	642.0	0.36	6.01	5.271	43.7	71
Africa	Cote d'Ivoire	22	25	32	1537.5	0.69	2.49	4.846	28.2	50
	Cameroon	147	25	52	1451.9	0.64	3.36	4.639	23.8	44
	Congo Democratic	20	42	34	462.8	2.89	4.10	6.018	76.6	56
	Comoros	30	54	53	1312.3	4.602	3.70	4.275	17.9	71

Country								
Ethiopia	34	12	37	767.6	9.85	1.81	4.081	27.3	80
Gabon	5	44	42	7413.8	2.65	19.37	3.72	3.4	11
Gambia	23	12	57	709.1	8.03	8.91	5.358	10.1	39
Kenya	35	17	44	1594.8	8.01	9.29	3.793	36.8	73
Liberia	37	10	40	694.3	12.42	2.03	4.513	40.9	49
Mali	38	18	48	827.0	1.76	9.44	5.968	49.7	58
Mozambique	21	25	38	426.2	9.772	3.17	5.179	62.4	65
Malawi	26	14	48	338.5	11.54	5.47	4.505	70.3	83
Namibia	7	**28**	52	5230.8	6.14	23.09	3.354	13.4	51
Nigeria	21	22	58	1968.4	16.52	6.01	5.457	53.5	51
Sierra Leone	60	6	33	499.5	18.22	4.32	4.359	52.2	58
Chad	49	15	30	662.5	3.7	6	5.846	38.4	77
Tonga	17	17	2	3959.1	7.44	1.00	3.595	1	77
Tanzania	29	25	38	958.4	5.32	1.94	4.95	49.1	67
Uganda	25	20	47	606.5	5.21	1.70	5.5	41.7	77
Zambia	7	37	52	1513.3	6.58	7.21	4.9	57.5	57
Zimbabwe	9	26	61	1333.4	0.91	4.94	3.7	21.4	68
Average	**31**	**23**	**43**	**1587**	**6**	**6.2**	**5**	**37**	**61**

Source: (WorldBank, 2019b)

According to Table 2.3, in West Asia and Latin America & Caribbean Countries, the services sector's contribution to the value-added GDP is higher than the other areas. In the recent decade's the services sector is considered the accelerator of economic and social development. The services sector is now the fastest-growing sector in the world economy because, in the developed nations, 73% share of output and employment comes from the services sector, and for middle-income countries, this ratio is 53%, and for low-income countries, it is 47 % (Ahmed & Ahsan, 2011). In South & South East Asia and Sub-Saharan Africa percentage of services sector to value-added of GDP is 47 %, 46%, and for Central Asia, it is 49%.

GDP per capita in West Asia and Latin America and Caribbean Countries is higher than other regions, while in these regions, inflation and unemployment rate are higher than others. The poverty headcount ratio is significantly higher in Sub Saharan Africa and South & South East Asia. Sub Saharan Africa and South & South East Asia have higher shares of agriculture sectors in the value-added GDP than others. Following the demographic characteristics, the fertility rate is higher in Sub Saharan Africa and South & South East Asia; in these two regions, the rural population's percentage is higher than the other regions.

By comparing Tables 2.1 and 2.2, it has views out that in Sub-Saharan Africa and South and Southeast Asia, gender inequality is higher. Most of the countries in these regions are agrarian and with low GDP per capita. The fertility rate and rural population rate of these regions are also very high, as in Table 2.2, the maternal mortality ratio and adolescent birth rate are higher, which is one of the primary reasons for the higher fertility rate in these regions. At the same time, these regions face their children's poor health due to their poor economic and demographic conditions. Latin America & Caribbean Countries have higher GDP per Capita and percentage of the services sector in the GDP value-added. However, this region showing the gender inequality index higher than West Asia, Central Asia, and less than the South & Southeast Asia and Sub-Saharan Africa.

On the other side, gender inequality is low in West Asia and Central Asia, but the inflation rate and unemployment rate are very high in these regions, which is more than 8 % of the total labor force. In these two regions, the fertility rate is low, maternal mortality and adolescent birth rates are also lower than in other regions, and face a small level of discrimination in employment and education. The global hunger index shows the average score, which is a sign of attention toward improving health in these regions.

In Latin America & Caribbean Countries, the gender inequality index is slightly better than the Sub Saharan Africa and South and Southeast Asia but near alarming situations. Economic and demographic status is reasonable, GDP per capita has a higher percentage of services in the value-added of GDP, but unemployment and inflation rate are also higher. In Latin America & Caribbean Countries prevalence of stunting, wasting, and underweight are more significant than in West Asia and Central Asia but lesser than the South and South East Asia and Sub-Saharan Africa.

CHAPTER 3: LITERATURE REVIEW

In this chapter, the literature review of previous studies provides comprehensive directions and guidance to scholars and researchers about the current research topic. Literature always helps to identify the gap in the existing literature and describes scholars,' and researchers' earlier published work in the related field (Sekaran & Leong, 1992). The current literature review attempts to describe the crucial features and measurement methods of women empowerment, its determinants, and the association with child health. This literature is reviewed in three sections: women empowerment, concepts, and measurement in the first section, determining women empowerment in the second section, and child health in the third section. These sections are as given below:

3.1 Women Empowerment

3.1.1 Conceptual/theoretical Debates on Women Empowerment

In the mid-1980s, empowerment was considered to challenge patriarchy. Patriarchy means men dominance, results in women's less control over material and intellectual resources. At that time, women empowerment defined as a goal to challenge the patriarchy ideology, the transformation of social structure to increase the individual ability to control one's life to get access over the material and intellectual resources (Bandura, 1982; Gibson, 1991; Rappaport, 1981; Rappaport, 1984, 1985; Wallerstein, 1992; Zimmerman & Rappaport, 1988).

In the 1990s, the term women empowerment was generally defined as an individual self-transformation process, transfer of power in social, economic, and political structures from superior to inferior ones (Women, 1995). Women considered empowered if they have involvement in welfare/well-being, have access to resources, proper awareness, and control over decision making (Congress, Organization, & UNICEF., 1994). At this point, welfare/wellbeing present all the social and economic opportunities with the active participation of women, access to resources mean open availability of funds without any gender biasness, awareness refers to knowledge about the attainment of gender equality and human right, and control over decision making describes ultimate power of decisions without any gender-based discrimination. The concept of empowerment has been defined in the literature in terms of power, autonomy, control, self-efficacy, and a means to achieve positive health outcomes for women and children (Mason 1995). So for, "Empowerment is the expansion of freedom of choice and action" (Blase & Anderson, 1995; Rowlands, 1997).

Women empowerment has expressed in the form of choices about marriage, the number of children, mobility, job, entertainment, and improvement in the quality of life (Medel-Anonuevo, 1995). Kabeer (1999)empowerment as increasing the people's abilities to make strategic life choices. She proposed three consistent dimensions resources-agency-achievement for the attainment of women empowerment. Resources included both material and nonmaterial resources. Agency refers to a process of decision making to set goals, motivation, and efforts. Resources and agency enable a person to make choices. Achievement means creating the potential to change the world through knowledge, skills development, self-confidence, self-esteem, autonomy, and freedom (Kabeer, 1999; Malhotra & Mather, 1997; Mehra, 1997; Rissel, 1994; Rodwell, 1996).

Amartya and Foster (1997) define capabilities as "the freedom that a person has regarding the choice of functioning's, given his/her features (conversion of characteristics into operation) and command over commodities.

At the beginning of 2000, women's empowerment was considered the transfer of power in all real domains. These domains categorized into education, employment, access to financial resources, family origin and community (Crow, 2000; Kishor, 2000; Presser & Sen, 2000)

Bennett (2002) defined empowerment and social inclusion. Bennett described empowerment as "enhancement of assets and capabilities," and social inclusion as "removing institutional barriers and enhancing incentives for access to assets and opportunity for development.

Power considered as someone's ability to make choices and express the concept of empowerment as a process by which people who have previously denied to get the ability to make choices as a means of achieving social and economic justice (Boehm & Staples, 2004; Naryan, 2002; Sen & Batliwala, 2000). In the structural context, empowerment presented to learn how to get access and control over resources(Johnson, Worell, & Chandler, 2005). Moghadam and Senftova (2005) and Alsop and Heinsohn (2005) explained empowerment as a process of enabling women to control their lives to access skills and resources and make meaningful and purposive choices themselves, family and, community. Cueva Beteta (2006)conceptualize empowerment as a process to get equality between men and women and to control of one's health Therefore, women's empowerment requires fundamental changes in institutions supporting patriarchal structures (Khattab & Sakr, 2009).

 Moreover, Tengland (2008) explained empowerment as the ability to control one's life compared to limited ability to maintain health. According to Tengland (2008) empowerment improved the ability to control the circumstances that affect one's health (physical or mental), home (where she lives), work (domestic or income), leisure time, and values (religious, political, and economic). However, it focuses on women since it encompasses some unique elements (Akram, 2018).

Bhukuth, Terrany, and Wulandari (2019) measured empowerment through entrepreneurship, believed that freedom of choices and decision making in business could be improved quality of life. Women empowerment improved the wellbeing of a women, wellbeing may be financial and social. A woman can be improved her quality of life being financially strong. Moreover, Autonomy, mobility and control over resources were considered the measure of women empowerment, and all these dimensions of women empowerment improved the self-efficacy and self-confidence(Ndaimani, 2018).

Gram, Morrison, and Skordis-Worrall (2019) developed a new typology by organizing the existing concepts of women empowerment. The said typology explained empowerment as collective or individual concept. It involved in the removal of internal psychological barriers (Self-Compassion) or external social barriers. Women Empowerment may come when a woman realizes her goal by herself or through the social awareness. Because when empowerment is related to freedom then freedom should be divided into direct and indirect freedom. Direct freedom is involved with the choices of individual while indirect freedom is related to society. Gram also focused that each measurement of women empowerment have its own direction and its totally mislead to sum up the these. Because objective measurement (quantitative) and subjective measurement (qualitative) cannot explained correctly if they unified.

Self-Compassion is a new measurement of women empowerment introduced by Samanta (2020) Samnta, believed that women is only empowered if she thinks faithfully for herself. It was exquisitely constructing the measurement of women empowerment, which was completely described what a woman want for herself. It explained a woman can be empowered through self-esteem, self-efficacy and self-awareness. Khalid, Samargandi, Shah, and Almandeel (2020)measured women empowerment through the provision of basic facilities, including education, health, housing services, Independence, and ownership of assets. Khalid developed a combine index of women empowerment along with the sub-dimensions index.

In the previous literature women empowerment was conceptualize through power(Mason, 1995; Mason & Smith, 2003) , freedom (Naryan, 2002; Rodwell, 1996; Sen & Batliwala, 2000), autonomy(Malhotra & Schuler, 2005) , decision making(Kabeer, 2005, 2011, 2012), mobility(Giele, 1977; Mehra, 1997; Moghadam & Senftova, 2005), self-efficacy and self-compassion(Bandura, 1982; Bhandari & Chhetri, 2013; Gram et al., 2019; Khalid et al., 2020; Nayak & Mahanta, 2008; Rappaport, 1981; Rappaport, 1984, 1985; Rodwell, 1996). It is concluded that women empowerment and their relationship with society intertwined with gender equality, class, race, ethnicity, age, culture and history. Power is known as with equity and fairness for women and men in access to resources, participation in decision-making and control over the circulation of resources and benefits. Gender equality is talked at these various levels with the aim of increasing equality between men and women and succeeding women's empowerment (Akter et al., 2017). Access to resources refers to mutually the means and the right to gain services, products, or commodities. Gender gaps in access to resources and services are the central problem for women's development. The process of empowerment contains mobilizing women to bridge these gaps. A basis of gender equality is the equal contribution of women in decision-making. Combined participation is also one of the critical aspects of women empowerment (Kabeer, 2005; Women, 2018b).

3.1.2 Dimensions/ Operational Definitions of Women Empowerment.

In previous literature, empowerment had defined as a goal, process, and outcomes measured through different dimensions. A few of the operational definitions of women empowerment are as follows:

Empowerment as a goal leads to increase in the ability to control one's life (Gibson, 1991; Tengland, 2008; Wallerstein, 1992), to improve the ability to change the world (Rodwell, 1996), to control individual or community health(Smith, Tang, & Nutbeam, 2006)

Empowerment is a self-transformation(Batliwala, 1995), transfer of political and social power (Women, 1995), to give power to the disempowered to enhance their abilities to make choices.

Empowerment means to enhance the abilities to make strategic life choices(Malhotra & Schuler, 2005) and to get control over one's life (Mishra & Tripathi, 2011). Empowerment process can be a catalyst for social changes (Kabeer, 2005), to get equality between men and women (Cueva Beteta, 2006) and ability to control life in the context of health, home, work, income, close relationships, leisure time and values (Tengland, 2008). Empowerment is expressed as process and outcomes, transfer of power to an oppressed group as a means of achieving social and economic justice (Boehm & Staples, 2004; Kabeer, 2005). Nayak and Mahanta (2008) examined how mothers' empowerment in India was linked to education and employment as an enabling factor for empowerment. They suggested women should be empowered simultaneously through several dimensions if they were to benefit across the whole aspects of decision making, media, self-esteem, and confidence.

Empowerment explained the ability to exercise choices in three interrelated dimensions resource, agency, and achievement (Kabeer, 1999). Resources are economic and included human and social are well served to enhance the ability to exercise choices. Change or provision of resources could change the ability to make choices. Agency is the ability to recognized one's goal and acts upon it. It is also expressed in the sense of motivation, purpose, and means to carry out activities for actualized the choices. Resource and agency makeup people's capabilities: that is their potential and living the lives they want. The achievement has been considered in terms of both the agency exercised and its consequences (Kabeer, 2001, 2002, 2003, 2011, 2012).

Table 3.1: Operational Definitions and Dimensions of Women Empowerment

Conceptualize Empowerment	Dimensions	Authors
As a Process to get control over one's life and ability to make choices and opportunities	Civil, political, and economic Participation, Education, employment, mobility, Health,	(Giele, 1977; Mehra, 1997; Moghadam & Senftova, 2005)

As a Goal to learn how to access and achieve control over resources	Community resources, collective decision making, resources mobilization skills,	(Zimmerman & Rappaport, 1988) 1995
As a goal to attain self-determination	Self-esteem Self-confidence Decision making	(Bandura, 1982; Bhandari & Chhetri, 2013; Nayak & Mahanta, 2008; Rappaport, 1981; Rappaport, 1984, 1985; Rodwell, 1996)
As a goal to self-transformation	Autonomy Freedom	(Naryan, 2002; Rodwell, 1996; Sen & Batliwala, 2000)
As a mean to achieve positive health outcomes as women and children	Autonym terms as power status, Agency (Decision Making)	(Mason, 1995; Mason & Smith, 2003)
As a process to transfer the power to disempower	Resource (Physical and Human) Agency (Decision Making) Outcomes	(Kabeer, 1999, 2001, 2002)
As a Goal to get control over one's life, body, and environment	Education, employment, access to financial assets, family origin, and community.	(Mishra & Tripathi, 2011)
As a process to control power and awareness	Autonomy Knowledge	(Malhotra & Schuler, 2005)
As a process to give power to disempowered to enhance their abilities to make choices	Education Employment Political Participation	(Kabeer, 2005, 2011, 2012)
As a change in the structural context	Internal and Intrapersonal skills, access to resources	(Johnson et al., 2005)
As a process and outcome	Social and economic justice	(Batliwala, 1994; Boehm & Staples, 2004)
As a process to make structural changes	Social, economic and social assets, Informal and formal institutions	(Alsop & Heinsohn, 2005)
As a goal to control one's health	Health (Physical and mental health)	(Smith et al., 2006)
As a goal to control one's life	Health (Physical and mental health), Home (where one is live), leisure time, to whom have a close relationship, values (religion, political, economic and social)	(Tengland, 2008)
The process to acquire power at an individual and collective level	Assets, Income, knowledge, literacy, (at an	(United Nations Development Fund for, 2008)

	individual level), leadership, access to opportunities (at community level)	
Process of binding resources and achievement	Decision Making	(Dhok & Thakre, 2016)
As a Process and Outcome	Decision Making Attitudes toward beating (Self-esteem) Attitudes toward Violence (Self-Confidence)	(Habibov, Barrett, & Chernyak, 2017)
The process of change covers personal and collective knowledge, behavior, institutions, and outcomes in the social and cultural context.	Economic Socio-Cultural Education Health	(Asaolu et al., 2018; Richardson, 2018)

The UNDP states that the GII reflects women's disadvantages relative to men in three dimensions—reproductive health, empowerment, and the labor market. Specifically, there is no information on women's participation in local government, women's participation, and income from informal sectors, asset ownership, gender-based violence, and community decision-making in GDI. The World Economic Forum in 2006 constructed the global Gender Gap Index (GGI) (Permanyer, 2013; UNDP, 2015).

In the Global Gender Gap Report (2012), the World Economic Forum specifies that their index's goal is to capture the gaps in outcome variables rather than the differences in input variables. The GGI measures five aspects of women's empowerment: economic participation, economic opportunity, political empowerment, educational attainment, and health and well-being. Criticisms of the GGI index are more about rich countries (OECD countries) while having minimal data on the developing countries, and similar to the GDI, it mainly focuses on economic aspects (Permanyer, 2013; UNDP, 2015).

It is challenging for a low-income country to rank high on the GGI. Women's Empowerment in Agriculture Index (WEAI) was developed by Alkire et al. (2013). The WEAI includes two sub-indices: the five domains of empowerment (5DE) and the Gender Parity Index. The first one reflects ''the percentage of women who have empowered in five domains of empowerment in agriculture'' or 5DE, which includes: (1) the decisions about agricultural production, (2) access to and decision-making power about productive resources, (3) control of the use of income, (4) leadership in the community, and (5) time allocation (Alkire et al., 2013; Alkire & Santos, 2014).

In a previous study, the Women's Empowerment Matrix had constructed by six dimensions—physical, socio-cultural, religious, economic, political, legal—and at six levels: individual, household, community, state, region, and globally (Charmes & Wieringa, 2003). Many scholars have recommended that measurements of women's empowerment should be carried out at three levels: household, community, and broader areas (national and international) (Cueva Beteta, 2006; Ismail, Mohd Rasdi, & Nadirah Abd. Jamal, 2011; Malhotra & Schuler, 2005).

Desai (2010) has pointed out the significant challenge facing in measuring women's empowerment. Because there is a lack of gender-disaggregated data of the most dimensions of empowerment. In contrast to Cueva Beteta (2006), who says that most current data lack measurement at the household level, Desai (2010) claims that most data only exist for the aggregate or household level, while data for the community, state, and region exists only for very few countries. Another challenge that Desai (2010) has pointed out is the measurement of women's empowerment by universal indicators, while women's empowerment is context-specific (Mosedale, 2005; Odutolu, Adedimeji, Odutolu, Baruwa, & Olatidoye, 2003).

The most difficult challenge is to measure the process and agency for women's empowerment. The process is measured by changes in variables such as education and employment over time. It also depends on the changes in behaviors (in fecundity or household decision-making) over time. Similarly, the agency is also challenging to measure. Since the agency implies that women's consciousnesses could transform, it would have to be estimated based on women's interpretations of what they perceived as changes in their knowledge and perspectives (Fetterman, Kaftarian, & Wandersman, 1996; Musonera & Heshmati, 2017).

Khan (2016) explained women's empowerment through poverty alleviation. The study focused on developing gender equality and women empowerment — the result based on Pakistan's secondary data. The sources of data were the United Nations Development Program 1998 (Khan, 2010). The dependent variable was poverty and literacy rate, gross primary enrollment, combined enrollment ratio, labor force, and mortality rate were the independent variable. The government and absence of infrastructure compulsory to cope with the problem were paved the way for NGOs to step to help the poor people and women in a particular provision of an environment free of all discrimination, violence, and exploitation. If social and political issues were not addressed, it was difficult to impose poverty (Farooq, Ahmed, & Jasra, 2008; Khan, Mann, Zafar, Hashmi, & Akhtar, 2010).

Measurements on agency can only complete through ethnographic studies or surveys at the local level (Desai, 2010). Pratley and Sandberg (2018) tested three measurement models of women empowerment: a simple composite index model, the functional scales model, and the five-dimensional model of empowerment by using microdata (DHS) of Sub-Saharan Africa. Economic, social, and psychological dimensions were used to measure women empowerment, and then further intimate partner violence was treated as separate dimensions. Husband abuse to wives and wives refusing to husbands has also been used as different dimensions to measure women's empowerment (Phan, 2016a; Upadhyay & Karasek, 2012).

The functional scales model favored over the simple composite model and variants of the five-dimension framework and preferred to these specifications. Tsiboe et al. (2018) developed the women empowerment index in agriculture using five domains income, production, and leadership. Further, it was explored one new thing to attach these three domains with times and resources. It has focused on some household preliminary issues such as household nutrition and food poverty (Khan, 2016).

This five-domain index of women empowerment was constructed by Alkire et al. (2013). OLS technique was applied to find out the effect of women empowerment on food poverty and household nutrition. This study found that women empowerment improves the household nutrition level and reduce food poverty (Alkire & Santos, 2014). Njoh and Akiwumi (2012) construct the women empowerment index using an indicator which was based on the Millennium Development Goals (MDGs), including the percentage of school-aged girls in school, female adult literacy rates, the female share of non-agricultural employment, and female representation in government (UNDPI, 2009).

Equal weights of each variable were used to construct the composite index of women empowerment. Data on fifty-four African countries were used to develop the relationship between women's empowerment and these countries' religions. Three religions Islam, Christians, and indigenous African religion were used to find the association between women's empowerment and beliefs. Regression analysis was employed and seen the positive association of all the four indicators of women empowerment with Christianity and a negative association with Islam (Ahmed, 1992).

Indigenous African religion showed a positive association with female adult literacy rates and female share of non-agricultural employment and a negative association with the percentage of school-aged girls in school and female representation in government. Njoh and Ananga (2016) tested the hypothesis that women empowerment enables them to attain development goals, which was the third of the eight Millennium Development Goals (MDGs). Indicators of women empowerment—women's literacy, the proportion of women with secondary education, the percentage of women with formal employment, and women's role in government have been used in this study (Kabeer, 2003; UNDPI, 2009).

Inequality, in access to land as the dependent variable and women's empowerment as the independent variable, was measured by four indicators—the study conducted on the fifty-four developing countries of Africa. The multivariant regression analysis has used to find the relationship between inequality in access to land and women empowerment. It found an inverse relationship between women's empowerment and gender inequality in land (Permanyer, 2013; UNDP, 2015).

Mishra (2014) measured disempowerment by using India's survey data. He defined disempowerment as a deprivation of choices. Four indicators used to measure disempowerment were fertility decisions, economic decisions, household decisions, and personal decisions. Multidimensional approaches had used in literature. First, it considered the weight of the decision's specific components in measuring overall disempowerment, and data has fixed the exogenously by principal components. The second was the disaggregation of the disempowerment measure for defining it as an additive in subgroups or regions' disempowerment measures. Multidimensional indicators have used to found the degree of disempowerment in India's two states from the North and the South (Mishra, 2014).

According to Lopez-Avila (2016), women empowerment was explained better against aggressive domestic violence than controlling ones. Women empowerment enables the women to put a voice against domestic violence rather than silently accept it. This study explored the relationship between women's empowerment and domestic violence in rural Colombia. Women's empowerment has been measured by social capital, self-esteem, and household decisions. Two Indices has constructed for women empowerment and disagreement against violence (Garcia-Moreno Claudia & Avni, 2016; Jamal, 2017)

Chung, Kantachote, Mallick, Polster, and Roets (2013) evaluated in their report gender-sensitive indicators across five dimensions--economic contribution, education, governance, health, and media. A financial contribution has been measured by market participation and resource equity. Educational measurement has been calculated by management by representation, electoral system, processes, and justice. Health was measured by access and utilization of health services, disease, prevention, environmental health, fertility, population growth, healthcare management health expenditures, maternal and infant health, mental health, risk factors, nutrition, and reproductive health. Media expressed in indicators such as equal treatment of media employees, similar news reporting coverage, the same expression of freedom of speech, and violence against women (García-Moreno Claudia et al., 2015; Gram et al., 2019; Khalid et al., 2020).

It is concluded that women empowerment has become an important issue during the last two decades. Augmentation in women empowerment is one of UN and other international organizations' techniques to decrease population growth rate and poverty alleviation. A significant share of the female population in the underdeveloped civilization, their status is not equal to those of men in most of the world (Ahmed, Creanga, Gillespie, & Tsui, 2010; Heaton, Huntsman, & Flake, 2005; Tijani & Yano, 2007). Women are an important part of the society, their participation in decision making through their participation in economic activities is meager. Working women contribute to the national income of the country and maintain a sustainable livelihood for the families, throughout the world. Globally, sixty percent of women worked unpaid (Ferrant et al., 2014). Hence two-third of women are poor in the world. (Bank, 2018; Nips, 2012). Pakistan is the second lowest country of the world in the ranking regard. In Pakistan, it is a common practice that daughters are deprived of inheritance in favor of sons (Sathar & Shahnaz, 2000).

Power is generally explained regarding control and influence over others (Kabeer, 1999, 2001, 2002). The control of men over men, men over women, and by dominant social, political and economic class over those who are marginalized(Kabeer, 2005, 2011, 2012). If people are continuously denied power and influence in a society, they begin to internalize this denial of authority. Rowlands (1998) used the term 'internalized oppression.' They have fewer opportunities and less choice in making decisions of their lives (Kritz & Adebusoye, 1999; Senarath & Gunawardena, 2009). There are many reasons for disempowerment of women in underdeveloped countries. Poverty is the primary reason of disempowerment. Reducing poverty through farming communities is under investigation among development circles of the world. These approaches improve the rural livelihood through the introduction of new technologies, community organization, awareness creation, capacity building, and human resource development. Agriculture is the only sector which utilized the natural resources appropriately (Alkire et al., 2013).

Previous literature, pointed women decisional power as a crucial factor for women empowerment. Because , in some cases, mothers have buying capacity, but they cannot take food-related decisions independently. In joint families, mother in law has more dominant power to make food decisions about their daughter-in-law and their grandchild. Reconization of descional power and acheivement of goals are essentional for women empowerment (Bhukuth et al., 2019; Gram et al., 2019; Jones et al., 2019; Khalid et al., 2020).

3.1.3 Determinants of Women Empowerment

Winter (1994) evaluated women empowerment through women's position in the labor market, employment rate, job provision on gender bases, and wage difference due to female, health facilities, and labor law. For the analyses, Brazil, Colombia, Chile, Costa Rica, Honduras, and Venezuela have used employment and earnings data from the national survey households. Policies and interventions had a substantial impact on women's empowerment in the employment sector. Another contribution has added by Tzannatos (1999) through the data on the female labor force participation obtained from the International Labor Organization data from 1950 to 1990 of several countries and areas. He also used identical indicators for women empowerment previously used by Winter (1994), described the women's positions in the labor market, and found that the women's empowerment delivered the active contribution in the labor market.

Kishor (1995) examined women empowerment through direct measures, the customary autonomy index, and the non-customary autonomy index using the Egypt Demographic and Health Survey (EDHS) of 1988. Customary autonomy index covered all decisions making in family planning, children's education, and marriages (reflects the traditional role of women). The non-Customary autonomy index included the autonomy in the general areas (reflects the nontraditional role of women). This study found a strong relationship between modernism, economic, and cultural factors with women empowerment as traditional and non-traditional roles.

Mason (1995) used five Asian countries (Pakistan, India, Malaysia, Thailand, and the Philippines) to measure the gender and family system in the social context. Women's characteristics, household characteristics, assets in the form of land, participation informal employment, and the wife position in front of husband strongly determined the women's empowerment. Women empowerment measured through the power of decision-making in household expenditures.

Kritz and Makinwa-Adebusoye (1999) used data from the survey of 1991 from some ethnic groups in Nigeria. They had determined women's decision-making authority through women's characteristics- ethnicity, age, health, education, employment, and vice versa. Ethnicity was a persuasive predictor in women's decision-making authority and is even more important than women's individual-level characteristics as a determinant of power. This ethnic effect occurred both by developing the levels of resources that women achieve and by improving the relationships between women's obtained characteristics to the family (Kritz & Makinwa-Adebusoye, 1999).

Bloom, Wypij, and Gupta (2001) measured women's autonomy through control over finances, decision-making power, and freedom of movement. All these measures significantly influence maternal health care (number of antenatal care visits) in India. Likewise, determinates of maternal health and women empowerment were examined by Linear and binary logistic regression. Economic Status, religion, employment status, live with the mother-in-law, the natal home location, contact with natal kin, one or more children dead, age, and education have a positive impact on control over finances, decision-making power, and freedom of movement. While control over finances, freedom of movement has persuasive and positive dependence on maternal health care, and the decision-making power has weak and detrimental reliance on maternal health care. Age and education also showed positive relationships with maternal health care, but women's autonomy has more influence rather than all other indicators (Chung et al., 2013; Kantachote, Mallick, Polster, & Roets, 2013; Nardo et al., 2005; Peterman, 2015).

Acharya, Bell, Simkhada, van Teijlingen, and Regmi (2010) analyzed how socioeconomic factors affect decision making autonomy of women in health care, daily and durable household purchasing, visiting family and relatives in Nepal by using survey data (NDHS) 2006.

Multivariable logistic regression examined the effect of women age, residence, ecological zone, development region, education, wealth quintile, employment on the past 12 months, number of living children on decision making: Age, profession, and number of living children have a positive impact on women's autonomy in all decision making.(Kabeer, 1999)

Chaudhuri (2010) determined the time and birth cohort trends of women's empowerment in eight countries of South Asia and Southeast Asia. Women empowerment has been measured through resources as economic participation, educational attainment, wage work, agency variables as fertility and desired female to the male sex ratio of living children, and outcome as the ideal female to the male sex ratio of living children.

A single index was constructed to represent the women's empowerment. The assessment of predictable cohort lines proved that the Philippines and Vietnam, both in South East Asia, had the highest education level, maximum economic participation rates, and low fertility rates. Cambodia has the maximum female to male ratio. Pakistan and Nepal have lower education; Pakistan and Bangladesh have the lowest economic participation rates and highest fertility rates; India has the lowest sex ratio (Chaudhuri, 2010).

Jeckoniah, Nombo, and Mdoe (2012) analyzed the association between women's participation in the onion value chain development and their empowerment in Tanzania. A composite index was constructed to measure women empowerment by personal autonomy, household decision making, domestic economic consultation, and freedom of movement. In Tanzania women in Simanjiro district had categorized in a medium level of empowerment.

Ordinal logistic regression analysis was employed to find the factors that determined the women empowerment of women participation in the onion value chain development activities. Empowerment was found to increase with educational attainment, age at first marriage, and women's income. Access to credit has a significant impact on both women participating in value chain programs and non-participants; access to extension services has not substantial for both program participants and non-participants (Jeckoniah et al., 2012).

Muhammad, Shaheen, Naqvi, and Zehra (2012) tried to examine the relationship between women's empowerment indicators and socioeconomic variables in rural Bangladesh. Many factors like a financial situation in the form of household wealth, demographic status demonstrated by age, and women's social status represent the women's empowerment. Moreover, women's exposure indicated in the way of media, while four dimensions like self-esteem, decision-making participation within household affairs, freedom of mobility, and control of resources, taken to measure the process of empowerment (Muhammad et al., 2012).

Khan and Noreen (2012) explored the socioeconomic determinants of women empowerment concerning the women who obtained the micro-credit. The sample size was 200 women who received a loan and 200 who did not get a loan through random sampling from the Bahawalpur, Pakistan. Women empowerment was measured by constructing a simple index based on five indicators related to child health, education, selection of spouse or children, purchase of essential goods, and the decision of household savings. Age, education of husband, father inherited assets, marital status, many sons alive, and amount of microfinance were determined as factors that influenced the women empowerment.

Three simple linear regression models were employed and followed by women empowerment, women who utilized loans by themselves, and empowerment of women who did not use credit by themselves. Women who used microcredit by themselves were considered more empowered than women who did not use loans by themselves. As well as microfinance was found as a significant explanatory variable of women empowerment along with the age of women, education of husband/head of household/father, number of sons, father's assets have a positive effect, and marital status has a negative impact on women empowerment (Khan & Noreen, 2012).

The study found a positive correlation between women's empowerment and domestic violence. This proved the theories that argue that men use force as a way to influence their power within the household. Social capital and self-esteem were significantly correlated with aggressive domestic violence, but women's household decisions showed less correlation with domestic violence (Donta, Nair, Begum, & Prakasam, 2016; Pambe, Gnoumou, & Kaboré, 2014).

Women's empowerment influenced by many socioeconomic and demographic factors. Earlier mother characteristics like age, education, wealth index, current and parent's Locality, and health determined the women's empowerment. It was assumed that these characteristics help the women be empowered by money earning capability, developing the confidence to face challenges, enhancing the ability to make decisions regarding themselves and their intimates (Bates, Schuler, Islam, & Islam, 2004; Pambe et al., 2014).

Women from a rural area and the Terai region have less autonomy in decision-making than other decision-making indicators. Development in regions has a different impact on decision making in visiting family or relative as compared to other decision makings. Western women were more likely to decide about their health care while they were less likely to purchase daily household needs. Women with more years of education had a positive association with autonomy in personal health care decision making. However, more years of schooling showed a non-significance impact on other types of decision-making and freedom (Becker, Fonseca-Becker, & Schenck-Yglesias, 2006; Hindin, 2006; Kritz & Adebusoye, 1999).

Alkire et al. (2013) presented the women's empowerment in agriculture index based on the five domains of women empowerment--production, resources, income, leadership and time, and gender parity index. WEAI has two sub-indices, one represents the empowerment, and the other was gender parity in Bangladesh, Guatemala, and Uganda. The addition of gender parity for measurement of the women empowerment was a new contribution. It was a weighted average of the five sub-index value of 0.746 and the gender parity sub-index value of 0.899. The score of the WEAI for the Western Highlands of Guatemala was 0.702. The weighted average of the five sub-index value of 0.690 and the gender parity sub-index value of 0.813. Women's empowerment in agriculture index (WEAI) for Uganda was 0.800, with five sub-index value of 0.789 and GPI value of 0.898.

Different age groups, personal education level, the highest grade of education completed, wealth quintile to which the household belongs, household hunger score have a significant effect on the women empowerment (Alkire et al., 2013).

Age has a positive association with empowerment in Bangladesh and Guatemala but showing no significant evidence in Uganda. Education has an insignificant impact in Bangladesh and Guatemala but had a significant in Uganda. Wealth had positive and significant in Bangladesh and Uganda but not significant in Guatemala. In all three regions, women's empowerment in agriculture had associated with decision-making and autonomy regarding religious faith, more significant decisions regarding family planning, and higher autonomy in protection from violence less likely to have the freedom to decide own healthcare (Alkire et al., 2013).

In most other studies, determinants of women empowerment were analyzed in more than one area in a single country and tried to explore the contextual difference of women empowerment in different regions. The studies by Jejeebhoy (2000) for Uttar Pradesh and Tamil Nadu in India and Jejeebhoy and Sathar (2001a) for the Uttar Pradesh and Tamil in India and Punjab in Pakistan, found traditional sources to be more important determinants of autonomy – namely, co-residence with a mother-in-law, size of dowry, age, and number/gender of children (Jejeebhoy & Sathar, 2001a).

Women's empowerment described as a multifaceted and multidimensional concept. That problem was addressed and challenged to measure empowerment. The gender equity or women's empowerment measures have not been discussed; the issues must be similar for women in agriculture (Malapit & Quisumbing, 2015; Sraboni, Malapit, Quisumbing, & Ahmed, 2014).

In Tamil Nadu, only age depicts as a strong determinant of empowerment. Education and work status were strongly predicted empowerment in all three sites less in Tamil Nadu. In Uttar Pradesh and Punjab, only secondary education mattered. For variables reflecting context, namely nationality, religion, and region, the only area was famous; they considered the area to proxy the cultural context, explicitly prevailing social establishments that complaint gender discrimination (Jejeebhoy & Sathar, 2001a).

Upadhyay et al. (2014) explained empowering the women through decision-making in their own life of the household. The primary data had used in this article. The data had collected from DHS or World Fertility Surveys (Upadhyay & Karasek, 2012). The dependent variable was decision-making. Independent variables were age, education, employment, household income, mobility/freedom of movement, general self-efficacy, and control by partner or family.

Recognized the women's experience of empowerment and its effects were an essential and early step in gender equity at the public level and in achieving the Millennium Development Goal, " Enhance the gender equality and empowering women" (UNDPI, 2009).

Sado, Spaho, and Hotchkiss (2014) proposed measurement of women empowerment through the utilization of health-care services for mothers and addressed the issues of regional disparities and health status for the antenatal and postnatal care. The data had collected from the 2008-09 Albania Demographic and Health Survey. The dependent variable was women's empowerment, and independent variables were household wealth, educational attainment, age, employment status, and household structural factors — the binary logistic regression model used in this article. Women's empowerment, known as a concept, was measured by many other social, cultural, and economic terms. In some studies, women empowerment is considered the determinant of the maternal health care utilization at the household and society levels. Both women's empowerment and antenatal and postnatal care usage were interlinked (Nosheen & Chaudhry, 2018; Palamuleni & Adebowale, 2014).

Assaad, Nazier, and Ramadan (2014a) presented women empowerment as an outcome of interest, influenced by individual and socio-demographic factors in Egypt. Women empowerment was measured through two dimensions decision-making power index and mobility index; both are the direct measurement. In this study outcome of interest was indicated by the determinants of women empowerment. Moreover, education, employment, poverty status, number of children, having an adult son, and a woman's husband, the age difference between women and husband, and characteristics of the father had considered the vital determinants of women empowerment.

This study comprised two groups in one group; only individual characteristics of households had predicted as the determinants of participation in decision-making and freedom of mobility, and in the second group along with different attributes of household's regional areas of Egypt were included. Education, employment, poverty, total children, all levels of higher education of women had a positive and significant impact on decision making power while higher education hurts mobility (Assaad et al., 2014a).

While the employee had a positive impact on both participation in decision making and freedom of mobility, the increasing total number of children has a positive impact on the other hand, if the adult child was son, then women husbands' behavior had an adverse affect on both decision making and movement. More differences between women and husband age reduced participation in decision making and progress. The poverty status of households negatively impacts the empowerment; according to the different income groups, women belong to the middle-income group with more empowerment (Assaad et al., 2014a).

According to Sharma and Shekhar (2015), South Asia women had less power in decision-making, which had commonly affected her ethnicity, level of deprivation, urban/rural livings, and education. Due to these issues, they tried to investigate the different levels of women empowerment and estimated the factors that were actively affecting the women empowerment in India, Nepal, and Bangladesh (Sharma & Shekhar, 2015).

Women empowerment was assessed by three dimensions, economic decision making, household decision making, and physical movement to construct a single index through using principal component analysis and categorized this index into three levels, low medium and higher (Sharma & Shekhar, 2015). Age, education levels, media exposure, occupation, marital duration, and wealth status were important factors for women empowerment. Socio-economic and demographic factors determined women's status in the household and the family; older women have more empowerment than younger. Women in urban areas seemed to be more empowered than women in rural areas (Sharma & Shekhar, 2015).

Phan (2016a) attempted to measure women empowerment on a household level by using the microdata of four countries Cambodia, Indonesia, Philippines, and Timor-Leste. Women empowerment was measured through four indicators, women's participation in employment, women's participation in decision-making, family planning, and women's education. Four aspects of women empowerment were based on twelve operationalized variables has calculated by factor scores (Becker et al., 2006; Jin, 1995).

Despite the previous studies, family planning had an insignificant relationship with women's empowerment. Women with higher education had more chances of participation in the labor force and got independence in household decision-making (Senarath & Gunawardena, 2009; Subaiya & Vanneman, 2016).

Musonera and Heshmati (2017) examined women empowerment in Rwanda by using survey data (DHS) 2010. Women empowerment indicated by two dimensions of decision-making index and self-esteem index (attitudes towards physical abuse of spouses) and then constructed a cumulative index by combining these two indices. Age in years, children ever born, regular exposure to media, employment for cash, household wealth had a positive association. Meanwhile, age at first marriage, residence in the rural area, and the spousal age difference had a negative relationship with all three indices of women empowerment. This study examined various aspects of women empowerment and then combined these aspects into a single index. After index construction, the study focused on the most important determinants of women empowerment. Media exposure and employment had a strong positive association with decision making and self-esteem. On the other hand, women who were above than nineteen years age at the time of first marriage had a strong negative association with decision making and self-esteem (Alkire et al., 2013; Anand & Sen, 1994; Chakrabarti, 2017; Charmes & Wieringa, 2003; Krishnan, 2010).

Haq, Jali, and Islam (2017) had evaluated the role of women empowerment in the rural areas of Pakistan. An Index was constructed through six indicators of women empowerment: involvement in household matters, freedom in mobility, labor force participation, decision-related to child health, decisions in everyday household expenditures, and freedom to cast a vote. The study also found the determinants of women empowerment. Educational status, working status, household members, and health status proved to be the strong predictor of women empowerment. Women empowerment found a negative relationship with women's household size and health conditions [5] and a positive relationship with rural women's education.

Akram (2018) explored four women empowerment indicators--healthcare, social contacts, and decision-making participation. The additive index method had used to construct the women empowerment index. Order Logit regression analysis was applied to establish the relationship between the women empowerment index and its determinants. Women empowerment influenced by the age and gender of the head of the household, being a relative

---

[5] Suffering from any disease or not from the last year

of husband and family size negatively. On the other hand, husband's education and aware-ness from media contributed to the enhancement of women empowerment.

Baig et al. (2018) measured women empowerment through four dimensions--self-esteem, participation in decision making, freedom of mobility, and control over resources. Indices of women empowerment were constructed through Cronbach's alpha technique. Development in the rural areas was measured through access to healthy food, electricity, mobile communication, utilization of health care facilities, availability of education, and proper agricultural market. Ordinary least square techniques were employed to find the impact of participation in decision making, freedom of mobility, and self-esteem on rural development. All these three indicators of women empowerment had significant and positive effects, while control over resources was insignificant for rural development(Baig et al., 2018).

O'Hara and Clement (2018) described empowerment at the individual as well as at the household level. They used the WEIA for evaluating the extent of women empowerment in Nepal. According to them, the agriculture development sector limits the measurement of women's empowerment.

The results have been described in the qualitative fieldwork and in quantitative analysis. In the quantitative analysis, empowerment correlation had regressed with age, education, household wealth, income, and household composition on individual empowerment measuring by (WEAI). In which household composition has significantly correlated with women empowerment. Meanwhile, qualitative findings described that the ordinary sense of empowerment and empowerment definitions had agency distinction (O'Hara & Clement, 2018).

In the context of different regions, women empowerment/women autonomy had similarities and differences highlighted in the study of Jejeebhoy and Sathar (2001a). Data has been collected from Pakistan (Punjab) and India (Uttar Pradesh and Tamil Nadu). Women's autonomy was measured by four dimensions; economic decision making, mobility, freedom from the threat from husband, access to and control over financial resources, and making a summary index of all these dimensions using regression coefficient scores (Jejeebhoy & Sathar, 2001a). Primary school enrollment and secondary school enrollment have more positive and significant relation with women autonomy in Tamil Nadu than Punjab and Uttar Pardesh. While wage work in the last 12 months has more significant in Uttar Pradesh. Age has the same consequence on women's autonomy in all regions, while number of surviving sons was positive and insignificant in Punjab and significant in Uttar Pardesh. In contrast, the number of surviving daughters was insignificant in all three regions; living with mother-in-law/extended family negatively obstructed all three areas and dowry had positive effects on women's autonomy in all three regions (Jejeebhoy & Sathar, 2001a).

When the three religions and regions have been pooled in a regression analysis, then it had seemed that religion was acting an essential role in promoting female autonomy. Muslim women experienced more significant restrictions on their independence than Hindu women (Al-shami, Razali, & Rashid, 2018). Microcredit had seemed to be an effective instrument to empower women who were deprived of financial assistance and support (Al-shami et al., 2018).

This study intended to measure women empowerment by seven indicators mobility, daily expenditures decisions, children's school decisions, health expenditures decisions, loan order, use decisions, and assets purchase. Access to Amanah Ikhtiar Malaysia (AIM) was used as a microcredit indicator to determine its effects on several aspects of empowerment in urban Malaysia (Al-shami et al., 2018).

Ayevbuomwan, Popoola, and Adeoti (2016) examined women empowerment in rural Nigeria, followed by multidimensional poverty measures, and constructed a multidimensional women empowerment index using different dimensions. Production followed by decision making autonomy in agriculture, resources by ownership of house and land, education and time use followed by to visit family, listening radio and water sources had used to construct a single index by PCA. According to this index, 43%, women in rural Nigeria were disempowered.

The study discovered that the women's age, household head, and employment in the skilled and unskilled sector had the probability of increasing rural women's empowerment. On the other hand, the gender of household head, work in agriculture and allied industry, household size, and location of rural women in the Northern region of Nigeria have the probability of decreasing women empowerment in rural Nigeria as a multidimensional approach (Ayevbuomwan et al., 2016).

In educated families, women have awareness, financial resources, decision-making power regarding food, family life, and the freedom to go outside to see doctors and do other essential tasks without any hesitation. So, women need empowerment from society to perform their responsibilities independently (Caldwell & Caldwell, 1991; Ferrant & Kolev, 2016).

In developing countries, the awareness about women's problem, respect, empowerment, and family health is necessary. Because, the men's mentality required to be changed for the power balance in society. Without power balance home, community and country got imbalance which effects on home issues, social problem and country's political, economic and social status. So, giving respect to women is their human right by husband, society and state (Bari, 2005; Quamruzzaman & Lange, 2016).

Health is wealth because health is the fundamental human right of every child. So, if family, society, and country need healthy babies, they must be providing freedom, respect, confidence, and awareness to the women (Akram, 2018; Akter et al., 2017). In the above studies, researchers highlighted to give freedom, respect, care, healthy life, develop self-confidence, and self-esteem to women, which is the fundamental human right of women. At the same time, these studies highlights an imbalance in home, society, and country. Furthermore, this study also creates awareness among women who do not understand the meaning of empowerment and are doing unethical activities at their home, society, and country.

3.2   Women Empowerment and Child Health

There is a strong relationship between women's empowerment and child health. Empowered women can do better care for their child's health. This has been evidenced by the previous literature review as follows:

Kar, Pascual, and Chickering (1999) had identified the factors which could empower women and mothers for social and health activities. In all the cultures and regions, women considered the prime caregivers and made bold decisions for their children's health. Women's involvement in social and fitness activities could be promoted through women's empowerment. The procedure contains a meta-analysis of forty cases across the world. That determined the role of women/mother empowerment in social and health promotion programs.

In the previous literature, a link between women's work and child malnutrition in developing countries was limited and ambiguous (Mugo, Zwi, Botfield, & Steiner, 2015). Some studies found maternal employment to improves child malnutrition(Lamontagne, Engle, & Zeitlin, 1998). In other studies found that work increases the risk of malnutrition and infant death (Abbi, Christian, Gujral, & Gopaldas, 1991; Basu, 1992; Glick & Sahn, 1998), or that it was not statistically significant (Lamontagne et al., 1998; Mugo et al., 2015). Most of the other studies provide different results depending on the health outcome(Ukwuani & Suchindran, 2003a) or the gender of the child (Bhattacharya, Currie, & Haider, 2006)

Desai and Johnson (2005) explained the relationship between women's decision making and child health. Women's decision-making affects the child's health through day-to-day savior, access to resources, and emergency care. Demographic and Health Survey of twelve developing countries had used for estimation. Height for age, immunization, and child mortality were used to measure child health. Four decisions at individual and community level (household purchases large and daily, health care, visiting friends) was used to measure women's decision-making power.

Women education, father education, were used as control variables. The positive relationship between women's empowerment and child health was captured in this study in a different extent for each country. In Nepal and India, the relationship between women's empowerment and child health was influential compared to Sub-Saharan Africa and lesser in Latin America and the Caribbean's countries (Desai & Johnson, 2005).

Pongou, Ezzati, and Salomon (2006) evaluated the household, community, and environmental factors to determine Cameroon's child health. These three factors have significant importance in changing child health in the male child at 13-59 months. Maternal education, maternal age at first birth, and maternal health-seeking behavior showed a dynamic role in improving child health and improved sanitation and clean water. On the community level children living in the urban area had a better nutritional status than children living in rural areas.

The household and child health's socio-economic status had an interlinked relationship with each other's, and it has been proved in the previous studies. All the socio-economic determinants of child health had found an association with the mother's socioeconomic status. Awareness with health care precautions and the mother's education, age, working status, age at the time of first birth, child immunization, and the total number of children have a stronger influence on the child's health (Arif & Arif, 2012; Kabeer, 1999).

Meshram et al. (2012)investigated the extent of undernutrition among under-five year children. The sample has been collected through stratified random sampling from India. Nutrition status among children was observed through stunting, wasting, and underweight, and for simplicity, a composite index (CIAF) had constructed. Assessment of all these indices was made through WHO standard criterion of standard deviation units (terms as z score). Analysis of variance techniques and multivariate logistic regression was used for the analysis. The proportion of children underweight, and stunt was higher in India, and 63% CIAF was found among them. Deficiency in total calorie availability and low standard of living found to be a higher risk factor for causing malnutrition among the children.

In Nepal (Kapilvastu), 60% of children had malnutrition, 87% of women below 20 years' age at the time of their first pregnancy were considered a critical cause of malnutrition in Nepal. In the household's deficiency of food, lack of immunization, and poor care-seeking behavior hurts children's health and statistically significant. Mother's education and age were the most important factors to control malnutrition in children under five years(Bhandari & Chhetri, 2013).

Sujarwoto and Tampubolon (2013) found a causal relationship between the mother's social capital and child health. They adopted the channel as the mother's contribution to social activities improves the child's health and good child health prompt these activities while sick child restricts these activities and participation. Cross-sectional data of family surveys were used for the analysis. Children's characteristics, mother characteristics, social and community aspects were taken as control variables while the IV instrument variable was included in the model — all instruments were found positively correlated with the mother's social capital while uncorrelated with child health. The mother's age and education and the age of a child had a strong association with the mother's social capital. Mother's with an older child having a higher social capital. Mothers belong to the wealthiest communities having higher social capital, and all these factors were found to have a strong relationship with child health. Social capital, in the form of active and prosperous communities, improves child health mainly adjusts the child's height for age and weight for age. All social activities improve the mother's health and knowledge, which improved the child's health in turn and social capital (Sujarwoto & Tampubolon, 2013).

Scantlan and Previdelli (2013) explained a framework and a health pathway between women empowerment and child nutritional status. Direct measures like decision making and experience of violence had used instead of indirect measures like education and labor force participation. Decision making leads a woman to get better health care practices, and if there is no violence, then women became free from depression, which they were getting from the domestic violence. Age was also predating as an essential determinant as women older than husbands had more empowerment and had a strong and positive impact on child health.

Socioeconomic determinants of malnutrition in children of under five years age have been studied in Bangladesh. Stunting, wasting, and underweight as the measure of malnutrition, and both urban and rural areas had used in a separate analysis. Binary logistic regression was employed to find the socioeconomic determinants of malnutrition. Birth intervals, mother's education, and wealth index had a significant impact on malnutrition. Wealth index showed its influence on malnutrition in rural areas as compared to the urban areas. Mother higher education, better body mass index and more birth interval found to be in a healthy relationship with malnutrition(Khan & Raza, 2014).

Khan and Raza (2016a) explained the factors of malnutrition in Indian children under a five-year age. The composite index of anthropometric failure has formulated to check the extent of malnutrition among the children. The logit model was employed to find the determinants of malnutrition. Age, low birth interval and breastfeeding caused to increase the malnutrition while mother education, better body mass index and good wealth status found to negatively related to malnutrition in both rural and urban children.

Goode and Mavromaras (2014) examined the effects of family income on child health in the different age group between 0 to 17 years. They explained three pathways through which family income affects the child health, parental health awareness, household sanitation settings and nutrition consumption severed as mediators for improving child health. Family income had an essential role in enhancing child health up to the age of 12. Mother's age, education, and father age education have the probability of improving child health under the different age groups. Children under the age of 9-12 have shown more probability to stay with good health with higher family income.

Ibrahim, Tripathi, and Kumar (2015) had developed a link between the direct indicators of women empowerment--decision making with the child's health status. Child health outcomes, child stunting, and child immunization had shown a strong relationship with decision making. Women's with more independence in the decision making related to health, purchasing, spending of earning, and visit their family and relative, had more likely to be better care about their family and their children and enjoying the better health.

In developing countries to achieve the targets of SDG, it is necessary to empower their women (Hasan & Uddin, 2016). Children's health-seeking behavior was considered a significant factor of women empowerment along with the health care of women and decision making in household purchases. Women's and their husband's education, age, age at first marriage, occupation of women, and locality had their critical roles to boost up the women empowerment in developing countries like Bangladesh(Hasan & Uddin, 2016).

The risk of death, morbidity, and undernutrition of children under five years age could improve through the improved source of drinking water, sanitation, and non-solid cooking fuel in Sub-Saharan and South Asia (Anand & Roy, 2016). In developing countries, most of the children facing poor environmental conditions, which were the leading cause of poor health, especially in sub-Saharan countries where the shortage of food along with inadequate sources of drinking water, sanitation, and cooking fuel adversely affects child health (Anand & Roy, 2016).

The most common dimensions of women empowerment used in previous literature had made from direct (decision-making) and indirect indicators (labor force participation, health and education) of women empowerment (Jamal, 2018a). Instead of making separate dimensions of women empowerment, a combined index had a strong and positive impact on child nutritional status (Jamal, 2018a).

Maternal health had a significant impact on child health (Ahsan & Maharaj, 2018). Investment in child health and parental human capital are complimentary. Mother height and child height were correlated with each other. Parental human capital, education, and health were associated with the child's birth outcome (Ahsan & Maharaj, 2018).

Community norms and beliefs affect the women's attitudes towards care and health of their own and their children. Community and household's level decision making related to health have more effects on the child's survival as well as mothers' age at childbirth; education and wealth index had a significant impact on a child's nutritional status in Nigeria (Akinyemi, Adedini, & Odimegwu, 2017).

Women's employment had not been significantly affected the malnutrition in most developing countries when it had used as a binary variable. Regarding women employment, different occupations had different effects on the nutritional status of children. Clerical, sales and domestic jobs were associated with malnutrition in 49 developing countries and actively reduced malnutrition risk. Women's employment is not a good indicator of women's empowerment because work increases women's money power but reduces the time of care for their children(Assaad et al., 2014a). On the other hand, most women do the job because of poverty, so it is not a good indicator of women's autonomy (Burroway, 2017).

In the city of India (Nagpur), it had found that under five-year children of any community constitutes one of the nutritional deficiencies (underweight, stunting, and wasting). After calculating the composite anthropometric failure index in that city, about 58.59% of children in the slum areas face malnutrition. In this area, malnutrition was highly associated with poor socioeconomic status, uneducated mother, low birth weight, birth order, small birth interval, limited breastfeeding, immunization status, and childhood injuries (Dhok &

Thakre, 2016).

Women who got more education had the probability to married in the age above 15 years

old and more likely to use the contraceptive measures to control the fertility rate—de-

creases in fertility and early marriages trend to improve child health in developing countries

(Uganda). Women with more education would trade-off child quantity for child quality.

Women with more education seem to trade-off additional fertility to increase the invest-

ments in the children, which in turn improves the child's health (Keats, 2018).

Father's involvement in child health care activities limits the mother's empowerment in

decision-making. This may be expressive of women's capability to repel the patriarchy and

male dominance when they control their decision-making processes, including childcare

decisions. For improving women empowerment, it is necessary to review the father's in-

volvement in child health care because the patriarchy and traditional gender roles may af-

fect parental involvement in children's health care (Murshid, 2016a; Ukwuani &

Suchindran, 2003a).

Female political representation appeared to the dimension of women empowerment, which

hurts infant death and positively associated with measles vaccinations. Both cross-sectional

and longitudinal data of fifty-one developing countries proved this relationship that

women's political representation improved child health by increasing the spending on

mothers' health as mothers are more sensitive and closely involved in child health care to

fathers (Quamruzzaman & Lange, 2016).

Ibrahim and Pandey (2014) measured women's empowerment through decision-making, which positively impacted child health. The sample size 22,462 children in Nigeria and 45,516 in India were collected for analysis. The involvement of women in decision making about child health practices has approved the strong predictor of child well-being. This study provides evidence for the relationship between the indicators of women's empowerment and child health outcomes (Ibrahim & Pandey, 2014).

Malapit, Kadiyala, Quisumbing, Cunningham, and Tyagi (2015) studied the association between mother empowerment, childcare practices, and child nutrition in Nepal's rural areas. They used a cross-sectional dataset to construct the Women's Empowerment in Agriculture Index's (WEAI) covering the five Domains of Empowerment (5DE). All these sub-indices have been used to investigate the association between mother empowerment and child nutritional status. Child nutritional status has been measured through three indicators of nutrition length-for-age, weight-for-age z-score, and weight-for-length z-score in rural Nepal. Results have suggested that all these empowerment dimensions may influence child nutrition more than others in specific contexts.

Siddhanta and Chattopadhyay (2017) studied the relationship between child health and women empowerment. Microdata (Demographic and Health Survey) of Eastern India and Bangladesh had used to determine how much women empowerment has its impact on child health. According to data, stunting was found among the children below five years in Eastern India compared to Bangladesh. Women Empowerment was measured through direct indicators (decision making and freedom of movement)—indirect indicators (education and work status). Participation in decision making and freedom of movement had a significant role in reducing the stunting among the children. Education also had shown its considerable role in reducing the stunting, but work status increased stunting among the children (Siddhanta & Chattopadhyay, 2017). Women with thin and obese health had more probability of being a stunted child than healthy-weight women(Black et al., 2013). According to wealth status, children are less likely to be stunt than the wealthiest household. Mothers age more than 20 years had less likely to be having a stunted child. Birth order more than one had a positive impact on stunting, more the birth order more the stunting among the children (Siddhanta & Chattopadhyay, 2017).

Endris et al. (2017) explained the causes of health problems in developing countries. Ethiopia was selected as a sample country where malnutrition was found to be the leading cause of hunger. The composite anthropometric index had constructed to measure the presence of malnutrition. Logistic regression was used to detect the factors that were the leading cause of malnutrition among under-five-year children. In rural areas, 48.5% of children were found to be malnourished. Educated mothers, a household with prosperous wealth status, and children with more birth intervals reduced malnutrition among the children. Region of residence and malnutrition have been seen in a close relationship. Powerful and educated mothers always remained in the position to look after their children in a better way(Jamal, 2018a).

Vonaesch et al. (2017) investigated the prevalence of stunning and risk factors in Sub-Saharan Africa. In this region, boys' children were found to be having more chances to be stunt as compared to the girl child but did not find any biological reason. Some other socioeconomic risk factors promote the possibilities of stunting in children, most important were the income status of families, mother education, sanitation condition, child age, and family structure. In this region, most stunt children were overweight and increased the chance to pause the child's growth in the early five years.

In Mozambique, the mother's age, education, and body mass index improve child health. The female child showed fewer chances to be malnourished than a male child, and household wealth and urban residence had confirmed as a good indicator of child health in the study of Deutsch and Silber (2017). Women Empowerment (WE) is a social network that focuses on providing events and communication to improve child health with the power of collaboration, engagement, and growth, women education, the right to vote freely, may take part in economic activities, may take part in every walk of life as independent citizens of the country, decision making, should be religiously free, etc. (Deutsch & Silber, 2017).

Tracey and Polachek (2018) indicated the significance of the relationship between child health and parent's investment, specifically focus on the role of fathers in childcaring, which in turn had a positive impact on different aspects of child health. In this study, the new thing was that the child who has their father's resemblance got more care and love from their fathers. Mothers provide general information about child health index used as a dependent variable. The father's involvement follows different indicators like the number of health care visits for illness, the number of emergency room visits, and the most extended stay in hospitals as dependent variables. The study found a positive and significant impact of the father's resemblance to child health by employing the two Least Square models. It had shown that a child had more similarities with her father at birth; father invests more than that child who had no analogy with their fathers.

In Uganda, women's schooling had decreased fertility, and this decrease, in return, enhance the child's health. Microdata (Demographic and Health Survey) of Uganda was used for analysis, and the Ordinary Least Square technique was employed for the outcome. As women completed their schooling to higher education, delay in their childbirth — women seeking for best employment status and focused on reducing the child quantity and increasing the child quality. Child health outcomes were found by observing that women with higher schooling better looked after their children, reducing the children's diseases and ratio of malnutrition among the children (Keats, 2018).

Roy et al. (2018) assessed the undernutrition status of children from West Bengal and India. Composite Index of Anthropometric Failure has been constructed of the children under five years to measure malnutrition. This was a cross-sectional study, and 142 samples were collected from the Nasibpur Primary Health Center, Singur. This study attempted to determine the factors that influence the Composite Index of Anthropometric Failure (CIAF). Composite Index of Anthropometric Failure had classified into seven groups, one of which was no failure. Overall, 36.1%, children were found to be having CIAF. Children belong to the Muslim religion, female sex, and mothers with low education were malnourished.

Ziba, Kalimbira, and Kalumikiza (2018) estimated the burden of aggregate anthropometric failure among the Malawian children. The study described the undernutrition status of under five-year children through the indicators of the composite index of anthropometric failure in the context of the most popular measures of anthropometric stunting, wasting, and underweight. CIAF was further divided into seven groups, one with no loss and the other six with failure.

Augsburg and Rodríguez-Lesmes (2018) examined the relationship between child health and sanitation coverage, focusing on their causal relationship. The height indicated child health for age (stunt growth), which was considered a significant cause of many diseases. Primary data was collected from India for analysis. A healthy relationship was found between child health and sanitation in the early years of children. Safe and better sanitation provision had a significant role in improving the child's health in height for age, weight for age, and weight for height.

In Nations, either rich or poor, health and gender inequalities are responsible for causing mortality and morbidity in children under five-year children. Like education, social factors played a positive role in enhancing child health through a pathway of health behavior, psychosocial environment, and nutritional diet (Spencer, 2018).

Jones et al. (2019) adapted the Kabeer (1999) framework of resource-agency-outcome to investigated three domains of women empowerment (human and social assets, intrinsic agency, and instrumental agency) in East Africa and explained the pathway (maternal BMI, Household Wealth) through which these domains affect the child health. They developed the path using the structural equation model concluded that social and human assets indirectly affect child health through the maternal body mass index. In contrast, the intrinsic agency directly affects the child's health in the low wealth household, and instrumental agency affects the child health in the higher wealth household. Maternal BMI and household wealth directly related to women empowerment and women empowerment had a positive and significant effect on child health.

In low- and middle-income countries, gender equity was considered a better way to empower their women. Empowered women or empowered mothers had positive health-seeking behavior for their children. Mothers always have a greater interest in the health of their children as compared to their father, and this hypothesis was tested by Ekbrand and Halleröd (2018) on the 49 low and middle-income countries and proved that countries with a high degree of gender equity in health and education had a low level of health and food deprivation. In poor communities of Sub-Saharan Africa, the prevalence of malnutrition in under five years children appears significantly. Many socioeconomic and biological factors got focused on how these factors could reduce malnutrition for curing this severe health deprivation. Besides all these factors, Ross-Suits (2010) explained the role of maternal autonomy in the reduction of malnutrition at household level by testing the 2004-2005 Tanzanian (Demographic and Health Survey) dataset. Furthermore, proved a positive and significant role of maternal autonomy in reducing malnutrition in poor communities.

Malnutrition is a common problem in developing countries during pregnancy. Women cannot get proper food, which is required during pregnancy, either they eat excessively or lack of nutrition's, vitamins, minerals, and iron deficiencies (Endris, Asefa, & Dube, 2017;

WHO, 2016, 2018). The main reason for malnutrition is lack of care, unavailability of food, unawareness about proper diet, expensive food prices which are not affordable by their husbands. The ultimate results of malnutrition are the stunting, wasting and underweight problems in their children (Dasgupta, Parthasarathi, Biswas, & Geethanjali, 2014).

Children having with low height for age are considered to be stunted, it caused due to malnutrition. Stunting is associated with households, social and economic conditions. Unfortunately, stunting is starting during the pregnancy because the mother was not treated well, and their health and food got ignored (UNICEF, 2019; Vonaesch et al., 2017). Also, in pregnancy women need more nourishing food full of vitamins, minerals, and irons to give healthy birth. Child health and child survival are ultimately related to health, diet, and care of mothers (WHO, 2016). So, a malnourished girl, less than 18 years cannot birth a healthy baby (WHO, 2011, 2016).

The malnutrition can cause wasting, which is a severe problem regarding weight for height in children. Women should care about their health during pregnancy and child health from their birth to five years (UNICEF, 2018). Women must notice about their children weight and height and compare it regularly with standard weight-height index recommend by doctors to avoid wasting problems in their children. If mothers feel their child weight and height is not matching with each other, then they must consult with doctors to take precautionary measures and medicines to reduce the risk of death in wasting children (Scantlan & Previdelli, 2013; WHO, 2016, 2018).

Underweight is less weight of child according to their age. It is very common in developing countries because women do not get proper food to maintain their health as well as their babies. Underweight is a serious health condition of a child because an underweight child may be a stunt and wast (WHO, 2018). According to the literature, 1.9 billion adults are overweight or obese, and 462 million were underweight (WHO, 2018). At the same time, 52 million children under five years were wasted, 17 million severely wasted, and 155 million were stunted, while 41 million are overweight or obese, around 45% of deaths among children under five years linked to undernutrition (WHO, 2018). In 2014, approximately 462 million adults worldwide were underweighted, while 1.9 billion were either overweight or obese (WHO, 2018). In 2016, an estimated 155 million children under the age of five years were suffering from stunting, while 41 million were overweight or obese (WHO, 2018). These mostly occur in low- and middle-income countries. (WHO, 2018).

3.3   Research Contribution

This study seeks to fill the research gap in three distinct and novel ways; first, this study estimates women empowerment in five domains and determining women empowerment's contextual factors.

In literature, women's empowerment has been defined as a process (Bates et al., 2004; Batliwala, 1993; Batliwala, 1994; Batliwala, 1995; Batliwala et al., 1995; Kabeer, 1999, 2001, 2002, 2011; Lee-Rife, 2010; Mosedale, 2005), while others see it as a goal (Kishor, 2000; Tengland, 2008; Zimmerman & Rappaport, 1988). Additionally, the understanding of women's empowerment becomes complicated by the interchangeable uses of carefully related terms like women's status, women's autonomy, and gender as research phenomena (Tengland, 2008).

It is challenging to define empowerment in a single dimension because it is a multidimensional process. Change does not occur in one step; it takes time, strategies, and planning. If a person who denied making choices and suddenly asked him/her to make choices, she/he cannot make choices in the right way and according to requirement until she/he is not aware of their capabilities, goals, self-efficacy, and their role in society.

Adapting the Kabeer (1999) , resource-agency-achievement framework, the present study explained empowerment as a process to recognized a complete responsibility and choices made by women. Furthermore, the process is a series of actions or steps need to get results in terms of five interlinked dimensions. Work status and awareness are the preconditions to implementation of decisions (agency) and then after decision making its outcomes can comes in terms of self-esteem and self-confidence. The people who have more ability to make choices in their daily lives may be more potent in one domain, but they may not be empowered in other domains (Kabeer, 2011, 2012). Furthermore, contextual factors have been used to determine women's empowerment.

Second, this study used to measure child health through the nutritional status of children under five years by using anthropometric measures- stunting(height-to-age), wasting(weight-to-height), underweight (weight-to-age), and a composite index of anthropometric failure instead of using sole measure used in previous studies (Beal et al., 2018; Hamad, Sarwar, Ranjha, & Ahmad, 2016; Jamal, 2018a; Mary, 2018a, 2018b; Shah, Selwyn, Luby, Merchant, & Bano, 2003; Siddhanta & Chattopadhyay, 2017; Teshome, Kogi-Makau, Getahun, & Taye, 2009; UNICEF, 2019; Vonaesch et al., 2017) and find out the impact of women empowerment on four different measures of child health instead of

finding only socioeconomic and demographic determinants of child health (Achakzai &
Khan, 2016; Hamad et al., 2016; Kanamori & Pullum, 2013; Khan & Raza, 2014, 2016a;
Kumar, Mittal, & Sharma, 2010; Laghari et al., 2015).

Moreover, existing empirical studies have focused mainly on South Asia and Sub-Saharan
Africa, leaving out Southeast Asia, Central Asia, West Asia, Latin America, and Caribbean
countries. Indeed, many child health-related risk factors need to be addressed in these
areas, and an attempt should include in the current study. Focusing on the importance and
need of regional study, the third part of this study covered regional analysis, which was not
done in the previous literature.

CHAPTER 4: THEORETICAL FRAMEWORK

This chapter is divided into two parts. The theoretical and conceptual framework for the measurement of women empowerment adapting the Kabeer's framework of empowerment, including the author's own suggested objective measures of women empowerment following the previous literature (figure 4.1) and determinants of women empowerment (figure 4.2), has been presented in the first part. The second part covers the theoretical and conceptual framework for child health and women empowerment following the theories of Health Services Utilization by Andersen and Newman and Grossman Demand for Health. Under these two pinning theories, the author' developed her conceptual framework to coherent the link between women empowerment and child health (figure 4.3).

4.1 Women Empowerment Theories

Women empowerment is a complex concept, and it is tough to gather enough data on women's empowerment at all levels to measure process, agency, and achievement. However, in this study, an effort was made to measure women's empowerment at the household level across the thirty-three developing countries using the latest available data from the Demographic and Health Surveys. In this study, an attempt has been made to capture the framework of women empowerment. Under the light of the previous approaches; the capabilities approach (Sen, 1993) and the Kabeer (2005) resource-agency-outcome approach, Kishore and Reid (2000) evidence-source-setting, and Sharaunga, Mudhara, and Bogale (2016), instance-resource-agency.

Theoretically and conceptually, the present study based on the following theories because the selected indicators for the measurement of women empowerment are described well through these theories

4.1a. Feminism

The questions were raised from the centuries how women ought to be viewed and treated in society? Moreover, how women are viewed and processed in the community? There is a gap between what should happen and what is happening. This gap could be filled by change, and to bring this change a movement, and ideology is obligatory. The name of progress and ideology to identify women's role and accept her individuality is called Feminism. A doctrine of Feminism was dividing by Jaggar (1983) into three main parts/theories as follows

   i.   Liberal feminism

  ii.   Marxist/Socialist feminisms

 iii.   Radical feminism

i.   Liberal Feminism

Liberal Feminism follows a woman as an individual, and this individual should be free to move, free in decisions, and every right should be shifted to women because men and women both possess 'reasons' and 'rationality.' There should be no discrimination based on sex anywhere. Liberal feminism was egalitarian and reformist, not against the established basic structure of society. Marry Wollstonecraft the great feminist raised her voice and wrote in her book " Vindication of the Rights of Women" (Janes, 2017;

Wollstonecraft, 1792) women are equally capable as men; they should have all the rights that men have and gave rise to the demand of equality and end of discrimination/ emancipation.

John Stuart Mill (Mill, 1869), Martha C. Nuasbaum (Nussbaum, 1997), Friedan and Steinem (Fox, 2006) and Susan Moler Okin (Okin, 1989) John Locke (Hirschmann & McClure, 2010), David Hume (Jacobson, 2010), Jeremy Benthan (Collard, 2006), has significant contribution in the liberalism and argued that men and women are not confined with public and private spheres categorically by sex. Women should have equal right to enter in the public area like men because the root cause of female injustice and oppression is that all the work of females in the informal sector is unpaid and the government has no interference (Marshall, 2006).

Liberal feminists favor reforms by governments for giving the rights to the oppressed part of society or the people with less power. Such reforms would be effective through the channels of political and legal platforms. These reforms raise a change in economic opportunity, sharing responsibilities, education, health, and mass media. For liberal feminists, the ideal level of gender equality can enable the individuals to accept the lifestyle that suits a person being a weak part of society, and sufficient for their well-being (Gorey, Daly, Richter, Gleason, & McCallum, 2003; MacKinnon, 1983).

Mill and Mill (1970) supported the work of women outside their homes. Women should be attained autonomy and freedom for educational facilities, workload, rewards, and share in politics.

Friedan (1981) reinforced the idea that society should constantly reduce gender differences and develop a more equitable social system. To reduce gender inequality, liberal feminists had proposed measures that include equal economic and educational opportunities in society. Therefore, state intervention is a prerequisite for women's movement (Mill & Mill, 1970).

ii.   Marxist/Socialist Feminism

The words Marxism and Socialism are not identical, but both the words collectively derived their ideas from the pioneering work of Karl Marx (Marx, 2000a). Both the terms Marxist and Socialist, when used with feminism, define an explicit nature of feminism. They both follow a society model where the difference between the two classes is at their central attention. In feminism, men and women are those two broad concerns. Both concerns deals with the issue of power and subordination in society. Men have usually enjoyed power over women in all known societies resulting in women's subordination and inferior status (Haraway, 1990; Riley, 1988).

In the case of Marxism, those classes which control the forces of production have enjoyed power over those who have no control over the production, distribution, and exchange. Marxism feminists considered capitalism as the root cause of women's oppression, in these societies, women play the role to maintain and reproduce the workforce in a cheap way, act as a reserve army of labor, and treated as "slave of the slave"(Marx & Engels, 1970).

Marxism does not make a separate case for the exploitation of women. Women are part of the depressed classes who would be liberated once the capitalist system. Before the capitalist society was matriarchal, properties were transferred throw mother. Center of production was family; men and women worked together (Williams & Williams, 1977). But after capitalist society became patriarchal, mother rights have overthrown. Center of production was factory, and women were confined to domestic work. There should be a need to develop a relationship between material conditions and power structure within the family (Marx & Engels, 1970).

Moreover, men worked in factories; men who earn more than their needs, started to invest it and generate more wealth. Economic determinism is a fundamental concept in Marxism. This means that the economy determines the nature of most things in society (Marx & Engels, 1970). The concept rests on the belief that society has an economic base and a superstructure, and this superstructure consists of a world of ideas which may include religion, art, and literature. In other words, in classical Marxist theory, economy, rather than patriarchy, is the prime factor. This gave more importance to men who began to control the means of production; on the other hand, thus, women confined their services for domestic work (Marx & Engels, 1970).

Moreover, the change in inheritance process from matriarchal to patriarchal became the root cause for the women's exploitation, and the institution of the family was well-thought-out as the place which settled a relation of supremacy and subsidiary between men and women (Voloshinov & Bachtin, 1986).

Marx and Engels, the overthrow of patriarchal and property right again transfer to women, women can obtain the freedom of social, political, economic, and personal action. Marxist feminists suggest economic equality between men, and there should be wages for women workers (Marx, 1973). According to Marx, women's work is not only productive but also creative. One of the flaws of this theory is that Marxist feminisms demand creating a classless society rather than a genderless society and unable to understand women's problems, including women's individuality (Marx, 2000b).

iii.   Radical Feminism

Till 1960, there was no distinct feminist view, but after the 1960s, few feminists believe that neither liberalism nor socialism can understand the women's problem. Men originate all these ideologies, and they designed to keep women as subordinate (Koedt, Levine, Rapone, & Koedt, 1973). There is a need for a systematic theory of women's oppression that originated from the oppressed (Echols, 1989).

Radical Feminism is an independent ideology to explain women rights without following liberal feminism and socialist feminism. However, during the same time, some feminists did not believe in reforming the system but radically rearrange it by displacing patriarchal power structures (Daly, 2016). These women supposed themselves as rebels, and their inspiration to improve women's condition arose in the context of their participation in necessary activities where they found themselves excluded from equal power by the men within these activities (Tong, 2009).

According to Radical feminists, the root cause of women's oppression was patriarchy. In her book-Sex Politics (1970), Kate Millet wrote that male supremacy and dominance were maintained in society by linking sex to gender and by confining women to private life (Millett, 2016). There should be a need to explain sex and gender should work in different ways. Sex is a biological identity, while gender determined the social role of an individual (Osmond & Thorne, 2009).

Male is strong, powerful, and independent, so males with masculine traits become men; on the other side, females are polite, loving, caring, and nurturing, so females with feminine qualities become women. Society artificially considers gender while the sex is biologically determined. Biological determinism "Biology is Destiny" this idea is challenged by radical feminists (Butler, 1986).

Shulamith Firestone wrote in her book The Dialectic of Sex (1970) that the root of women oppression lies in the reproductive roles of men and women. To liberate women, they need to be 'freed' from these roles by replacing biological reproduction with artificial reproductive techniques (Firestone, 2003). Gender roles can be changed because these artificial reproductive roles cause the most harm and disadvantages to women. Division of labor is based on gender; men will work in the public sphere and participate in politics, doing business and entering the police, army, and military (Firestone, 2003).

On the other hand, women are going to the private sphere and become part of domestic's work (unpaid work), rearing children, and take care of their families. Men get the advantage of their paid work, which gives them power and dominance; meanwhile, women working in private sphere remained unpaid (Ferrant, Pesando, & Nowacka, 2014), and their work gives them sub-ordinance and inferior status. Radical feminists have a moderate approach and extreme approach; according to moderate approach the solution to overthrow this male dominance is to de-link the sex and gender, destroy all forms of male biasness and establish a genderless society (Crow, 2000).

4.2   Capability Approach and "Development as Empowerment"

Amartya Sen's terminology terms, the Capability Approach distinguishes between capabilities or capability and functioning: "The concept of 'functioning,' which has distinctly Aristotelian roots, reflects the various things a person may value of doing or being (Amartya & Foster, 1997; Sen, 1993). The value of functioning may vary from simple ones, such as being adequately nourished and being free from avoidable disease, to very complex activities or personal states, such as taking part in the life of the community and having self-respect. A person's 'capability' refers to the alternative combinations of functioning that are feasible for her to achieve" (Amartya & Foster, 1997; Sen, 1993).

Real numbers can represent the number or degree of work each person likes, and upon completion, his or her actual achievements can be viewed as an active vector. The capabilities sets consist of alternate feature vectors from which they can select. The 'capability set' would consist of the alternative functioning vectors from which she can choose. (Amartya & Foster, 1997; Sen, 1993). An individual's mix of jobs reflects their first accomplishments, while a combination of capabilities represents the freedom to perform: other sets of jobs that humans can choose from (Amartya & Foster, 1997; Sen, 1993).

4.3   Conceptual Framework: Women Empowerment and its Determinants

The conceptual framework was developed with the consideration of previous studies and the theoretical framework. The conceptual framework develops the relationship between the study (Sekaran & Leong, 1992). Figure 2.1 represents the conceptual framework for the present study, which indicates women empowerment.

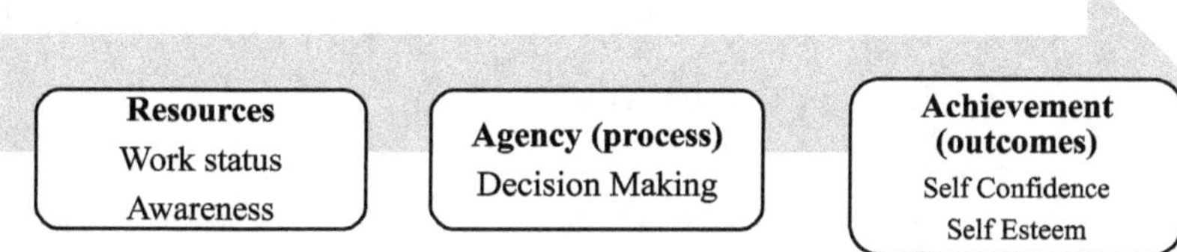

Figure 4.1: Conceptual Framework of Women Empowerment (Kabeer, 1999, 2005; Kishore & Reid, 2000; Sen, 1993)

This study documented five domains of women empowerment by following the resource-agency-outcome approach(Kabeer, 1999), resources are necessary for the self-transfor-mation, agency for self-determination, and achievement in the form of self-esteem and self-confidence. This study defined women empowerment as a process of self-transformation and self-determination through work status, awareness, the participation in decision mak-ing, having self-esteem and self-confidence following the Kabeer's resource-agency-achievement approach

1. Resources: Work status and awareness are essential for self-transformation (Naryan, 2002; Rissel, 1994; Rodwell, 1996; Sen & Batliwala, 2000) means transforming of one's thoughts, actions and behavior, evidenced as pre-conditions of change.

2. Agency: Participation in decision making is necessary for self-determination(Bandura, 1982; Rappaport, 1981; Rappaport, 1984, 1985). It is a process (agency) by which one

84

can control life, believe to control one's destiny, and enable a person to make meaningful and purposive choices.

3. Achievement: Self-esteem provide worth and believe in acting in the right ways (Batliwala et al., 1995; Frankenberg & Thomas, 2001). Self-confidence and self-esteem (Habibov et al., 2017; Jamal, 2017; Jamal, 2018a) provide worth and assurance in one's judgment, ability, and power.

In light of previous literature, women empowerment has been determined through socioeconomic characteristics like age, education, occupation, wealth, marital status, and microcredit. In this study, an attempt has been made to find out the contextual factors(Batool 2018, Toufique 2016), women characteristics, husband characteristics, and household characteristics in a single model to determine women empowerment in the five regions (South and Southeast Asia, West Asia, Central Asia, Latin America, and Caribbean Countries and Sub-Saharan Africa).

In the present study, the factors of women empowerment have divided into five parts; in part one, all the outcomes of interests like women's health, women's education, age difference with husband, and age at first birth are included (Assaad et al., 2014a; Ibrahim & Pandey, 2014). In the next four parts, determinants have chosen, directly and indirectly affecting women's empowerment, which is related to family, husband, household, parents, locality, and children.

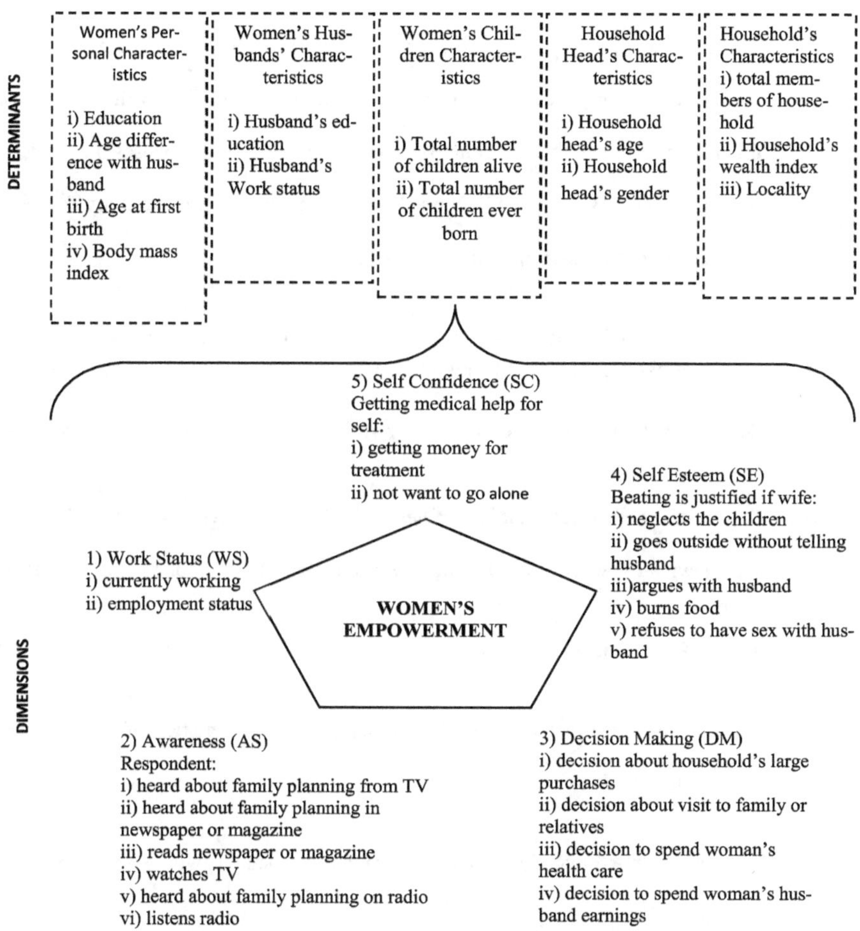

Figure 4.2: Dimensions and determinants of women's empowerment (Mahmud et al., 2012)

Women Empowerment and Child Health

This framework aims to formulate a mechanism through which child health is influenced by women empowerment and other related control variables. Many theories conceptualize the demand and supply for health, but the present study only focuses on the demand side following health services utilization theories because the present study focused on how women empowerment improves child health.

    i.   Model of Health Services Utilization by Andersen and Newman
   ii.   Grossman Model of Demand for Health

4.4   Andersen and Newman Framework of Health Services Utilization

A person's need, access, and use of health facilities was precise in the model of Anderson and Newman Framework of health services in 1973 through four stages(Andersen, 1995).

i.   Predisposing Factors

Predisposing factors are the socio-demographic characteristics of persons that happen before their illness.

a) Social Frame: Education, occupation, ethnicity, social networks, social interactions, and culture

b) Health Beliefs: Attitudes, values, and knowledge that people have concerning and towards the health care system

c) Demographic: Age and Gender

ii.   Enabling Factors

Enabling factors are the valuable aspects of the family or person to obtain care.

a) At Personal/Family Level: It is the understanding of the resources and their access like health services, income, and health insurance to better health.

 b) At Community Level: At the community level, it is the availability of personal health services, time spent on health, etc.

c) Possible additions: These factors are related to genetic and psychological characteristics.

iii.   Need Factors

Need factors are the sudden appearance of disease, and health problems and require the immediate help and functions of health care services. "Perceived need factors help to know care-seeking and observance to medical treatment, while assessed need base factors further carefully needed the kind and amount of treatment that provided to a patient from medical care provider (Andersen, 1995)."

● Perceived: "How people view their general health and functional state, as well as how they experience symptoms of illness, pain, and worries about their health and whether or not they judge their problems to be of sufficient importance and magnitude to seek profes-sional help (Andersen, 1995)."

● Evaluated: "Represents professional judgment about people's health status and their need for medical care (Andersen, 1995)."

iv. **Environment**

It refers to

a) General Health care system

b) External Health care systems

4.5   Grossman Model of Demand for Health

Grossman Model of Demand for health is the standard model for the demand for health and healthcare utilization (Grossman, 1972). This model is mainly focused on the three leading roles of health

i.   Health is consumption good; it contributes directly to the individual's utility function each period. Being healthy is valuable in and of itself

ii. Health is input into production. It generates productive time, which is useful for producing more health.

iii. Health is a form of capital. Unlike the home right, it endures from period to period. It can accumulate or depreciate over time. So, an improvement in health today can lead to better health tomorrow.

In this model, health is regarded as capital, and increases capital due to investment in health (such as health services or spending time on health activities) and depreciates due to factors such as age. People used health as consumption good (Grosman, 1972). A good meal at a certain level of consumption means that it is more effective than bad health. For example, a frustrated person will not be more efficient than a hearty man than he is not frustrated (Grossman, 1972).

On the other hand, the demand for health is based on health as an investment commodity. Health manages the total time available for work and non-work, such as the ability to make money. The days of poor health will bring them more discomfort, and these days cannot make money. Therefore, increasing health can make better use of time, which can be measured by money. This may be a return on investment in health. In addition to the two main reasons mentioned above for good health, health is also crucial for determining longevity (Grossman, 1972).

After Grossman's perceptual work, some theoretical studies have been carried out (Cropper, 1977; Wolfe, Jaffa, Wilson and, 1985), and more recent studies (Ehrlich & Chuma, 1990; Eisenring, 1999), but the model has retained.

The theoretical correlation between health needs (i.e., health standards/stocks) and medical needs (i.e., health investments/health insurance) on the one hand and changes in health, age, education, income, and lifetime wages, on the other hand, has compared to pure consumption models (comparison of empirical results of pure investment models), research has not reported (Gerdtham & Johannesson, 1999; Nocera & Zweifel, 1998; Wagstaff, 1993; Zweifel & Breyer). Husband used income, education, gender, and age as explanatory variables to estimate the demand for health equation. These studies have empirically tested the results obtained from the model of Grossman, 1972.

4.6   Conceptual Framework of Child Health

In this study, child health was measured by a composite index of anthropometric failure, which was constructed of three sub-indicators of malnutrition (stunting, wasting, and underweight). Malnutrition causes many diseases (Helminthic, infections, Injuries, Acute respiratory infections, including pneumonia) and increases deaths in children under five years. The conceptual framework of child health based on Anderson and Newman's model and Grossman model. These models are a more consistent tool for the study of health. According to the conceptual framework, child health (measured by nutrition level) is a function of four sets of factors: predisposing (demographic and social) factors, enabling factors (economic) factors, need-based factors, and environment.

i.   Predisposing Factors

Anderson and Newman's model has adopted evaluating the relationship between child health and predisposing factors (father education, father age, mother education, total children ever born) have an association to improve the child's health. Most children have more propensities to be ill compared to other children because of predisposing factors. Intake of nutrition predicted by individual characteristics—Mother characteristics, father characteristics, number of children, and total household size. Children with specific father/mother characteristics are more likely to have good health or bad health, depending on nutrition intake.

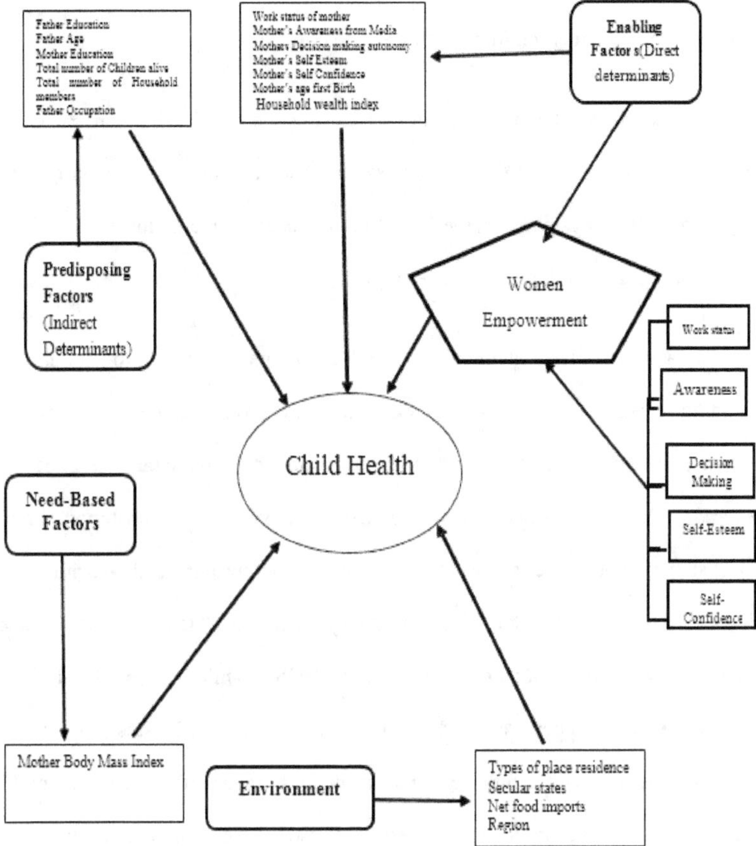

Figure 4.3: Child Health Model (Anderson & Newman, 1973)

ii.   Enabling Factors

The relationship between child health and enabling factors may lead to improve child health. These factors must be available to enable the family to act on a cost or satisfy a nutrition intake need. Enabling factors allows the family to provide all sources to their children that make their children with good health.

Women empowerment and child health are closely related to each other. Enabling factors (mother's work status, mother's awareness from media, mother's decision-making autonomy, mother's self-esteem, mother's self-confidence) enable a mother to be healthy and sturdy care of their children in a better way.

As more as women have autonomy in the decision making related to health, purchasing, spending of earning, and about to visit their family and relative, they can be more likely to be better care about their family and their children and enjoying the better health(Ibrahim & Pandey, 2014). Work status of women has an ambiguous relationship with child nutritional status; some studies support this relationship in improving child nutritional status for Nigeria (Ukwuani & Suchindran, 2003b), Pakistan (Jamal, 2018b), and India (Bhattacharya et al., 2006; Lamontagne et al., 1998). While some studies have proved a negative relationship between work status and child nutritional status (Lamontagne et al., 1998), Awareness with health care precautions has higher influence on the child's nutritional status(Arif & Arif, 2012). Women's self-esteem has a significant role in enhancing women behavior and attitude towards the family and children's care (Jamal, 2018b). Bases on work status and awareness, household decision-making, self-esteem, self-confidence and household wealth, emerged from the qualitative research process in determining child health (Scantlan & Previdelli, 2013).

iii.   **Need-Based Factors**

Need-based factors are perceived factors, how people view their general health status, and feel the pain of worries and face diseases. In the present model, mother body at first birth significantly influence child health.

iv.   **Environment**

Environment and child health are correlated with each other, place of living, secular states, net food imports and regions have an essential role in determining child health.

Table 4.1: Summary of Theoretical Framework

Variables	Description	Citations
Dependent Variables		
Child Health	Stunting (height for age)	(Beal et al., 2018; Hamad et al., 2016; Mary, 2018a, 2018b; Shah et al., 2003; Siddhanta & Chattopadhyay, 2017)
	Wasting (weight for height)	(Khan & Raza, 2014; Messelu & Trueha, 2016)
	Underweight (weight for age)	(Müller & Krawinkel, 2005; Solanki, Patel, Shah, & Singh, 2014)
	CIAF (Composite Index of Anthropometric Failure)	(Dhok & Thakre, 2016; Khan & Raza, 2016)
Independent Variables		
Predisposing Factors	Father Education	(Ahsan & Maharaj, 2018; Akinyemi et al., 2017)
	Father Age	(Burroway, 2017; Keats, 2018)
	Mother Education	(Bushra & Wajiha, 2015; Ibrahim et al., 2015)
	Father Occupation	(Goode & Mavromaras, 2014)
	Total children ever Born	(Arif & Arif, 2012)

	Total number of Household members	(Goode & Mavromaras, 2014; Khan & Raza, 2016a)
Enabling Factors	Women Empowerment Index	(Deutsch & Silber, 2017; Jamal, 2017)
	Work status of the mother	(Siddhanta & Chattopadh-yay, 2017)
	Mother's Awareness from Media	(Meshram et al., 2012; Sujarwoto & Tampubolon, 2013)
	Mothers Decision making Autonomy	(Desai & Johnson, 2005; Pokhrel & Sauerborn, 2004)
	Mother's Self Esteem	(Deutsch & Silber, 2017)
	Mother's Self Confidence	New Contribution
	Household Wealth index	(Jones et al., 2019; Tong, 2009)
	Mother's age at first Birth	(Pongou et al., 2006)
Need-Based Factors	Mother Body Mass Index	(Jones et al., 2019; Khan & Raza, 2014, 2016a)
Environment	Locality	(Ekbrand & Halleröd, 2018; Tong, 2009)
	Secular State	New Contribution
	Net Food Imports	New Contribution
	Region	New Contribution

CHAPTER 5: METHODOLOGY

This chapter deals with model specification, variables, source of data, and sets of countries selected for the current study.   The present chapter is based on the methodology with model specification, data, variables, and analytical techniques applied to found women empowerment(dimensions), constructions of composite women empowerment index, and to predict the determinants of women empowerment.   After that, it presents the analytical techniques employed to determine the relationship between women's empowerment and child health.

5.1   Data Collection and Set of Countries

For this study, data has accessed from the nationally representative Demographic and Health Surveys. DHS data is best for comparable study across the countries. DHS comes and modifies from World Fertility Surveys and Contraceptive Prevalence Surveys executed in the 1970s and 1980s. Since 1984, The Demographic and Health Surveys (DHS) Database has provided technical assistance to more than 300 demographic and health surveys in over 90 countries in Africa, Central Asia, West Asia, Southeast Asia and Southeast Asia, Latin America and Caribbean's. According to the previous surveys, collecting data for the DHS is original and comparable population-based on fertility, contraception, reproductive health, maternal health, immunization and survival, HIV/AIDS; maternal mortality, child mortality, malaria, and nutrition status of women and children in developing economies.

The primary objective and methodology of DHS Program are to expand and improve the data collection and use of data by host countries and for the policymakers. The Core questionnaires used for Demographic and Health Surveys cover a broader range of population and health topics.

Demographic and Health Surveys collect primary data using three plentiful types of questionnaires. A household questionnaire, men questionnaire, and women questionnaire. A household questionnaire is used to collect information on characteristics of the household's residence unit and data related to women and children's height and weight in the household. It is also used to identify members of the household who are eligible for an individual interview. Eligible respondents are then interviewed using an individual questionnaire as women and men questionnaires.

In a majority of DHS surveys, eligible individuals include women of reproductive age (15-49) and men age 15-59, or in some cases 15-54. In some countries, only women interviewed. Individual questionnaires include information on fertility, family planning, and maternal and child health.

DHS program sanctioned the data for research, and it is straightforward to access the required surveys at no cost(DHS Program). It is required to register on the DHS program and submitted the proposal along with the list of countries. The same process has been followed and got the latest datasets. Moreover, finally, access to the data sets was officially granted by the Demographic and Health Survey program.

The current study thirty-three, developing countries have chosen from the five different regions, Central Asia, Latin America and the Caribbean, West Asia, South, and Southeast Asia and Sub Saharan Africa. Countries set to be selected according to data available on the same questions related to women's work status, awareness, decision-making, self-esteem, self-confidence, stunting, wasting, and underweight. This study tried to extract the same indicators of women empowerment and child health from the DHS survey across the developing countries. Finally, data on the same indicators extracted from DHS's latest yearly survey on thirty-three countries. The description of countries selected for analysis is given in Table 5.1

Table 5.1: Selectin of Countries from Developing Regions

Regions	Developing Economies	Ever Married Women 15-49	Years
West Asia	Azerbaijan	8444	2005-2006
	Jordan	11352	2011-2012
	Armenia	6116	2015-2016
Central Asia	Tajikistan	9656	2011-2012
	Kyrgyz republic	8208	2011-2012
	Pakistan	13558	2012-2013
South and Southeast Asia	Timor Leste	13137	2009-2010
	Cambodia	17578	2013-2014
	India	124385	2005-2006
	Nepal	12674	2010-2011
Latin America and Caribbean	Haiti	14287	2011-2012
	Honduras	22757	2011-2012
	Peru	23888	2011-2012
	Guatemala	25914	2014-2015
Sub-Saharan Africa	Ethiopia	15683	2015-2016
	Gabon	8422	2011-2012
	Gambia	10233	2011-2012
	Comoros	5329	2011-2012
	Congo Democratic	18827	2013-2014
	Cote d 'ivoire	10060	2011-2012
	Cameroon	15426	2010-2011
	Chad	18623	2013-2014

Kenya	31079	2013-2014
Malawi	24562	2011-2012
Mozambique	13745	2012-2013
Namibia	10018	2015-2016
Nigeria	38948	2010-2011
Sierra Leon	16658	2012-2013
Tanzania	13266	2010-2011
Tonga	9480	2012-2013
Uganda	8674	2015-2016
Zimbabwe	9171	2013-2014
Burkina Faso	17087	2013-2014

Source: Demographic and Health Surveys, N=33

5.2   Measuring Women Empowerment

The measurement of women's empowerment is still a debate in the literature. Kabeer (1999); (Kabeer, 2005) has measured empowerment via three-dimensional resource-agency-achievement/outcome. Agency is referred to as a process through which choices are made to become effective, and resources are used to enable peoples to make choices, and achievement refers to the agency's outcome. Empowerment is best to define as a "process through which a powerless get the power of making choices" previously denied. Therefore, empowerment is measured as a process and followed the three dimensions of Kabeer (2005).

The recent DHS survey for developing countries has explored the direct and indirect indicators of women empowerment. The focus is on getting the most direct indicators related to women empowerment, followed by five dimensions. Due to the lack of data on all indicators of women empowerment and child health, an attempt has been made to sort the countries that have same indicators of women empowerment. These five dimensions are employed to present women empowerment in different aspects and construct a composite women empowerment.

5.2.1. Work Status (Resources)

This dimension of women empowerment covers the working status and employment status (job nature). The work status of women improves her financially and enables her to spend more money on her family. Work status has been considered as an economic resource (pre-conditions) of women empowerment. Access to such resources reflects that women may govern distribution and exchange on different institutional grounds (Abrar ul Haq, Jali, & Islam, 2018; Alkire et al., 2013; Njoh & Ananga, 2016; Phan, 2016).

5.2.2. Awareness (Resources)

This is the second dimension covering the pre-condition (resources) of women empowerment, such as access to media (newspaper, radio, TV) and this media exposure can increase the women's knowledge and learning. Resources include economic resources and human and social resources to enhance the ability to exercise choice. In the broader sense, resources are developed through a mixer of social interactions lead in the various institutional grounds that make up a society (family, market, community) (Chung et al., 2013; Muhammad et al., 2012; Tadesse et al., 2013).

5.2.3. Decision Making (Agency)

This third dimension of women empowerment relates to the agency—the capability to determine one's goal and act upon it. Agency comprises the meaning of motivation and purpose that individuals can conduct their activities, their sense of agency, or the 'power within.' Agency in the sense of 'power to' expresses people's capacity to determine their own life choices and follow their own goals while disagreeing with others. Moreover, the agency also executed a negative logic 'power over' capacity of manager/officer/husband/parents to override others' agency through violence, strength, and threat. Here, the agency in the sense of 'power to' relating to women's own-life choices has taken following the women's decision relating husband earning, her health care, large household purchases, and visiting her relative/friends.

From previous literature, decision-making is the most frequently used indicator of women empowerment by researchers. It is direct indicator of women empowerment and a process by which we can easily find out how much a woman has autonomy in her choices. Each indicator has four choices: women alone, women and husband, only husband, and by someone other. Women who decide by themselves have a higher score for measuring women's empowerment. (Acharya et al., 2010; Assaad et al., 2014; Bloom et al., 2001; Jejeebhoy & Sathar, 2001; Lopez-Avila, 2016; Mahmud et al., 2012).

5.2.4. Self Esteem (Agency)

This agency dimension refers to 'power within' in the sense of motivation regarding their self-respect/self-esteem. It has measured by beating is justified by the husband or not if the wife argues with husband, wife burns food, neglects children, goes outside without telling, and refuses to have sex. Women who agree with all these beatings have not a sense of self-respect and are not able to think, decide and do better for their selves.

Self Esteem is a significant variable for measuring women empowerment. Women's self-respect, dignity, and self-worth are the enabling factors for a woman to know what she is? What does she want to do? Furthermore, what is she doing? Every woman has a right to think about her self-respect, but unfortunately, in the developing societies, women are a submissive group always respects their husbands' orders, children, and family members (Jejeebhoy & Sathar, 2001; Lopez-Avila, 2016; Mahmud et al., 2012; Musonera & Heshmati, 2017; Tadesse et al., 2013.

5.2.5. Self Confidence (Outcome)

Self-confidence is the outcome indicator of women empowerment. This dimension reflects the self-confidence of women. Women's self-confidence indicates their ability to go outside for medical care alone and get money for their treatment. Two indicators measure it-- women want to go alone for her medical care and get money for her treatment. In previous literature, no one researcher used this indicator.

The composite index of women empowerment has been constructed by combining five women empowerment dimensions in a single index. Jeckoniah et al. (2012); (Musonera & Heshmati, 2017) included composite women empowerment in their studies and measures personal autonomy, household decision making, domestic economic consultation, and free-dom of movement to construct a Composite women empowerment index. Variables used for the construction of women empowerment described in Table 5.2

Table 5.2: Measurement Scale of Dimensions of Women Empowerment

Dimensions	Description	Measurement Scale in DHS Data
Work Status (WS)	Respondent is currently Working	No=0, Yes=1
	Respondent's Employment Status	0=did not work, 1=unskilled manual 2=Skilled manual, 3=household domestic, 4=agricultural - self-employed, 5=clerical 6=agricultural – employee, 7=sales, 8=services 9=professional/technical/managerial
Awareness (AW)	Respondent Watching TV	0=not at all, 1= almost daily, 2=at least once a week
	Respondent reading Newspaper/ Magazines	0=not at all, 1= almost daily, 2=at least once a week
	Respondent listening to a radio	0=not at all, 1= almost daily, 2=at least once a week
	Heard about family planning on radio	not at all=0, 1= less than once a week 2=at least once a week, 3= almost daily
	Heard about family planning on TV	not at all=0, 1= less than once a week 2=at least once a week, 3= almost daily
	Heard about family planning from newspapers	not at all=0, 1= less than once a week 2=at least once a week, 3= almost daily
Decision Making (DM)	The decision to spends about women's Husband earnings	0=Husband has no earnings, 1=Someone else, 2=Husband/partner alone, 3=Respondent and husband/partner 4=Respondent alone
	The decision to women's Health	1=Someone else, 2=Husband/partner alone

		3=Respondent and husband/partner, 4=Respondent alone
	The decision about large household purchases	1=Someone else, 2=Husband/partner alone 3=Respondent and husband/partner, 4=Respondent alone
	The decision about visits to family or relatives	1=Someone else, 2=Husband/partner alone 3=Respondent and husband/partner, 4=Respondent alone
	Beating justified if wife argues with husband	0= Yes justified, 1= Not justified
	Beating justified if wife neglects children	0= Yes justified, 1= Not justified
Self Esteem (SE)	Beating justified if Without telling husband	0= Yes justified, 1= Not justified
	Beating justified if the wife refuses to have sex with the husband	0= Yes justified, 1= Not justified
	Beating justified if a wife burns food	0= Yes justified, 1= Not justified
Self Confidence (SC)	Getting medical help for self: want to go alone	0=Big Problem, 1=Not a big problem
	Getting medical help for self: Getting money for treatment money	0=Big Problem, 1=Not a big problem

Source: Demographic and Health Survey (DHS-V 2003 – 2008, DHS-VI 2008 – 2013, DHS-7 2013 – 2018)

5.3 Principal Component Analysis and Factor Analysis used for Construction of Women Empowerment Dimensions

Factor analysis is used to discover the data infrastructure that monitors the response of a survey. Since there is no prior theory for the preparation of these reactions, it is thought that any individual indicator can be associated with any factor. Therefore, the model used a correlation between the factor and the original variable (factor load) to explain the latent factors' structure. In the analysis, Verimix technology has been used to maximize the correlation and reduce the correlation between different factors by using SPSS 21. The same technique was used by Tadesse, Teklie, Yazew, and Gebreselassie (2013).

Factor analysis (FA) is used to extract a set of components or factors from a group of variables "p" to determine which variables or factors are most different in the variable "p". In other words, it is used to subtract one set of p variables from one set of basic superordinate dimensions. These essential factors can be derived from the correlation between the variables, p. Each element is evaluated as a weighted sum of the p variable p. So, the ith factor is

$$F_I = W_{I1}S_1 + W_{I2}S_2 + W_IS_3 + \ldots\ldots\ldots\ldots W_{IP}S_P \qquad (5.1)$$

W_{ip} is the weight for m_{th} principal component and P_{th} variables. S variables used in factor analysis.

These factors will be referred to as a subdivision of women's empowerment scores. The five factors measuring women's empowerment in the factor analysis were excluded from the 19 variables, and these factors represent an exact proportion. The criteria used to confirm the factor analysis variability should show a higher weight (in most cases greater than 0.52) and test that the divergence factors reasonably represent the original variable. An element score for each of these five factors was extracted from these nineteen variables and found the central variable.

Since all these factors relate to women empowerment, they were combined into a single index. A similar procedure had implemented in earlier research (Antony & Rao, 2007; Hightower, 1978; Sekhar, Indrayan, & Gupta, 1991).

5.3.1   The Construction of the Sub-indices of Women Empowerment Index

Each sub-index of women empowerment based on the latest DHS survey of thirty-three countries has developed using factor analysis of nineteen variables, compiled and computed. Each index relates to different dimensions of women empowerment.

The steps have taken(DeCoster, 1998; Sakar, Keskin, & Unver, 2011; Sekhar et al., 1991):

i.   Identification of variables that cannot explain they can be mapped out by communalities.

ii.   Transformation variables, when the distribution is non-linear, then the assumptions of the various parametric techniques (e.g., Pearson correlation, ANOVA) are met.

iii.   Factor analysis can be sensitive to outliers, so remove outliers,

iv.   For very low and very high correlation, check the correlation matrix for multicollinearity.

v.   Factorability of the correlation matrix has checked.

vi.   Calculating the factor scores for the Index formation.

5.3.2. Testing the Suitability of a Factor Analysis

Before, it was used in factor analysis to confirm the correlation of multi-line problems. Factor analysis is useful for given multiline variables. Besides, various terrain loads often exceed standard errors, reducing its consistency, and making it difficult to label. In this study, Kaiser Meyer-Olkin (KMO), a measure of sampling adequacy (MSA), was used to detect multiple letters in the data to perform factor analysis. More specifically, the sampling relationships predicted whether the data could be significantly reduced in correlation and partial correlation (Williams, Onsman, & Brown, 2010). The KMO scale compares the coefficient of correlation coefficient with that of the coefficient of partial correlation. If variables already have common factors, the partial correlation coefficient should be smaller than the coefficient of correlation (Hill, 2011). For our data, the value is 0.736, indicating that factor analysis is possible (Table 5.3). The spherical test gives another test of the robustness of the relationship between variables. (Bartlett, 1954).

Table 5.3: KMO Measure of Sampling Adequacy and Bartlett's Test of Sphericity

KMO and Bartlett's Test		
Kaiser-Meyer-Olkin Measure of Sampling Adequacy.		0.736
Bartlett's Test of Sphericity	Approx. Chi-Square	2138734
	df	171
	Sig.	0.00

The null hypothesis that the population correlation matrix variables are uncorrelated checked by Bartlett's test of sphericity test. The results showed a significant level of 0.00, which is small to reject the hypothesis (the probability should be less than 0.05 to reject the null). According to these results, factor analysis is appropriate for this data set.

5.3.3. Dimensions of Women Empowerment: An outcome of Factor Analysis

The nineteen variables have been included in the factor analysis. Before applying the factor analysis, all these variables were standardized. The results have presented in Table 5.4. The number of factors extracted can be defined by choice and by default settings in SPSS that can help to decide the number of factors. One of the most commonly used techniques is Kaiser's criterion or eigenvalue rule. Under this rule, only factors with eigenvalues (the variances extracted by the factors) of 1.0 or more have been extracted into five variables.

A graphical method, known as the Cattell (1966) scree test (Figure 1), has been used to check the factor analysis's validity. After examining the scree plot, only five factors were extracted. Five variables relating to employment were reduced or extracted into factor 1 named " work status". Six variables relating to awareness from media have extracted into factor 2 named as "awareness" Four variables relating to household decisions have extracted into factor 3 named as "decision making". Five variables relating to self-respect have extracted into factor 4 named as "self-esteem". Two variables relating to female confidence has extracted into factor 5 named as "self-confidence".

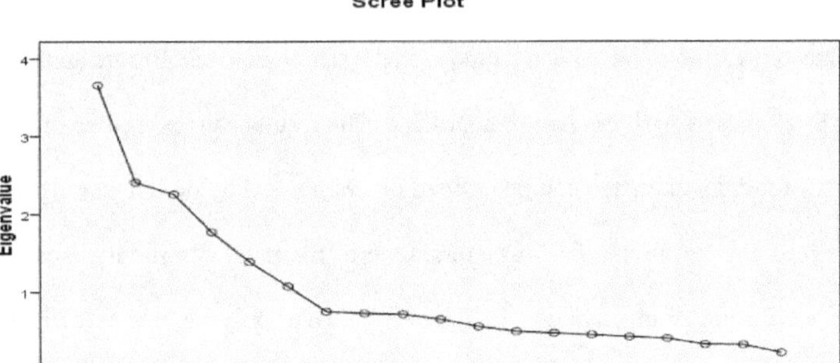

Figure 5.1: Scree Plot of Eigenvalues of Factors of Women Empowerment

The results of PCA using varimax rotation has presented in Table 5.2. Five factors/dimensions of women empowerment explain 60.451 percent of the total variance in the data. This first factor used to measure women's work status a reliable indicator of women empowerment. This factor explains 9.31 percent of the variance and explains the variations about the respondent currently working or not and respondent employment Status

For the second factor, the respondent's awareness level has been judged through how and how much time she heard about family planning from TV,newspaper/magazine or listen or from the radio. The respondent watching TV shows strong positive loadings compared to radio, or newspaper/magazine. This dimension explains 12.681 percent of the variance. This factor represents women's awareness from media, which is considered as the second most important dimension.

109

The third factor explains for 11.87 percent of the variations and explains the variations in the decision to spend women's health care, decided to spend on health services, about domestic consumptions, and freedom to visits their relatives or friends. This factor is a measure of the participation in decision making to represent the third dimension of women empowerment.

For the fourth factor explained, the response of the women against beating is justified if wife argues with husband, beating is justified if wife neglects children, beating is justified if the wife goes outside without husband showed higher positive loadings, as compared to beating is justified if wife refuses to have sex with husband, beating is justified if wife burns food. Loading results from an orthogonal rotation are correlation coefficients of each variable with the factor, so they naturally range from -1 to +1. The self-esteem explains 19.27 percent of the total variation. This factor is a reasonable representation of self-esteem. It means that better women empowerment indicated by high self-esteem.

The fifth factor explains 7.30 percent of the variance about variables, getting medical help for self: not wanting to go alone, getting medical help for self, and getting money for treatment. This factor is used to measure the fifth dimension of women empowerment, named as self-confidence. The same factor analysis had used in previous studies (Phan, 2016; Rathirani & Semasinghe, 2015; Williams, 2005).

Table 5.4: Results of PCA: Varimax Rotation Factor Matrix

Sr.	Variables	Work Status	Aware ness	Decision Making	Self Esteem	Self Confidence	Communalities
1	Beating is Justified if Wife Argues with husband				0.814		0.674

No.	Item					
2	Beating is Justified if Wife neglects the Children			0.827		0.690
3	Beating is Justified if Wife goes outside without telling Husband			0.817		0.682
4	Beating is Justified if Wife refuses to have sex with husband			0.713		0.535
5	Beating is Justified if Wife Burns Food			0.741		0.557
6	Respondent currently working	0.919				0.855
7	Respondent Employment Status	0.909				0.833
8	Respondent read newspaper or magazine		0.664			0.488
9	Respondent listen radio		0.526			0.402
10	Respondent Watching TV		0.653			0.504
11	Heard about family planning on radio last few		0.581			0.432
12	Heard about family planning from TV		0.734			0.582
13	Heard family planning in newspaper/magazine		0.711			0.521
14	Decision to spend women's husband earnings		0.668			0.464
15	Decision to spend women's Health Care		0.751			0.576
16	Decision about household Large purchases		0.811			0.663
17	Decided to their relatives		0.755			0.586
18	Getting medical help for self: not want to go alone				0.833	0.724
19	Getting medical help for self: Getting Money for treatment				0.844	

5.3.4. Construction of Combine Women Empowerment Index

As a first step in forming a single index, factor score coefficients(component scores) have been estimated through the regression method. Factor scores are the scores of each dimension of women empowerment. For calculating the factor scores for a given case for a given factor, the case's standardized score on each variable has multiplied by the corresponding factor loading of the variable for the given factor and summed these products. This calculation was carried out using SPSS 21 and factor scores as variables in subsequent calculations.

The five factors explained 60.45 percent of the total variation, with the first, second, third, fourth, and fifth factors explaining 19.27 percent, 12.68 percent, 11.88per cent, 9.31 percent, and 7.31 percent, respectively. Therefore, the importance of the factors in measuring overall women empowerment is not the same. For the combined women empowerment index, the proportion of the percentages of factors(scores) used as weights on the factor score coefficients

$$CWEI = (19.277/60.451) \text{ (Factor 1 score)} + (12.681/60.451) \text{ (Factor 2 score)} + (11.876/60.451) \text{ (Factor 3 score)} + (9.310/60.451) \text{ (Factor 4 score)} + (7.307/60.451) \text{ (Factor 5 score)}. \tag{5.2}$$

This single index measures the women empowerment of thirty-three developing economies from the five different regions. The value of the index can be positive or negative, making it difficult to interpret. Therefore, a Standardized Index (SI) has developed, the value of which can range from 1-5, using the formula:

$$CWEI = WEI\text{-}(min) / max\text{-}(min) \tag{5.3}$$

A similar technique was used in previous studies by (Antony & Rao, 2007; Hightower, 1978; Krishnan, 2011; Sekhar et al., 1991).

Classification of Combined women empowerment into three Groups

This combine women empowerment is then further divided into three groups as followed (Brajesh & Shekhar, 2015; Jeckoniah et al., 2012) by frequency distribution formula[6]

- Low women empowerment Index ranged between 1.27 to 2.36

- Medium women empowerment index ranged between 2.36 to 3.45

- High women empowerment Index ranged between 3.45 to 4.54

5.4   Description of Explanatory Variables

The independent variables have been categorized into women's personal characteristics, women's husband characteristics, women's children, head of household characteristics, and household characteristics. They are explained here.

i.   Women Education

Women Education means the number of schooling years categorized into no education, primary, middle and higher education. Women's education is the most important determinant to enhance women's empowerment at every level. Women empowerment is increasing with the increase in education, and higher education has shown as a positive contributor in enhancing women empowerment. Education always strengthens women's position in her family, empowered in decision-making, and can be a part of the labor force. All the education categories ultimately improve self-esteem and self-confidence—the authors also

---

[6] $i \leq$ H-L/k
Where i=class interval, H= highest number, L= Lower Number and k=number of groups

supported this association (Assaad et al., 2014a; Brajesh & Shekhar, 2015; Gupta & Yesudian, 2006; Jeckoniah et al., 2012) .

ii.   Age Difference with Husband

Age is the socio-demographic characteristic that has a substantial impact on every aspect of a woman's life. Women pass through different stages of her life from her birth to her death. This study found the impact of women's age difference with their husbands, categorized as older than husbands, equal with husbands and younger than husbands. Women of older age showing a strong relationship with empowerment. It is defined as older women have more experience and foresee power rather than young women.

iii.   Age at First Birth

Women Empowerment and age at first marriage have a negative relationship. A woman who is older at her first birth seems to be less empowered. In previous studies, age at first marriage was used to find its impact on women empowerment instead of age at first birth. (Brajesh & Shekhar, 2015; Jeckoniah et al., 2012); Musonera and Heshmati (2017) found an inverse relationship between age at first marriage and women empowerment (Brajesh & Shekhar, 2015; Jeckoniah et al., 2012). the current research used age at first birth to predict women empowerment instead of age at first marriage because the age at first birth means a woman's age to become a mother. After becoming a mother, women have the honor and better position in the families in developing countries than women who have not children or have children at a late age(Harwood, Yalçinkaya, Citlak, & Leyendecker, 2006;

Vedam et al., 2017). Due to these reasons in this study, age at first birth is considered a strong determinant of women empowerment.

iv.   Body Mass Index

Body mass index is a good indicator of health. Normal body mass index indicates the absence of illness and diseases. Normal body mass index is necessary for the complete mental, physical, and social welfare of women. In this study, health of women has been measured by women's body mass index. There is a significant and positive relationship between women's body mass index and women empowerment. In the previous study (Abrar-ul-Haq et al., 2017), women's health showing a strong relationship with women empowerment.

v.   Husband Education

Education has a central role in achieving sustainable and equal societies, nations, and the world. Educational provides better learning about human rights that should be available for every person independent of their gender. Education of husband is categorized by no education, primary, middle, and higher education. Education of husband has a positive relationship with women empowerment, but the study by Noreen (2011) found husband education and women empowerment in negative relationships. Still, Brajesh and Shekhar (2015) and Akram (2018) predict a positive relationship between women empowerment and the education of husbands.

vi.　Husband Employment Status

Husband's employment status means the husband is working or not working. Women whose husbands are working have better financial and authorized status than those whose husbands are not working.

vii.　Total Number of Children Alive

When the number of children increased, women face difficulties in managing household responsibilities, taking care of their children even then she cannot take care of themselves. Due to all of these inside the family, her value, respect, and influence on decision making decreased. Assaad et al. (2014a) predict a negative relationship between the number of children and women empowerment. Brajesh and Shekhar (2015) depict a direct positive effect of increase in children's number on women empowerment.

viii.　Total Number of Children Ever Born

The total number of children ever born consider as the fertility rate of a woman. According to the literature, women fertility negatively affects women empowerment. Baig et al. (2018) proved a negative relationship between women empowerment and children ever born. On the contrary, a positive association between women empowerment and children born has observed in some studies (Brajesh & Shekhar, 2015); Musonera and Heshmati (2017).

ix.   Gender of Head of Household

In this study, the gender of the household, as male found a negative relationship with women empowerment, males as a head of household are more authorized and try to minimize women's role and autonomy. Ayevbuomwan et al. (2016) explained the negative relationship between women empowerment and female gender as a head of household while Maqsood, Ullah, and Farooq (2015) measured and Baig et al. (2018) found a positive relationship with female gender as a head of household.

x.   Age of Head of Household

The head of the household is categorized into five groups below 25 years, 25-35 years, 35-45 years, 45-55 years, and above than 55 years. Age of head of household below than 55 have a positive relationship with women empowerment. Ayevbuomwan et al. (2016) proved a positive relationship between women empowerment and age of head of household while Akram (2018) predict the inverse association between them.

xi.   Total Member of Household

The total number of households mentions to a set of people or the sum of people residing in the same house. In a household with more members, women of that house seem to be less empowered than the houses where the household members are less than five. Akram (2018) and Abrar ul Haq, Jali, and Islam (2018) measure women empowerment through employment and decision-making and proved that more household members negatively impact women empowerment.

xii.   Household Wealth Index

The wealth index is an important factor in determining women's empowerment. It describes the wellbeing and living standards of a country. The wealth index is categorized as the poorest, poorer, middle, richer, and richest. The household wealth index has a positive relationship with women empowerment. Women belong to the richest households seem to be more empowered. Women empowerment measured by decision making index and self-esteem using Rwanda data(Musonera & Heshmati, 2017). While, measured by economic, social, health, and education dimensions and construct index using Nigeria data(Brajesh & Shekhar, 2015). Gupta and Yesudian (2006) measured women's empowerment by women's mobility and household decision-making and constructed the index. Akram (2018) measured women empowerment by empowerment in healthcare, empowerment in social contacts, empowerment in household decision making, and empowerment in financial decision-making by using Pakistan data and depict the direct effect of wealth index on women empowerment.

xiii.   Locality

Locality means the location of the household, which is categorized into rural areas and urban areas. Women living in urban areas seem to be more empowered as compared to women living in rural areas. The studies prove the positive relationship of urban locality on women empowerment(Brajesh & Shekhar, 2015; Musonera & Heshmati, 2017).

5.5   Econometric Analysis

5.5.1   Chi-square Test Statistics

It has been used to analyze the association between dependent and independent variables. Hypothesis testing: Ho: There was a significant association between the dependent variable and independent variables. To test the null hypothesis, we can compare with it given by (i=1, 2....n, j=1, 2,3,...m). From this calculated and tabulated values with degree of free-dom (n-1) (m-1), we decide about Ho's rejection that says there was no significant associ-ation between two variables. We reject Ho if greater than or if p-value less than level of significance, otherwise we do not reject Ho.

Steps of Chi-Square

- State hypothesis (i.e., null, and alternative hypothesis)
- Select the desired level of significance (alpha level of significance)
- Check the statistics
- Compute the calculated value
- Obtain the critical (tabulated) value
- Interpret the test

5.5.2   Ordinary Least Square Method

There are many econometric techniques to estimate the parameters of the connection be-tween dependent and independent variables. However, for current research, ordinal least 'square' method has been used to estimate the determinants of women empowerment dimensions. The following reasons are behind for choosing this method

The parameters estimates obtained by OLS have some optimal properties(Gujarati & Porter, 1999; Stone & Brooks, 1990)

- The OLS is a smooth method relative to other statistical techniques data
- The data used for analysis is not excessive.
- A variety of economic relationships can be evaluated, but this method and gives satisfactory results.
- All the steps of this are straightforward and easy to understand.
- For all other statistical techniques, this method is essential.

For the current study, the multiple regression method has to be considered for econometric analyses that are the relationship between one dependent and more than two independent variables. (Greene, 2000; Gujarati, 2003; Long, Long, & Freese, 2006).

Models

Dimensions of women empowerment were examined by using the following functions Model 1, 2, 3, 4, and 5 are estimated by OLS technique

$$WS = \alpha_0 + \alpha_1 WE + \alpha_2 ADH + \alpha_3 AFB + \alpha_4 BMI + \alpha_5 HE + \alpha_6 HES + \alpha_7 GHH +$$
$$\alpha_8 AHH + \alpha_9 TNCA + +\alpha_{10} TNCEB + \alpha_{11} THM + \alpha_{12} WI + \alpha_{13} PR + \mu_i \quad \textbf{(5.4)}$$

$$AW = \gamma_0 + \gamma_1 WE + \gamma_2 ADH + \gamma_3 AFB + \gamma_4 BMI + \gamma_5 HE + \gamma_6 HES + \gamma_7 GHH +$$
$$\gamma_8 AHH + \gamma_9 TNCA + \gamma_{10} TNCEB + \gamma_{11} THM + \gamma_{12} WI + \gamma_{13} PR + \mu_i \quad \textbf{(5.5)}$$

$$DM = \delta_0 + \delta_1 WE + \delta_2 ADH + \delta_3 AFB + \delta_4 BMI + \delta_5 HE + \delta_6 HES + \delta_7 GHH +$$

$$\delta_8 AHH + \delta_9 TNCA + \delta_{10} TNCEB + \delta_{11} THM + \delta_{12} WI + \delta_{13} PR + \mu_i \qquad (5.6)$$

$$SE = \beta_0 + \beta_1 WE + \beta_2 ADH + \beta_3 AFB + \beta_4 BMI + \beta_5 HE + \beta_6 HES + \beta_7 GHH +$$

$$\beta_8 AHH + \beta_9 TNCA + \beta_{10} TNCEB + \beta_{11} THM + \beta_{12} WI + \beta_{13} PR + \mu_i \qquad (5.7)$$

$$SC = \theta_0 + \theta_1 WE + \theta_2 ADH + \theta_3 AB + \theta_4 BMI + \theta_5 HE + \theta_6 HES + \theta_7 GHH +$$

$$\theta_8 AHH + \theta_9 TNCA + \theta_{10} TNCEB + \theta_{11} THM + \theta_{12} WI + \theta_{13} PR + \mu_i \qquad (5.8)$$

Sum of the squared residuals in all these models of OLS is minimized. Estimates βs of all the models are unbiased, had minimum variance, consistent, and normally distributed. The description and measurement of explanatory variables used in the empirical models declared above are listed in Table no. 5.5.

Table 5.5: Measurement Scales of Variables

Characteristics	Variables	Measurement scales
	Women Education (WE)	0=No Education 1=Primary 2=Secondary 3=Higher
Women personal characteristics	Age difference with husband (ADH)	0=Older than husband 1=Equal with husband 2=Younger than husband
	Age at first birth (AFB)	0=Less than 20 Years 1=20-25 2=Above than 30
	Body Mass Index (BMI)	0=less than 18.5 kg/m2 1=more than 18.5 kg/m2
Husband Characteristics	Husband Education (HE)	0=No Education 1=Primary 2=Secondary 3=Higher
	Husband Employment Status (HES)	0=Did not Work 1=Did Work
Women Children Information's	Total Number of Children alive (TCA)	Discrete
	Total number of children ever born (TCEB)	Discrete
	Gender (GHH)	0=Male

Household Head's Characteristics	Age (AHH)	1=Female 0=Below 25 1=25-35 2=35-45 3=45-55 4=Above than 55
	Total member of the household (THM)	Discrete
Household's Characteristics	Household Wealth Index (WI)	0=Poorest 1=Poorer 2=Middle 3=Richer 4=Richest
	Locality (PR)	1=Urban 0=Rural
Macro-Economic Factors Net food Imports countries		1=Yes 0=No
Secular States		1=Yes 0=No
Regions South and Southeast Asia		1=Yes, 0=Otherwise
Central Asia		Yes, 0=Otherwise
West Asia		Yes, 0=Otherwise
Latin America and Caribbean's Countries		Yes, 0=Otherwise
Sub-Saharan Africa		Yes, 0=Otherwise

Source: Demographic and Health Surveys(DHS-V 2003 – 2008, DHS-VI 2008 – 2013, DHS-7 2013 – 2018)

5.5.3 Ordinal Logistic Regression

Logistic regression can be useful when we are trying to model a dependent variable according to one or more independent variables, as it has two consequences for the variable. When a response variable has more than two categories in its natural order or arrangement. In statistics, the required logarithm model (also known as the required logistic regression or proportional odds model) is the regression model, depending on the variable. It is reasonable to think of more precise response models with more than two possible values.

The most common logistic regression method is the proportional probability model. According to several cube variables, the relative probability model's basic idea is to reproduce explicit variables based on the most commonly entered shadow points. We can consider three levels of logic models, each consisting of a gradient of variables of interest. This means that we can adjust the values, but the actual distance between the categories is unknown. The empowerment level of women is low to high.

Assumptions of Ordinal Regression

• The dependent variable should be measured at the ordinal level.

• Ordinal independent variables must be either continuous or categorical.

• There is no multicollinearity.

• Each independent variable has an identical effect at each cumulative split of the ordinal dependent variable.

• The relationship between each pair of outcome groups is the same.

• The effects of any explanatory variables are consistent or proportional across the different thresholds.

5.5.3a. The Model of Ordinal Logistic Regression

$$\ln(\theta_j) = \alpha_j + \beta_1 X_1 + \beta_2 X_2 + \ldots\ldots\ldots\ldots + \beta_9 X_9 \qquad (5.9)$$

Where the number of categories aggregates j, this is the part we want to discover. Response to abortion is considered a combination of three additional systemic responses, but there is clear and deliberate management of these responses, such as empowering low, medium, and high. If we know that a series contains a specific class, a special model tells us how independent variables relate to large or small ones.

In order to deal with an ordered categorical variable, the use of an ordered logit (an OL-OGIT) or ordered probit (an OPROBIT) model is more appropriate (Greene, 2000; Gujarati, 2003; Long et al., 2006). Therefore, in order to investigate the determinants of composite women empowerment index, the concept of 'ordered' modes women and the selected model is an OLOGIT model and its various extensions.

Assuming that the composite Women empowerment is an ordered discrete variable with j categories (low, medium and high), an OLOGIT model (in terms of probability) can be written as (Long, 1997):

$$\Pr(y_i > j \mid X) = g(X_i \beta') = \frac{\exp(X_i \beta' - \phi_j)}{1 + \exp(X_i \beta' - \phi_j)} \quad j = 1,....,m-1 \qquad \textbf{Equation 5.10}$$

where X_i is a (k×1) vector of observed non-random explanatory variables; β is a (k×1) vector of unknown parameters to be estimated; m is the number of categories of the ordinal dependent variable. The parameters of the model (β) and the cut-points (ϕ_1 and ϕ_2) are estimated by the method of maximum likelihood (Long et al., 2006). In equation (9), it is assumed the effects of explanatory variables on the level of severity are assumed to be fixed across observations. However, this may not be true as the effect of an explanatory variable may vary across observations. Some recent studies have suggested employing random parameters models (Anastasopoulos & Mannering, 2009; Ben-Akiva et al., 2002; McFadden & Train, 2000).

5.5.3b. Estimation by Ordered Logistic Model

$$CWEI = \alpha_0 + \alpha_1 WE + \alpha_2 ADH + \alpha_3 AFB + \alpha_4 BMI + \alpha_5 HE + \alpha_6 HES + \alpha_7 GHH + \alpha_8 AHH +$$

$$\alpha_9 TNCA + +\alpha_{10} TNCEB + \alpha_{11} THM + \alpha_{12} WI + \alpha_{13} PR + \alpha_{14} Ri + \mu_i \qquad \textbf{(5.11)}$$

R1= South and Southeast Asia

R2= Central Asia

R3= West Asia

R4=Latin America and the Caribbean

R5= Sub-Saharan Africa

5.5.3c. Models

$$CWEI = \alpha_0 + \alpha_1 WE + \alpha_2 ADH + \alpha_3 AFB + \alpha_4 BMI + \alpha_5 HE + \alpha_6 HES + \alpha_7 GHH + \alpha_8 AHH + \alpha_9 TNCA + +\alpha_{10} TNCEB + \alpha_{11} THM + \alpha_{12} WI + \alpha_{13} PR + \alpha_{14} R1 + \mu_i$$
$$\textbf{(5.12)}$$

$$CWEI = \gamma_0 + \gamma_1 WE + \gamma_2 ADH + \gamma_3 AFB + \gamma_4 BMI + \gamma_5 HE + \gamma_6 HES + \gamma_7 GHH + \gamma_8 AHH + \gamma_9 TNCA + \gamma_{10} TNCEB + \gamma_{11} THM + \gamma_{12} WI + \gamma_{13} PR + \gamma_{14} R2 + \mu_i$$
$$\textbf{(5.13)}$$

$$CWEI = \delta_0 + \delta_1 WE + \delta_2 ADH + \delta_3 AFB + \delta_4 BMI + \delta_5 HE + \delta_6 HES + \delta_7 GHH + \delta_8 AHH + \delta_9 TNCA + \delta_{10} TNCEB + \delta_{11} THM + \delta_{12} WI + \delta_{13} PR + \delta_{14} R3 + \mu_i$$
$$\textbf{(5.14)}$$

$$CWEI = \beta_0 + \beta_1 WE + \beta_2 ADH + \beta_3 AFB + \beta_4 BMI + \beta_5 HE + \beta_6 HES + \beta_7 GHH + \beta_8 AHH + \beta_9 TNCA + \beta_{10} TNCEB + \beta_{11} THM + \beta_{12} WI + \beta_{13} PR + \beta_{14} R4 + \mu_i$$
$$\textbf{(5.15)}$$

$$CWEI = \theta_0 + \theta_1 WE + \theta_2 ADH + \theta_3 AFB + \theta_4 BMI + \theta_5 HE + \theta_6 HES + \theta_7 GHH + \theta_8 AHH + \theta_9 TNCA + \theta_{10} TNCEB + \theta_{11} THM + \theta_{12} WI + \theta_{13} PR + \theta_{15} R5 + \mu_i$$
$$\textbf{(5.16)}$$

5.6   Women Empowerment and Child Health

The principal purpose of this research is to recognize the direct link of women empower-ment with child health. The empirical model is motivated by Andersen's and Newman and Grossman (1972) models with modification.

5.6.1. Economic Framework and Model Estimation of Child Health

Household is a multiperson family unit assumed to produce and consume vector of com-modities (Yi), constituted by Becker (1965) and Strauss and Thomas (1995) in their theo-ries of time allocation and revised theories of choice household's utility function is

$$U = U(Y_i \; ..... \; Y_n) \tag{5.17}$$

Subject to the resource allocation

$$\sum P_i Y_i = 1 = W + V \tag{5.18}$$

Yi are the market commodities purchased, and pi is the market price, 'I'is money income, W is wage, and V is income from other sources (Juster and Stafford, 1985; Aguiar and Hurst, 2007; Aguiar et al., 2012). Households usually will be maximizing their utility by combining the time and market good to produce more necessary public goods (healthy children), which directly affect the human capital accumulations for the household and nations. The new utility function of household's is now represented as

$$U = f(Y_i, \; N_i, \; L_i) \tag{5.19}$$

The household is then assumed to produce a vector of commodities Ni. These commodities are associated with different activities related to nurturing and rearing children to enhance their nutritional status (Becker and Lewis, 1973; Willis, 1973; Grossman, 1972a; Becker, 2007b). The good nutritional status is estimated by standardizing anthropometric measures (stunting, wasting, and underweight). Therefore, the household utility function is maximized subject to different constraints, including time-specific nutrition and income (Strauss and Thomas 1995). Following the work of Grossman (1972) general health production function, the reduced form production function of health (nutritional status) of a child in a household could derive as (Garcia and Alderman 1989, Khan 2013, Khan 2014, Haroon (2018).

$$Hi = f\,(WE_{mpi},\ M_i,\ Fr_i,\ F_i,\ H_i,\ C_i)\ \ i = 1,\ 2 \tag{5.20}$$

Hi is health (nutritional status), which depended on the vector of health inputs, women/mother's empowerment (WEmp), mother's characteristics (Mi), fertility rate (FRi,) father characteristics (Fi), household's characteristic (Hi)and country characteristics. This study focuses on developing the relationship between health outcome (nutritional status) and empowerment and parents' and households' characteristics.

The production function of health (5) presents the economics of non-market activities, which is more important and plays a role of the vector of inputs for producing market goods Becker (1973, 1974, 1981, 1991). Investment of time in a child's health is a human capital formation, which becomes the life cycle earnings and productivity(Browning et al., 2014).

5.6.2. Model Specification of Women Empowerment and Child Health

We take our theoretical model on the data by the following binary logistic regression model

$$CH = \beta_0 + \beta_1 WE + \beta_2 ADH + \beta_3 AFB + \beta_4 BMI + \beta_5 HE + \beta_6 HES + \beta_7 GHH + \beta_8 AHH + \beta_9 TNCA + \beta_{10} TNCEB + \beta_{11} THM + \beta_{12} WI + \beta_{13} PR + \beta_{14} R4 + \mu_i$$

$$(5.21)$$

Table 5.6: Operational Definition of Variables and Measurement Scale

Variables	Description	Measurement Scale
Dependent Variables		
Child Health	Stunting (height for age)	1=Stunting (z scores <−2 SD), 0=Otherwise
	Wasting (weight for height)	1=Wasting (z scores <−2 SD), 0=Otherwise
	Underweight (weight for age)	1=Underweight ((z scores <−2 SD), 0=Otherwise
	CIAF (Composite Index of Anthropometric Failure)	1=Yes, 0=No
Independent Variables		
Predisposing Factors	Father Education	0=No Éducation 1=Primary 2=Secondary 3=Higher
	Father Age	Discrete
	Mother Education	0=No Éducation 1=Primary 2=Secondary 3=Higher
	Father Employment	1=Employed 0=not Employed
	Total children ever Born	Discrete
	Total number of Household members	Discrete
Enabling Factors	Women Empowerment Index	Continuous
	Work status of the mother Index	Continuous
	Mother's Awareness from Media Index	Continuous
	Mothers Decision making Index	Continuous

	Mother's Self Esteem Index	Continuous
	Mother's Self Confidence Index	Continuous
Need-Based Factors	Mother Body Mass Index	0=less than 18.5 kg/m2 1= more than 18.5 kg/m2
	Mother's age at first Birth	0=Less than 20 Years 1=20-25 2=Above than 30
Environment	Locality	1=Urban, 0=Rural
	Secular State	1= Secular, 0= Otherwise
	Net Food Imports	1=Net food importer,0=Otherwise
	Household Wealth index	0=Poorer 1=Middle 2=Richer 3=Richest

Note: SD=Standard Deviation

5.6.3 Binary Logistic Model

This study determines that child health will be evaluated using the Binary logistic model (Ibrahim & Pandey, 2014). The dependent variable in logistic regression is usually distributed; that is, the dependent variable can value 1 for the probability of success or 0 for failure probability. This type of variable is called the Bernoulli variable (or binary). Although logistic regression is not implemented more often and is not discussed here, its application extends to include cases where the dependent variable is greater than the two states called multinationals or called multidimensionally (Tabachnick & Fidell, 1996).

As mentioned earlier, there are independent variables or predictive logistic slopes that can take any form. This means the distribution of independent variables in binary logistic regression is not the same. It does not usually need to be divided into groups, united, or vice versa. The relationship between the predictor and the response variable is not a linear function in the logistic regression. Instead, the logistic regression function is used which is given as

$$\theta(x) = e^{(\alpha+\beta_1 x_1 + \beta_2 x_2 + \dots + \beta_k x_k)} / 1 + e^{(\alpha+\beta_1 x_1 + \beta_{2} x_2 + \dots + \beta_k x_k)} \qquad (5.22)$$

Where a = the constants of the equation and b = the coefficient of the predictor variables.

Now we find the link function for which the logistic regression model is a generalized linear model (GLM). For this model the making response 1 is

$$P(S)/P(F) = \theta(x)/(1-\theta(x)) = e^{(\alpha+\beta_1 x_1 + \beta_2 x_2 + \dots + \beta_k x_k)} \qquad (5.23)$$

The log adds has a linear relationship

$$\text{Log}[\theta(x)/(1-\theta(x))] = \alpha + \beta x + \beta_2 x_2 + \dots + \beta_k x_k \qquad (5.24)$$

Thus, the appropriate link in the log-odds transformation, the logistic. The logistic regression model id is given by

$$\text{Log it}[\theta(x)] = \log[\theta(x)/(1-\theta(x))] = \alpha + \beta x + \beta_2 x_2 + \dots + \beta_k x_k \qquad (5.25)$$

The permanents in this model, α, $\beta 1$, $\beta 2 \dots \beta k$ can no longer be estimated by least squares, but are found using the maximum like hood method (Cox & Snell, 1989). Logistic regression calculates the probability of success over the probability of failure; therefore, the analysis result is in the form of an odds ratio. Logistic regression also provides knowledge of the relationship and strengths among the variable.

CHAPTER 6: WOMEN EMPOWERMENT IN DEVELOPING ECONOMIES: AN AGGREGATED ANALYSES

This chapter deals with the data analytical and econometric analysis and interpretations of socio-economic determinants of women empowerment. This chapter explains five dimensions of women empowerment extracted through factor analysis and their determinants using the Chi-Square test and linear regression. Then composite women empowerment index and its predictors have been evaluating through Chi-Square test and Ordered Logit Regression

6.1 Extents of Women Empowerment (Dimensions) in Developing Economies

The extent of women empowerment varies in developing economies regarding its dimensions. This variation among the developing economies occurs due to variations in their socioeconomic factors at household and macro levels. However, the primary cause of this variation is a gender difference in rules and regulations due to this gender differences in rules and regulation have its effects on both developed and developing economies and their women ("Women, Business and the Law 2018," 2018). The extent of women empowerment status in developing economies regarding its dimensions are explained in Table 6.1.

.

Table 6.1: Countries' Ranking with Empowerment Status (Qualitative)

Country	Work Status (%)	Rank	Country	Aware-ness (%)	Rank	Country	Decision Making (%)	Rank	Country	Self Esteem (%)	Rank	Country	Self Confi-dence (%)	Rank
Uganda	59.1	1	Guatemala	18.8	1	Cambodia	82.1	1	Nepal	99.6	1	Gambia	78.1	1
Burkina Faso	43.4	2	Namibia	16.9	2	Armenia	72.9	2	Peru	99	2	Jordan	76.7	2
Nepal	41.4	3	Jordan	16.5	3	Kyrgyz republic	68.9	3	Guatemala	94.4	3	Namibia	75.4	3
Tanzania	40.4	4	Peru	13.5	4	Timor Lestee	67.4	4	Honduras	90.8	4	Kenya	72.9	4
Kenya	33.3	5	India	13.4	5	Zimbabwe	66.5	5	Malawi	90.5	5	Mozambique	69.7	5
Sierra Leon	29	6	Tajikistan	13.2	6	Peru	63.1	6	Haiti	90.3	6	Uganda	64	6
Malawi	25.5	7	Honduras	12.8	7	Ethiopia	61.9	7	Mozambique	87.8	7	Nigeria	61	7
Namibia	23.1	8	Kenya	12.5	8	Namibia	60.9	8	Armenia	87.2	8	Kyrgyz republic	56.9	8
Cambodia	20.8	9	Kyrgyz republic	11.6	9	Haiti	53.6	9	Namibia	77.9	9	Haiti	55.4	9
Tonga	20.8	10	Tanzania	9.3	10	Jordan	53.4	10	Zimbabwe	75.2	10	Malawi	55.2	10
Mozambique	17.9	11	Gabon	8.6	11	Gabon	48.8	11	Jordan	75.1	11	Tanzania	54.8	11
Honduras	17.8	12	Nepal	8.2	12	Honduras	48	12	Tonga	71.4	12	Honduras	54.5	12
Guatemala	17.4	13	Haiti	7.5	13	Guatemala	47	13	Comoros	68.7	13	Zimbabwe	54.1	13
Timor Lestee	16.8	14	Timor Lestee	6.9	14	Azerbaijan	41.8	14	Nigeria	67.9	14	Tajikistan	52.7	14
Armenia	16.1	15	Uganda	6.6	15	Tajikistan	39.7	15	Burkina Faso	64.2	15	Burkina Faso	49.5	15
Comoros	16	16	Azerbaijan	6.2	16	Comoros	39.6	16	Kenya	64.1	16	Timor Lestee	47.3	16
Congo Democratic	15.7	17	Cambodia	4.8	17	Kenya	39.3	17	India	64	17	Tonga	45.6	17
Gabon	15.6	18	Mozambique	4.8	18	Mozambique	38.4	18	Cameroon	63.4	18	Ethiopia	43.7	18
Haiti	14.6	19	Nigeria	4.5	19	India	38.2	19	Kyrgyz republic	62	19	Pakistan	43	19
Nigeria	14.3	20	Cameroon	4	20	Nepal	38.2	20	Pakistan	59.4	20	Nepal	42.6	20

Country	Value	Rank	Country	Value	Rank	Country	Value	Rank	Country	Value	Rank	Country	Value	Rank
India	14	21	Malawi	3.3	21	Congo Democratic	36.9	21	Gabon	57.9	21	Comoros	40.4	21
Gambia	13.6	22	Burkina Faso	3.1	22	Pakistan	33.1	22	Cambodia	57.7	22	Azerbaijan	38.3	22
Azerbaijan	13.5	23	Comoros	3	23	Malawi	31.1	23	Cote d I Voire	57.2	23	Cote d I Voire	34.5	23
Tajikistan	13.5	24	Cote d'Ivoire	2.5	24	Uganda	27.7	24	Uganda	55.9	24	Cambodia	32.9	24
Kyrgyz republic	13.3	25	Ethiopia	2.2	25	Sierra Leon	26.3	25	Azerbaijan	50.2	25	Gabon	31.4	25
Jordan	10.7	26	Gambia	2.1	26	Cameroon	25.9	26	Tanzania	49.9	26	Cameroon	29.9	26
Cote d I Voire	10.2	27	Armenia	1.9	27	Gambia	22.7	27	Ethiopia	49.6	27	Congo Democratic	27.3	27
Cameroon	10	28	Zimbabwe	1.9	28	Chad	21.6	28	Gambia	46.9	28	Chad	24	28
Ethiopia	7.4	29	Sierra Leon	1.7	29	Tanzania	20.1	29	Tajikistan	40.4	29	Sierra Leone	14.1	29
Pakistan	7	30	Pakistan	1.5	30	Tonga	19	30	Sierra Leon	37.5	30	India	9.2	30
Chad	4.1	31	Tonga	1.1	31	Cote d I voire	18.9	31	Chad	35.6	31	Peru	0	31
Zimbabwe	2.1	32	Chad	0.8	32	Nigeria	17.3	32	Congo Democratic	35.3	32	Guatemala	0	32
Peru	0.1	33	Congo Democratic	0.5	33	Burkina Faso	7.8	33	Timor Lestee	16.4	33	Armenia		33

Source: Demographic and Health Surveys(DHS-V   2003 – 2008, DHS-VI 2008 – 2013, DHS-7   2013 – 2018)

Regarding women employment/work status—amongst the 33 developing economies—Uganda, Burkina Faso, and Nepal are respectively ranked 1st, 2nd, and 3rd (at the top; showing higher empowerment regarding work status) whereas Chad, Zimbabwe, and Peru are respectively ranked 31st, 32nd, and 33rd (at the bottom; showing lower empowerment regarding work status).

Regarding women's awareness status, Guatemala, Namibia, and Jorden have shown relatively higher while Tonga, Chad, and Congo Democratic have recorded lower empowerment. In contrast with Cote d'Ivoire, Nigeria, and Burkina Faso, women's participation in decision making is meagre, and Cambodia, Armenia, and the Kyrgyz Republic are far better concerning this dimension of women empowerment.

For self-esteem, women enjoy higher empowerment status in Nepal, Peru, and Guatemala, while receiving lower status in Chad, Congo Democratic, and Timor Leste. Women's empowerment is better for self-confidence in Gambia, Jorden, and Namibia, while the status is the worst in Peru, Guatemala, and Armenia.

6.2 Extents of Composite Women Empowerment Index (CWEI) in Developing Economies

As different dimensions of women empowerment, there is a different extent of composite women empowerment index in developing economies in Table 6.2.

Table 6.2: Countries' Ranking to Women Empowerment Status (Quantitative)

Country	Less Empowered (%)	Rank	Country	Moderately Empowered (%)	Rank	Country	High Empowered (%)	Rank	Country	CWEI Mean Score	Rank
Chad	38.9	1	Peru	87.4	1	Namibia	44.6	1	Tonga	4.08	1
Pakistan	30	2	Tonga	83.4	2	Haiti	39	2	Peru	3.79	2
Tajikistan	25.5	3	Zimbabwe	83	3	Nepal	38.8	3	Honduras	3.4093	3
Ethiopia	23.4	4	Gambia	82.5	4	Honduras	38.7	4	Nepal	3.3673	4
Congo Democratic	20.9	5	Jordan	82.2	5	Kenya	36.5	5	Haiti	3.3644	5
Azerbaijan	19.5	6	Burkina Faso	82	6	Cambodia	29.4	6	Guatemala	3.2891	6
Sierra Leon	19.1	7	Armenia	81.2	7	Uganda	26.6	7	Namibia	3.2874	7
Timor Lestee	17.2	8	Timor Lestee	79.1	8	Guatemala	23	8	Kenya	3.2466	8
Cote d I voire	16	9	India	79	9	Mozambique	22	9	Cambodia	3.2389	9
India	14	10	Cameroon	77.6	10	Malawi	21.2	10	Armenia	3.2171	10
Nigeria	12.9	11	Sierra Leon	77.5	11	Kyrgyz Republic	20.4	11	Malawi	3.2118	11
Cameroon	10	12	Comoros	77.3	12	Tanzania	19.2	12	Uganda	3.1692	12
Tanzania	8.5	13	Malawi	77	13	Nigeria	18.9	13	Mozambique	3.1515	13
Gabon	8	14	Cote d I voire	76.8	14	Gabon	17.6	14	Jordan	3.1377	14
Comoros	7.9	15	Congo Democratic	75.8	15	Armenia	16.7	15	Zimbabwe	3.1317	15
Gambia	7.6	16	Mozambique	75.6	16	Jordan	16.1	16	Azerbaijan	3.1037	16
Burkina Faso	7.6	17	Guatemala	75.5	17	Zimbabwe	15.1	17	Tanzania	3.0321	17
Kyrgyz republic	7.2	18	Gabon	74.4	18	Comoros	14.8	18	Burkina Faso	3.0312	18
Tonga	5.9	19	Kyrgyz republic	72.4	19	Peru	12.4	19	Gabon	3.0286	19
Kenya	5.2	20	Tanzania	72.3	20	Cameroon	12.4	20	Kyrgyz republic	3.0061	20
Namibia	4.1	21	Azerbaijan	70.1	21	Ethiopia	11.5	21	Cameroon	2.9889	21
Uganda	4.1	22	Uganda	69.3	22	Tonga	10.6	22	Comoros	2.9584	22

Country	Value	Rank	Country	Value	Rank	Country	Value	Rank	Country	Value	Rank
Mozambique	2.5	23	Cambodia	68.3	23	Azerbaijan	10.4	23	Gambia	2.9568	23
Cambodia	2.4	24	Nigeria	68.2	24	Burkina Faso	10.4	24	Nigeria	2.9243	24
Armenia	2.1	25	Pakistan	66	25	Tajikistan	10.3	25	Cote d I voire	2.8632	25
Zimbabwe	1.9	26	Ethiopia	65.1	26	Gambia	10	26	Tajikistan	2.8369	26
Malawi	1.8	27	Tajikistan	64.2	27	Cote d I Voire	7.2	27	India	2.8285	27
Jordan	1.6	28	Nepal	61	28	India	7	28	Ethiopia	2.8265	28
Guatemala	1.5	29	Haiti	60.2	29	Pakistan	4	29	Sierra Leon	2.7714	29
Honduras	1.3	30	Honduras	60	30	Timor Lestee	3.6	30	Congo Democratic	2.732	30
Haiti	0.8	31	Chad	59.8	31	Congo Demo-cratic	3.4	31	Timor Les-tee	2.7316	31
Nepal	0.2	32	Kenya	58.2	32	Sierra Leon	3.4	32	Pakistan	2.6554	32
Peru	0.2	33	Namibia	51.3	33	Chad	1.3	33	Chad	2.5221	33

Source: Demographic and Health Surveys(DHS-V   2003 – 2008, DHS-VI 2008 – 2013, DHS-7   2013 –2018

Regarding composite women empowerment index (CWEI) score (constructed as a multi-dimensional and quantitative measure of women empowerment), Tonga, Peru, and Honduras has respectively ranked 1st, 2nd, and 3rd (top scorers; showing higher empowerment status of women) whereas Timor Leste, Pakistan, and Chad are respectively ranked 31st, 32nd, and 33rd (least scorers; showing lower empowerment status of women).

6.3   Determinants of Women Empowerment: Bivariate Analyses

Bivariate analyses have performed through the Chi-Square test and presented in Table 6.3, Table 6.4, Table 6.5, Table 6.6, Table 6.7, Table 6.8. Results consistent with the literature and determine how women's characteristics, husband characteristics, total children, head of household characteristics, and overall household characteristics play a prime role in determining women empowerment. Women empowerment is a dynamic process; it is not easy to comprise women empowerment in a single dimension. In this study, an attempt has made to explain more than one aspect of women's inclusion through which women can be empowering.

6.3.1   Women Levels of Work Status and its Determinants

Chi-square test results (Table 6.3) show that women's socioeconomic background, household family members, and households are significantly associated with all three levels of women's dimension (work status) of women empowerment. All components found to be significantly associated (at a 5% level; $p < 0.05$) with the work status measures resources (pre-conditions) of women empowerment(Brajesh & Shekhar, 2015; Guinée, 2014).

Table 6.3: Bivariate Analysis of Women's Work Status and Characteristics of Women and Her Households of Members and Households

Characteristics	Work Status				Character.	Work Status			
	L	M	H	Number		L	M	H	Number
Women Characteristics	%	%	%	New		%	%	%	
Women Education					**Age of Head of Household**				
No Education	40	42	18	121195	Below 25	50	34	15	22780
Primary	40	41	19	101178	25-35	46	36	19	93716
Secondary	58	27	15	109771	35-45	43	37	20	106185
Higher Education	50	13	37	27901	45-55	47	34	19	74633
Women Body Mass Index					Above than 55	51	31	18	62734
less than 18.5 kg/m2	49	34	17	37052	**Women Children Characteristics**				
equal or more than 18.5kg/m2	49	33	18	237878	**Total number of Children Alive**				
Age Difference with Husband					=< 4	47	34	19	86288
Older than Husband	41	38	21	6629	>4	46	37	18	273768
Equal with husband	48	33	19	162822	**Total number of Children Ever Born**				
Younger than Husband	46	36	18	189872	=< 4	55	29	17	86288
					>4	44	37	19	273768
Respondent Age at First Birth					**Household's Characteristics**				
Below 20	46	36	19	301611	**Total Household Members**				
20-30	46	30	24	22094	=< 5	46	35	19	326334
Above 30	54	29	17	36351	>5	47	36	17	33028
Husband Characteristics					**Wealth Index of household**				
Education					poorest	43	41	16	69512
No Education	39	42	19	84803	poorer	43	38	19	68991
Primary	40	40	20	92633	middle	45	36	20	70250
Secondary	53	31	16	135212	richer	48	34	18	73012
Higher Education	55	20	26	42597	richest	53	27	20	78291
Husband Employment status					**Locality**				
Did not Work	50	22	29	13986	Rural	47	39	15	225189
Did Work	45	36	19	337216	Urban	49	29	22	134867
Household Head's Characteristics									
Gender of head of household									
Female	40	34	26	307563	Total	46	35	19.718.	360056
Male	44	37	19	52493					

Notes: chi-square ($\chi 2$) have significance level $p < 0.05$ at 95% Class Intervals, L=Low, Medium=M, High=H

6.3.2 Women's Levels of Awareness Status and its Determinants

Chi-square test result (Table 6.4) shows that socioeconomics and demographic factors of women, household's family members, and homes are significantly associated with all three levels of women's dimension (awareness) of women empowerment. All characteristics found to be significantly associated (at a 5% level; $p < 0.05$) with the awareness measures resources (pre-conditions) of women empowerment(Khan, 2018; Sebayang, Efendi, & Astutik, 2017).

Table 6.4: Bivariate Analysis of Women's Awareness and Characteristics of Women and Her Household's Members and Households

Character.	Awareness				Character.	Awareness			
	Low	M	H	Number		L	M	H	Number
Women Characteristics	%	%	%			%	%	%	
Women Education					**Age of Head of Household**				
No Education	84	16	0	121195	Below 25	69	26	5	22780
Primary	64	31	4	101178	25-35	61	32	7	93716
Secondary	37	48	15	109771	35-45	59	33	8	106185
Higher Education	18	51	31	27901	45-55	57	34	9	74633
Women Body Mass Index					Above than 55	55	30	15	62734
less than 18.5 kg/m2	68	27	5	37052	**Women Children Characteristics**				
equal or more than	54	36	10	237878	Total number of Children Alive				
Age Difference with Husband					=< 4	54	36	1000	86288
Older than Husband	57	34	9	6629	>4	69	27	5	273768
equal with husband	56	35	9	162822	Total number of Children Ever Born				
Younger than Husband	62	31	7	189872	=< 4	51	38	11	86288
					>4	62	31	7	273768
Respondent Age at First Birth					**Household's Characteristics**				
Below 20	61	32	7	301611	Total Household Members				
20-30	44	41	16	22094	=>5	58	33	9	326334
Above 30	51	38	11	36351	>5	66	28	6	33028
Husband Characteristics					**Wealth Index of household**				
Husband Education					poorest	84	15	1	69512
No Education	85	14	1	84803	poorer	74	23	3	68991
Primary	67	29	4	92633	middle	64	32	5	70250
Secondary	47	42	11	135212	richer	50	41	9	73012

Character.	L	M	H	Number	Character.	L	M	H	Number
Higher Education	28	48	24	42597	richest	28	50	22	78291
Husband Employment status					**Locality**				
Did not Work	64	30	6	13986	Rural	71	25	42	25189
Did Work	59	33	8	337216	Urban	40	45	15	134867
Household Head's Characteristics									
Gender of the head of household									
Female	59	33	8	307563	**Total**	59 66059.1	32	9	360056
Male	58	33	9	52493					

Notes: chi-square ($\chi2$) have significance level p < 0.05 at 95% Class Intervals, L=Low, Medium=M, High=H

6.3.3 Women's Levels of Participation Making and its Determinants

Chi-square test result (Table 6.5) shows that socio-economics and demographic character-istics of women, household's family members, and households are significantly associated with all three levels of women's dimension (decision making). All components found to be significantly associated (at a 5% level; p < 0.05) with the decision-making measures agency (a process of change) of women empowerment(Acharya et al., 2010; Asaolu et al., 2018).

Table 6.5: Bivariate Analysis of Women's Decision making and Characteristics of Women and Her Household's Members and Households

Character.	Decision Making				Character.	Decision Making			
	L	M	H	Number		L	M	H	Number
Women Characteristics	%	%	%			%	%	%	
Women Education					**Age of Head of Household**				
No Education	4	64	32	121195	< 25	2	60	38	22780
Primary	3	57	40	101178	25-35	1	59	40	93716
Secondary	6	51	43	109771	35-45	2	57	41	106185
Higher Education	4	47	49	27901	45-55	6	55	39	74633
Women Body Mass Index					>55	11	56	33	62734
less than 18.5 kg/m2	7	56	37	37052	**Women Children Characteristics**				
equal or more than 18.5kg/m2	4	55	41	237878	**Total number of Children Alive**				
Age Difference with Husband					=< 4	4	54	42	86288
Older than Husband	3	46	52	6629	>4	5	62	32	273768
Equal with husband	6	53	41	162822	Total number of Children Ever Born				
	3	60	37	189872	=< 4	10	56	35	86288

Characteristic	L	M	H	N	Characteristic	L	M	H	N
Younger than Husband					>4	3	57	40	273768
Respondent Age at First Birth					**Household's Characteristics**				
Below 20	3	57	39	301611	Total Household Members				
20-30	3	53	45	22094	=< 5	3	56	41	326334
Above 30	12	55	33	36351	>5	12	64	24	33028
Husband Characteristics					**Wealth Index of household**				
Education					poorest	4	60	37	69512
No Education	3	66	31	84803	poorer	4	58	38	68991
Primary	2	57	41	92633	middle	5	57	39	70250
Secondary	6	52	42	135212	richer	5	56	40	73012
Higher Education	6	53	42	42597	richest	4	55	41	78291
Husband Employment status					**Locality**				
Did not Work	7	59	35	13986	Rural	5	59	37	225189
Did Work	4	57	39	337216	Urban	4	54	43	134867
Household Head's Characteristics									
Gender of head of household									
Female	4	46	50	307563	**Total**	4.2	57	39	360056
Male	4	59	37	52493					

Notes: chi-square ($\chi2$) have significance level p < 0.05 at 95% Class Intervals ,L=Low, Medium=M, High=H

6.3.4 Women's Levels of Self Esteem and its Determinants

Cross-tabulation result (Table 6.6) shows that women's socioeconomic and demographic factors, household's family members, and households are significantly associated with all three levels of women's dimension (self-esteem) of women empowerment. All characteristics found to be significantly associated (at a 5% level; p < 0.05) with the self-esteem measures outcome (achievement) of women empowerment(Chung et al., 2013; Lopez-Avila, 2016).

Table 6.6: Bivariate Analysis of Women's Self Esteem and Characteristics of Women and Her Household's Members and Households

Characteristics	Self Esteem				Characteristics	Self Esteem			
	L	M	H	Number		L	M	H	Number
Women Characteristics	%	%	%			%	%	%	
Women Education					**Age of Head of Household**				
No Education	23	22	56	121195	Below than 25	15	19	6	22780
Primary	14	19	67	101178	25-35	15	19	66	93716
Secondary	11	19	70	109771	35-45	15	19	66	106185
Higher Education	4	10	86	27901	45-55	16	19	65	74633
Women Body Mass Index					>55	1	20	64	62734
less than 18.5 kg/m2	20	23	57	37052	**Women Children Characteristics**				
equal or more than 18.5kg/m218.5kg/m2	14	19	67	237878	Total number of Children Alive				
Age Difference with Husband					=< 4	13	18	69	86288
Older than Husband	13	17	70	6629	>4	19	21	59	273768
Equal with husband	14	19	67	162822	Total number of Children Ever Born				
Younger than Husband	16	20	64	189872	=< 4	13	18	69	86288
					>4	16	20	64	273768
Respondent Age at First Birth					**Household's Characteristics**				
Below 20	16	19	65	301611	Total Household Members				
20-30	11	17	72	22094	=< 5	15	19	67	326334
Above 30	14	18	68	36351	>5	21	22	57	33028
Husband Characteristics					**Wealth Index of household**				
Education					poorest	21	22	58	69512
No Education	23	22	54	84803	poorer	19	21	60	68991
Primary	14	18	68	92633	middle	17	21	62	70250
Secondary	13	20	67	135212	richer	13	19	67	73012
Higher Education	8	13	78	42597	richest	8	14	79	78291
Husband Employment status					**Locality**				
Did not Work	16	22	62	13986	Rural	19	21	61	225189
Did Work	16	19	65	337216	Urban	10	17	74	134867
Household Head's Characteristics									
Gender of head of household									
Female	13	18	69	307563	**Total**	15	19	65	360056
Male	13	19	65	52493					

Notes: chi-square (χ2) have significance level p < 0.05 at 95% Class Intervals ,L=Low, Medium=M, High=H

6.3.5 Women's Levels of Self-Confidence and its Determinants

Chi-test result (Table 6.7) shows that socioeconomic and demographic factors of women, the household's family members, and households are significantly associated with all three levels of women's dimension (self-confidence) of women empowerment. All characteristics found to be significantly associated (at a 5% level; $p < 0.05$) with the self-confidence measures outcome (achievement) of women empowerment.

Table 6.7: Bivariate Analysis of Women's Self Confidence and Characteristics of Women and Her Household's Members and Households

Characteristics	Self Confidence				Characteristics	Self Confidence			
	L	M	H	Num-		L	M	H	Num-
Women Characteristics	%	%	%			%	%	%	ber
Women Education					**Age of Head of Household**				
No Education	12	57	30	121195	Below than	9	52	40	22780
Primary	9	51	40	101178	25-35	13	48	40	93716
Secondary	21	39	40	109771	35-45	15	47	38	106185
Higher Education	27	26	48	27901	45-55	16	47	37	74633
Women Body Mass Index					>55	19	47	35	62734
less than 18.5 kg/m2	27	49	24	37052	**Women Children Characteristics**				
equal or more than	17	45	38	237878	Total number of Children Alive				
Age Difference with Husband					=< 4	18	45	36	86288
Older than Husband	12	54	34	6629	>4	9	52	40	273768
Equal with husband	17	47	36	162822	Total number of Children Ever Born				
Younger than Husband	14	47	39	189872	=< 4	17	43	39	86288
					>4	14	49	37	273768
Respondent Age at First Birth					**Household's Characteristics**				
Below 20	15	48	37	301611	Total Household Members				
20-30	19	41	40	22094	=< 5	16%	47	37	326334
Above 30	17	44	40	36351	>5	11%	49	40	33028
Husband Characteristics					**Wealth Index of household**				
Education					poorest	7	64	29	69512
No Education	10	59	32	84803	poorer	9	57	34	68991
Primary	9	52	39	92633	middle	13	50	37	70250
Secondary	20	43	37	135212	richer	18	42	41	73012
Higher Education	25	28	47	42597	richest	28	27	45	

Characteristic	L	M	H	Number	Character	L		M	H	Number
Husband Employment status					**Locality**					
Did not Work	6	47	47	13986	Rural	5		59	37	225189
Did Work	16	47	37	337216	Urban	4		54	43	134867
Household Head's Characteristics										
Gender of the head of household										
Female	16	42	42	307563	**Total**	15	4	47	38	360056
Male	11	48	41	52493						

Notes: chi-square ($\chi 2$) have significance level p < 0.05 at 95% Class Intervals ,L=Low,Medium=M,High=H

6.3.6 Women's Levels of Empowerment Index and its Determinants

Association between the composite women empowerment index with its predictors has been found by using chi-square statistics. The results are interpreting in Table 6.8. Women's body mass index equal to or more than 18.5kg/m2 shows the association with medium and higher empowerment compared to women with lower body mass index. Women younger than husbands have an association with medium and higher empowerment compared to the same age as the husband and older than the husband(Bhukuth et al., 2019; Sebayang, Efendi, & Astutik, 2019; Sheikhsoha, 2016).

Table 6.8: Bivariate Analysis of Composite Women Empowerment Index and Characteristics of Women and Her Household's Members and Households

Characteristics	CWEI				Character.	CWEI			
	L	M	H	Number		L	M	H	Number
Women Characteristics	%	%	%			%	%	%	
Women Education					**Age of Head of Household**				
No Education	18	76	6	121195	Below	11	75	14	22780
Primary	8	75	17	101178	25-35	10	72	18	93716
Secondary	7	71	22	109771	35-45	9	72	18	106185
Higher Education	1	55	43	27901	45-55	11	72	17	74633
Women Body Mass Index					>55	13	73	14	62734
less than 18.5 kg/m2	17	76	7	37052	**Women Children Characteristics**				
equal or more than	9	72	18	237878	Total number of Children Alive				
Age Difference with Husband					=< 4	9	71	20	86288

Older than Husband	7	69	24	6629	>4	14	75	11	273768
Equal with husband	10	72	18	162822	**Total number of Children Ever Born**				
Younger than Husband	11	73	15	189872	=< 4	11	71	18	86288
					>4	11	74	16	273768
Respondent Age at First Birth					**Household's Characteristics**				
Below 19	11	73	16	301611	**Total Household Members**				
20-30	7	65	28	22094	=< 5	10	72	18	326334
Above 30	12	71	17	36351	>5	17	75	8	33028
Husband Characteristics					**Wealth Index of household**				
Education					poorest	17	77	6	69512
No Education	18	76	6	84803	poorer	14	77	10	68991
Primary	8	75	17	92633	middle	11	75	14	70250
Secondary	9	72	19	135212	richer	8	72	20	73012
Higher Education	5	62	33	42597	richest	4	63	38	78291
Husband Employment status					**Locality**				
Did not Work	11	72	18	13986	Rural	13	75	12	225189
Did Work	10	73	17	337216	Urban	6	69	25	134867
Household Head's Characteristics									
Gender of head of household									
Female	11	74	15	307563	**Total**	10	73	17	360056
Male	8	67	25	52493					

Women below than 19 years at her first birth seem to have an association with medium and higher empowerment than other age groups. Women's empowerment is significantly associated with the employment status of her husband. Women whose husbands are working seem to be more empowered than those whose husbands are not working, in the households where the head of household is female showing association with medium and with higher empowerment as compared to those where the head of household is male(Ayevbuomwan et al., 2016; Maqsood et al., 2015).

Age of head of household is showing association with women empowerment. Women belong to the house where the head of household was in the age of 25-45 years seems to be more empowered than other age groups of the head of households.

Women who have total children alive less than four have the probability of being medium, and higher empowerment than those who have more than four children. Women who have children ever born below and equal to four reported having medium empowerment and higher empowerment than those who have more than four children ever born.

The wealth status of the household has a strong association between women's empowerment. According to households' wealth index, women who belong to richer and richest households seem to have more medium and higher empowerment than those who belong to poorer, poorest, and middle wealth statuses(Pambe et al., 2014). Households have the total number of household members less than or equal with five, showing a higher association with a medium level of empowerment than the household with more than five household members. Locality wise women lived in urban areas with more association with higher empowerment levels than the women residing in rural areas(Jejeebhoy & Sathar, 2001b).

6.4   Dimensions and Determinants of Women Empowerment: Linear Regression Analysis

Table 6.9 presented the regression analyses of five dimensions of women empowerment individually and explained five sets of regression. In these sets of regressions: work status, self-esteem, awareness, decision making, and self-confidence are taken separately as dependent variables and regress with their determinants. Linear Regression analyses for determinants of women empowerment are as follows:

6.4.1 Women Characteristics

a   Women Education

In the regression analysis, higher education enormously resolute each dimension of women empowerment. Having a higher, secondary, or primary education seems to be more empowered than illiterate women empowerment. Results indicate that women with higher levels of education are more empowered compared to less educated women. Education also enhances the awareness level of women about their rights (Saraft and Yano, 2007). In this regard, Parveen and Leonhäuser (2005) argued that education and skill improved women's socio-economic condition and made them able to demand and protect their rights more effectively. Furthermore, in her views, education helped tackle the socio-cultural norms that hinder their wellbeing (Ahmad & Sultan, 2004; Heaton, Huntsman, & Flake, 2005; Sridevi, 2005), explored in their independent studies that education has a significant influence on women's empowerment.

b.   Age difference with Husband

The age of a woman and her husband has compared, and it was categorized into women older than husband, younger than husband, and have the same age. In the regression analysis, women older than husbands and younger than husbands positively and significantly influence the work status. It seems that age difference with husband has a positive and have influence on women's work status compared to equal age with husband (reference category).

Meanwhile, women older than husbands positively and significantly affect awareness, decision-making, and self-esteem. In comparison, these dimensions negatively associated with women younger than their husbands compared to the same age with husbands (reference category). Self-confidence positively related to women's age difference with their husbands either she is older than husband or younger than the husband compared to same age with her husband.

In all these sets of regression, women older than husbands and younger than husbands indicate a statistically significant relationship with women empowerment. In this order, Solomon and Adekoya (2006), in their research in Nigeria showed that older women had enormous decision-making power than younger ones; however younger women also attain this status gradually as they grow up. Besides this, Tareque, Haque, Mostofa, and Islam (2007) indicated that younger wives are kept under tight control than elder wives because they are careful and more trustworthy than the younger ones. Studies conducted by (Ahmad & Sultan, 2004; Frankenberg & Thomas, 2001; Heaton et al., 2005); Jejeebhoy (2000) support the argument that age/conjugal age was one of the critical determinants of women's empowerment.

Table 6.9: Socioeconomics Determinates of Women Empowerment (Sub-Indices)

Socio-Economics and Demographic Characteristics	Model 1	Model 2	Model 3	Model 4	Model 5
	Work Status	Awareness	Decision Making	Self Esteem	Self-Confidence
(Constant)	2.236***	.927***	4.354***	4.745**	3.785***
	(0.015)	(0.013)	(0.015)	(0.015)	(0.016)
Women Characteristics					
Women Education (No Education is reference category)					
Primary	0.007***	0.356***	0.213***	0.103***	0.258**
	(0.006)	(0.005)	(0.005)	(0.006)	(0.006)
Secondary	-.237***	0.717***	0.232***	0.049***	0.171**

	(0.006)	(0.005)	(0.006)	(0.006)	(0.006)
Higher	0.220***	1.035***	0.433***	0.255***	0.215**
	(0.010)	(0.008)	(0.009)	(0.010)	(0.010)
Age Difference with Husband (Equal age is reference category)					
Older than husband	0.090***	0.068***	0.227***	0.044***	0.042**
	(0.014)	(0.012)	(0.014)	(0.014)	(0.015)
Younger than Husband	0.023***	-0.031***	-0.027***	-0.020***	0.121**
	(0.004)	(0.003)	(0.004)	(0.004)	(0.004)
Age at First Birth (Below than 19 is reference category)					
20-30	-.050***	0.054***	0.049***	0.006	0.010**
	(0.007)	(0.006)	(0.007)	(0.007)	(0.007)
Above 30	0.008	0.056***	-.004	-.023***	0.041
	(0.009)	(0.007)	(0.008)	(0.009)	(0.009)
Women Body Mass Index (less than 18.5 kg/m2 is reference category)					
Body Mass Index	0.031***	0.044***	0.070***	0.097***	0.383**
	(0.006)	(0.005)	(0.005)	(0.006)	(0.006)
Husband Characteristics					
Husband's Education (No education is reference Category)					
Primary	0.016***	0.126***	0.112***	0.147***	0.039**
	(0.006)	(0.005)	(0.006)	(0.006)	(0.003)
Secondary Education	-0.160***	0.138***	-.012***	0.023***	0.154**
	(0.005)	(0.005)	(0.006)	(0.006)	(0.007)
Higher Education	-0.144***	0.240***	-.098***	0.052***	-0.09***
	(0.004)	(0.007)	(0.005)	(0.009)	(0.004)
Husband Employment status (Did not work as reference category)					
Did work	0.164***	0.156***	0.118	0.007**	-.236***
	(0.011)	(0.009)	(0.011)	(0.004)	(0.012)
Household Head's Characteristics					
Gender of the head of household (Male is reference category)					
Female	0.063***	-0.073***	0.305***	0.048**	0.176***
	(0.005)	(0.005)	(0.005)	(0.011)	(0.006)
Age of Head of Household (Above than 55 is reference category)					
25-35	0.086***	-0.026***	0.204***	0.001	0.132***
	(0.005)	(0.005)	(0.005)	(0.006)	(0.006)
35-45	0.119***	0.007***	0.187***	-0.026**	0.079***
	(0.005)	(0.004)	(0.005)	(0.005)	(0.006)
45-55	0.057***	0.020***	0.097***	-0.026	0.053***
	(0.006)	(0.005)	(0.006)	(0.005)	(0.006)
Women Children Characteristics					
Total Number of Children Alive (>4 is reference Category)					
Total no. children alive	-.062***	-.119***	-.240***	-.074***	0.233***
<=4	(0.004)	(0.004)	(0.004)	(0.005)	(0.005)

Total Number of Children Ever Born (>4 is reference Category)

Children Ever Born	0.151***	0.001	0.335***	0.043**	-.060***
<=4	(0.005)	(0.004)	(0.005)	(0.005)	(0.005)

Household's Characteristics

Wealth Index (Poorest is reference category)

Poorer	0.065***	0.133***	-.027***	0.009	0.006
	(0.006)	(0.005)	(0.006)	(0.006)	(0.007)
Middle	0.091***	0.286***	-.009	-.002	-.026
	(0.006)	(0.005)	(0.006)	(0.006)	(0.007)
richer	0.109***	0.476***	-.023***	0.061** *	-.103***
	(0.007)	(0.005)	(0.006)	(0.007)	(0.007)
Richest	0.137***	0.745***	-.007	0.19***	-.103***
	(0.007)	(0.006)	(0.007)	(0.008)	(0.007)

Total number of Household Members (>5 is reference Category)

Total Household members	0.032***	0.062***	-.323***	-0.046**	0.024***
<=5	(0.007)	(0.006)	(0.007)	(0.008)	(0.008)

Locality (Rural is reference category)

Urban	-0.86***	0.137***	0.117***	0.11***	0.011***
	(0.005)	(0.004)	(0.005)	(0.005)	(0.005)

Notes: Significance level <0.01=***,Significant level <0.005=** and Significance level <0.10=*
Standard Error ()

c.   Women Age at Her First Birth

In the regression analysis, the woman's age at first birth was significant in determining

women's different dimensions. Women age at first birth in the range of 20-30 years has a

positive impact on the dimensions; awareness, decision making, self-esteem and self-con-

fidence compared to it has a negative impact on work status. Whereas having age at first birth above than thirty years old was positively associated with awareness and negatively squeezed self-esteem compared to the reference category. Furthermore, at the same time, work status, and self-confidence showed positive and significant association with the age above thirty.

Women age at first birth has used in this study instead of age at first marriage. In developing countries, women who become a mother at an earlier age have a different position in the family as compared to women who become a mother at older age. For work status earlier age for birth become a hurdle for women because, with the responsibility of a child, a woman could not work correctly. However, at the same time earlier age at birth (20-30) increase the self-esteem and decision making power of women(Sebayang et al., 2017).

d.   Women Body Mass Index

Women's body mass index was showing a strong relationship with all dimensions of women empowerment. Women body mass index strongly determined work status, awareness, decision making, self-esteem, and self-confidence. All these dimensions of women empowerment are positively affected by women's body mass index equal to or greater than $18.5 kg/m_2$. It seems to be that women with good health are more empowered as compared to those who are in poor health. Abrar ul Haq et al. (2018) and measure women's health as she was suffering from any severe disease or not and showing adverse effects on women empowerment however in this, while in this study body mass index was used for measuring the women's health.

6.4.2   Women Husband's Characteristics

a.   Husband's Education

Husband education with higher levels is negatively related to women's work status, decision making, and self-confidence while positively associated with awareness and self-esteem. Husband with higher education has adversely related to women empowerment in previous studies (Noreen, 2011; Sathar & Shahnaz, 2000). The education of women husbands greatly influenced the women empowerment measured by decision making. This result also included in the studies of Brajesh and Shekhar (2015), and Akram (2018). All these studies predict that husband education has a valuable role in enhancing women empowerment(Abekah-Nkrumah, 2013; Moonzwe Davis et al., 2014; Phan, 2016b; Presser & Sen, 2000; Upadhyay et al., 2014; Upadhyay & Karasek, 2012).

b.   Employment Status of Husband

The husband's employment status 'did work' positively influences work status, awareness, self-esteem, and decision making, but it harms self-confidence. Most of the women demand to have a spouse to be work or earn more for comfortable livings. The husband is either healthy or wealthy could be meet all the financial needs of the wife, and the family. Such an admirable act of husband gives care and comfort to a woman, but she was dependent on her husband to provide resources for her and family use. At the same time, she avoids going outside independently and loses her self-confidence. Husband with good working status, good awareness, and broadened mind level increase her wife's awareness level and respect her. In this way, a woman has access to media endowed or awareness to be empowered(Acharya et al., 2010; Senarath & Gunawardena, 2009; Tadesse et al., 2013; Upadhyay & Karasek, 2010), proved the same negative relationship between decision making and the husband's employment status.

6.4.3 Household Head of Household Characteristics

a. Gender of Head of Household

Female as head of household showing a significant and robust contribution to determine women empowerment in all its dimensions. Female as head of household has a positive impact on work status, self-esteem, decision making and self-confidence. Female as head of household negatively affects the second dimension of women empowerment measured by awareness instead of the male head of household. Ayevbuomwan et al. (2016) explained negative relationship between women empowerment and female gender as a head of household while Maqsood et al. (2015) measured women empowerment by the use of contraceptive by using the data of Seven Sisters South Asian and Baig et al. (2018) women empowerment measured through an index by using the data of Pakistan (Muzaffargarh) found positive relationship with female gender as a head of household.

b. Age of Head of Household

Age of head of household is separated into different groups to assess which age group of head of household more likely to influence women empowerment. Households where the household's age head was between 25 to 45 positively and strongly associated with women's work status. Although all age groups positively associated with work status as compared to the head of households above 55 years old. However, the age of 25 to 35 seems to be highly significant with the work status of women. While all age groups below 55 years have a positive impact on awareness compared to age above 55. Decision-making, which is the third dimension of women empowerment, was positively associated with all age groups below 55 years but statistically significant with the age group between 25 to 35 years. The age of head of household in the age group from 25 to 35 has a negative influence on awareness but age between 35-45 years was highly significant than age above 55. Age in the range of 35 to 45 and 45 to 55 have a negative but insignificant impact on self-esteem. Self-confidence positively related to all age groups of the head of households below 55 years old as compared to age above 55.

6.4.4. Women's children Characteristics

a. Total Number of Children Alive

Work status, awareness, decision making, and self-esteem are negatively associated with the total number of children alive below or equal to four, while self-confidence is positively associated with the total number of children alive. Assaad et al. (2014a) and Baig et al. (2018) predict a negative relationship between women empowerment and many children alive while (Brajesh & Shekhar, 2015) found favorable for women empowerment with many children alive below or equal to four.

b.   Children Ever Born

The total number of children ever born below or equal than four is positively associated with work status, awareness, and decision-making. The total number of children ever born below or equal to four is negatively associated with self-esteem and self-confidence. Musonera and Heshmati (2017) found a negative relationship between self-esteem and children ever born.

6.4.5. Household Characteristics

a.   Household Wealth Index

Household wealth has appeared to be one of the most important determinants of women empowerment, which is significantly determining all dimensions of women empowerment. Work status and awareness of women seen to improve with the improvement in household's wealth status. Self-confidence has a negative association with the wealth status of households. Meanwhile, women empowerment measured by decision making gradually increases with the wealth of households and positively associated with the wealthiest households. Musonera and Heshmati (2017) proved a positive relationship between women decision making index and self-esteem with richest wealth status index; Brajesh and Shekhar (2015), Gupta and Yesudian (2006), and Akram (2018) found women's mobility, participation in household decision making and health care positively affected by higher wealth status of households. Decision-making is a power that is indeed related to self-confidence, education, knowledge, and family support by households' wealth.

b.   Total Household Member

Total numbers of household members are positively associated with awareness and self-confidence while negatively associated with self-esteem, decision-making, and self-confidence. Women's empowerment is decreasing with the increase in the total member of households. Akram (2018) and Abrar ul Haq et al. (2018) found women empowerment measured by household affairs, freedom of movement, daily household expenditure, child health, women's participation have a negative relationship with the total number of household members.

c.   Locality

The work status of women residing in urban areas is negatively affected by locality compared to women residing in rural areas. On the other side, women empowerment measured by self-esteem, awareness, decision making, and self-confidence is positively and significantly determined by the urban Localites compared to the rural Locality. Brajesh and Shekhar (2015); Musonera and Heshmati (2017) proved the same significant results of urban locality on self-esteem and decision making.

6.5   The Role of Regions in determining Women Empowerment: Ordered Logit Regression Analysis

In the parameter estimates of ordered logistic regression, standard errors, p-values (Sig.), and odds ratios shown in Table 6.10. The thresholds shown at the top of the parameter estimates output, and they indicate where the dependent variable has cut to make the three groups observed for women empowerment. The threshold coefficients represent the intercepts, precisely the point (in terms of a logit) where women empowerment has predicted into the three categories. By taking the exponent of the combined estimate relative to a given predictor, i.e. $e^{\beta j}$ considering it is to obtain a view of the standard odds ratio that describes the corresponding odds for Xj differing by one unit. Table 6.10 presented six models of ordered logistics regression; in the first model, women's empowerment is regress with women's characteristics, women's number of children, women's husbands' characteristics, head of household characteristics, and household characteristics. After that, in the next five model's variable of the region has included to evaluate the impact of region on women empowerment.

Table 6.10: Socioeconomics Determinants of Women Empowerment Index

	Model Without Regions	Model with Region1	Model with Region2	Model with Region3	Model with Region4	Model with Region5
	Estimates (Std.Error)	Estimates (Std.Error)	Estimates (Std.Error)	Estimate (Std.Error)	Estimates (Std.Error)	Estimates (Std. Error)
Intercept 1	-.376*** (0.049)	-0.665*** (0.049)	-.385*** (0.049)	-.366*** (0.049)	-.340*** (0.049)	-.069 (0.049)
Intercept2	3.922*** (0.050)	3.731*** (0.050)	3.934*** (0.050)	3.937*** (0.050)	4.0555*** (0.050)	4.264*** (0.050)
Women's Personal Characteristics						
Education (No education is reference category)						
Primary	0.823*** (0.014)	0.663*** (0.014)	0 .838*** (0.014)	0.830*** (0.014)	0.650*** (0.014)	0.800*** (0.014)
Secondary	0.885*** (0.015)	0.760*** (0.015)	0.974*** (0.015)	0.944*** (0.015)	0.814*** (0.015)	0.942*** (0.015)
Higher	1.859*** (0.022)	1.678*** (0.022)	1.996*** (0.022)	1.972*** (0.022)	1.829*** (0.022)	1.959*** (0.022)
Age Difference with Husband (Older than the husband is reference category)						

Same Age	-0.443*** (0.033)	-0.379*** (0.033)	-0.430*** (0.033)	-0.438*** (0.033)	-0.196*** (0.033)	-0.490*** (0.033)
Younger than Husband	-0.472*** (0.033)	-0.467*** (0.033)	-0.476*** (0.033)	-0.467*** (0.033)	-0.292*** (0.033)	-0.584*** (0.033)

Women Body Mass Index (less than 18.5 kg/m2 is reference category)

Body Mass Index (>18.5Kg/m2)	0.426*** (0.013)	0.170*** (0.014)	0.447*** (0.013)	0.446*** (0.013)	0.325*** (0.013)	0.338*** (0.013)

Age at First Birth (above than 30 is reference category)

Less than 19 Years	0.132*** (0.017)	.0.127*** (0.017)	0.139*** (0.017)	0.128*** (0.017)	0.082*** (0.017)	0.149*** (0.017)
20-30	0.324*** (0.023)	0.341*** (0.023)	0.307*** (0.023)	0.330*** (0.023)	0.292*** (0.023)	0.343*** (0.023)

Women's Husband Characteristics

Education (No education is reference category)

Primary	0.450*** (0.015)	0..447*** (0.015)	0.451*** (0.015)	0.453*** (0.015)	0.320*** (0.015)	0.499*** (0.015)
Secondary	-.014 (0.015)	0.105*** (0.015)	0.023 (0.015)	0.012 (0.015)	0.031*** (0.015)	0.091*** (0.015)
Higher	0.043*** (0.020)	0.147*** (0.015)	0.118*** (0.020)	0.058*** (0.020)	0.112*** (0.021)	0.140*** (0.020)

Husband's Employment Status (Did not work is reference category)

Did Work	0.266*** (0.020)	0.429*** (0.027)	0.266*** (0.026)	0.257*** (0.026)	0.147*** (0.027)	0.403*** (0.026)

Women Children Information's

Total Children alive (Children above than four is reference category)

=<4	0.316*** (0.010)	0.416*** (0.011)	0.314*** (0.010)	0.325*** (0.010)	0.267*** (0.010)	0.406*** (0.011)

Children Ever Born(More than 4 is reference category)

=<4	-0.247*** (0.013)	-0.262*** (0.012)	-0.265*** (0.012)	-0.268*** (0.012)	-0.297*** (0.012)	-0.273*** (0.012)

Household Characteristics

Household Wealth Index (Poorest is reference category)

Poorer	0.146*** (0.015)	0.189*** (.015)	0.138*** (0.015)	0.142*** (0.015)	0.174*** (0.015)	0.271*** (0.015)
Middle	0.330*** (0.015)	0.419*** (0.015)	0.312*** (0.015)	0.310*** (0.015)	0.381*** (0.015)	0.514*** (0.015)

Richer	0.598*** (0.016)	0.741 *** (0.016)	0.565*** (0.016)	0.549*** (0.016)	0.686*** (0.016)	0.854*** (0.016)
Richest	0.963*** (0.018)	1.186*** (0.018)	.897*** (0.018)	0.866*** (0.018)	1.088*** (0.018)	1.426*** (0.017)
Locality (Urban is reference category)						
Urban	0.265*** (0.011)	0.232*** (0.011)	0.240*** (0.011)	0.302*** (0.011)	0.220*** (0.011)	0.286*** (0.011)
Total Number of Household members (Above than 5 is reference category)						
=<5	0.329*** (0.017)	0.333*** (0.017)	0.314*** (0.017)	0.336*** (0.017)	0.328*** (0.017)	0.331*** (0.017)
Regions						
South and Southeast Asia		-0.800*** (0.010)				
Central Asia		0.887*** (0.023)				
West Asia			.479*** (0.020)			
Latin America and the Caribbean					1.238*** (0.015)	
Sub-Saharan Africa						-0.498*** (.010)
Pseudo R-Square						
Cox and Snell	0.137	0.158	0.142	0.139	0.160	0.145
Nagelkerke	0.174	0.201	0.180	0.176	0.204	0.185
McFadden	0.096	0.112	0.099	0.097	0.113	0.102

Notes: Significance level <0.01=***,Significant level <0.005=** and Significance level <0.10=*

Standard Error ()

6.5.1. Women Characteristics

Women's characteristics are the essential factors of women empowerment. In Table 6.10, the association among composite women empowerment index and her characteristics has described as follows:

a.   Age Difference with Husband

As compared to the reference category (older than husband), females of the same age with husbands and females younger than husbands negatively affect the composite women empowerment index in all the sets of models. The same relationship has discussed in previous study and proved the strong relationship between age difference between husband and wife with women empowerment(Batool & Jadoon, 2018).

b.   Women Body Mass Index

As compared to the women with lower body mass index, the women with higher body mass index more likely to be empowered in all models. Body mass index is the indicator of the health. With good body mass index means a woman pertains good health. Body mass index has favourably increased the composite women empowerment index. Previous studies proved this relationship(Heslehurst et al., 2019; Jo et al., 2015; Mei et al., 2018; Tigga & Sen, 2016).

c.   Age at First Birth

Women's age is a critical determinant as it also indicates the age of women at her marriage and the age at her first birth. As discussed earlier, older women have more probability of being empowered; in this regard age at her first birth also plays a very imperative role in determining women's empowerment. Age at her first birth indicate how early she become mother and a mother seem to be more empowered in developing countries as compared to those women who do not have children(Samari, 2017). Women were having the aged below 19 years old, and in the range, 20-30 years seem to be more likely to empower than the women above 30 years old.

6.5.2   Women's Husband Characteristics

Results revealed that husband characteristics have a substantial influence on the composite women empowerment index. The relationship between women empowerment and husband characteristics has explained as follows:

a.   Husband Employment Status

According to the husband's employment status, only the women who were married to an employed husband have more probability of being empowered than a woman married to a husband who did not work. According to results, working husbands have a substantial impact on the composite women empowerment index.   Husbands did not work harms women's empowerment as results shown in all of the models in Table 6.10.

b.   Husband's Education

Husband education has a positive impact on women empowerment. All categories of husband education were a positive and significant impact on women empowerment compared to uneducated husbands. Husband education play a crucial role in empowering a women. Educated husbands are broad minded and like to involve ttheir wives in decision making and give them the respect(Akter et al., 2017; Furuta & Salway, 2006; Sebayang et al., 2017; Sundström, Paxton, Wang, & Lindberg, 2017).

6.5.3   Head of Household Characteristics

Characteristics of the head of households are essential to determine women empowerment inside of households. In this framework, age and gender of households showing a strong relationship with women empowerment.

a.   Gender of Head of Household

Women belong to households where the female was the head of households and are more likely to be empowered than the households where the males were the head of households. Females as head of households, respect the women's decisions inside the households and give them the equal opportunity to participate in all decision-making. Females as head of households also reduce the gender inequality in the family, which maximizes women's self-efficacy and self-confidence in the households.

b.   Age of Head of Household

According to results age of head of households indicate an inverse relationship with women empowerment. Head of households whose age is less than 25 years shown a significant role in enhancing the women empowerment. Women empowerment is positively affected by the age of 25 to 55 years as compared to the households where the age of head was above than 55 years old in all the models(Ayevbuomwan et al., 2016).

6.5.4   Women Children Information's

a.   Total number of Children Alive

Women's total number of children alive and women empowerment is closely related to each other. Results in the Table 6.10 indicate that women who have children equal to or below four are more likely to be empowered than the women whose children are more than four in all sets of models(Assaad, Nazier, & Ramadan, 2014b).

b.   Children Ever Born

There exists a strong association between the total number of children ever born and women empowerment. With the evidence of results, women empowerment seems to decreased if total children ever born were less than four children. Women with more children have more power to participate in household decisions making; her work status has improved, increased their self-confidence and self-esteem.

6.5.5   Household Characteristics

a.   Wealth Status of Households

As compared to the reference category (the poorest households), a gradual increase in coefficients of the composite index of women empowerment observed, as well as wealth status (index) improved. That is, the women belonging to the poorer category were more likely to be empowered as compared to the poorest category(reference). Likewise, the women belonging to the middle, richer, and richest households were more empowered than those who belong to the poorest households. It is evident from various studies that economic well-being matters/translates into women's participation in labor force, decision-making, high awareness, self-confidence, and self-esteem. Women belong to households with better wealth status have a relatively high likelihood to be empowered as compared to houses with low wealth status. (Mahmud et al., 2012)

b.   Locality

Results indicate that women living in rural areas seem to be less empowered than women living in urban areas. Urbanization has a positive consequence on empowerment, which means that by the urbanization women can get a better opportunity for herself and aware about the role of empowerment because urban women have more education and know about all law and rights to decide any matters in a better way as compared to the women living in rural areas.

d.   Total Number of Household Members

Women living in the household where the total number of household members was less than or equal to five seem to be more empowered than the women living in the household more than five household members.

6.5.6   Regions

When regions used as a dummy variable for capturing their effects toward composite women empowerment index, then it was found that Central Asia, West Asia, and Latin

America, and the Caribbean have a positive and substantial effect on the composite women

empowerment index than two regions South and Southeast Asia and Sub-Saharan Africa.

CHAPTER 7: WOMEN EMPOWERMENT IN DEVELOPING ECONOMIES: DISAGGREGATED ANALYSIS

In this chapter, the empowerment of women has measured through the principal components' analysis, specifically in Asia (South and Southeast, Central and West Asia), Latin America and the Caribbean, and areas of sub-Saharan Africa. Then, women's empowerment factors have discovered through the Ordinary Least Square method in each region. The latest Demographic and Health Survey of each country has used for regression. The data describe a large amount of information about women's characteristics, the characteristics of the woman's husband, children of women, the characteristics of the head of the household, and the characteristics of the household.

7.1 Descriptive Analysis

The descriptive analysis has a vital role in any research. The descriptive analysis and summary of the variables used in regression analyses presented in Table 6.1. Region-wise explanation of the personal characteristics of women, her husband, women's children, head of household and characteristics of households are described as follows:

7.1.1 Women's Personal Characteristics

According to the target group of women, which has selected for this study described by their education, age, body mass index and, age at her first birth of women. Data showed that in South and Southeast Asia, 32% of women have no education, and 40% of women have secondary education. The ratio of higher education is meagre in South and South

Asia, which is only 9% compared to Central Asia and West Asia, where the ratio of higher education is 29% and 23%, respectively. Meanwhile, in Latin America and Sub-Saharan Africa, higher education rates are 13% and 5%.

Table 7.1: Descriptive and Summary of the Variables Used in the Regression

Independent Variables	South and Southeast Asia		Central Asia		West Asia		Latin America and the Caribbean		Sub-Saharan Africa	
	N	%	N	%	N	%	N	%	N	%
Women Characteristics										
Women Education										
No Education	58,425	32	162	1	5,388	11	7,941	8	103,927	32
Primary	32,674	18	359	2	3,696	8	39,205	41	109,758	33
Secondary	73,220	40	12,203	68	27,761	58	36,683	38	99,255	30
Higher Education	17,000	9	5,140	29	10,829	23	12,389	13	15,336	5
Women Body Mass Index										
less than 18.5 kg/m2	40,916	27	1,501	8	769	2	3,850	4	24,419	11
equal or more than 18.5kg/m2	112,969	73	16,224	92	42,017	98	84,963	96	192,940	89
Women's Age										
15-25	73,320	40	7,659	43	11,542	24	40,973	43	145,292	44
26-35	56,116	31	4,817	27	17,243	36	27,199	28	100,740	31
36-45	40,925	23	3,960	22	14,343	30	21,165	22	63,948	19
Above than 45	10,971	6	1,428	8	4,546	10	6,881	7	18,334	6
Respondent Age at First Birth										
10-15	10,964	6	27	0	871	2	5,552	6	33,176	10
16-20	64,003	35	5,278	30	15,169	32	35,501	37	126,132	38
21-25	38,457	21	5,284	30	16,895	35	17,314	18	48,162	15
26-30	9,594	5	935	5	5,106	11	5,023	5	11,069	3
31-35	1,736	1	198	1	1,104	2	1,307	1	2,240	1
36-40	277	0	43	0	238	1	286	0	324	0
41-45	35	0	8	0	25	0	27	0	36	0
>45	56,266	31	6,091	34	8,266	17	31,208	32	108,593	33
Husband Characteristics										
Husband's Age										
15-25	14,497	11	1,350	11	2,070	5	8,095	15	17,884	9
26-35	47,259	36	4,331	37	13,861	33	18,532	33	65,939	32
36-45	41,550	32	3,743	32	14,161	34	16,830	30	62,847	31
46-55	22,435	17	2,243	19	9,379	22	9,536	17	36,830	18
56-65	3,877	3	139	1	1,783	4	1,982	4	14,342	7

Above than 65	714	0	32	0	509	1	492	1	5,461	3
Education										
No Education	31,005	23	60	0	3,877	9	5,649	9	75,113	34
Primary	26,234	19	117	1	4,800	11	29,651	45	60,789	28
Secondary	61,423	45	7,809	60	25,339	59	24,982	38	65,761	30
Higher Education	19,079	14	5,036	39	8,801	21	5,625	9	17,223	8
Household Head's Characteristics										
Gender of the head of household										
Female	27,332	15	3,879	22	5,739	12	29,709	31	90,595	28
Male	154,000	85	13,985	78	41,935	88	66,509	69	237,719	72
Age of Head of Household										
15-25	7,133	4	373	2	1,315	3	6,247	6	23,515	7
26-35	34,548	22	1,787	10	10,583	22	19,622	20	80,212	24
36-45	54,157	29	4,727	26	14,253	30	28,299	29	92,088	28
46-55	44,064	23	5,797	32	12,495	26	22,896	24	68,855	21
56-65	27,677	13	2,833	16	5,043	11	11,596	12	39,214	12
=>66	13,753	8	2347	13	2,985	8	7,558	8	24,406	7
Women Children Characteristics Number of Children Ever Born										
0-3	78,641	43	8,290	46	14,359	30	47,870	50	131,296	40
4-6	59,086	33	4,922	28	18,179	38	27,697	29	124,324	38
More than 6	43,605	24	2,652	26	15,136	32	20,651	21	71,852	22
Household's Characteristics										
Total Household Members										
>=5	167,014	92	16,173	91	46,489	98	91,973	96	288,833	88
6-9	13,422	7	1,676	9	1,112	2	4,186	4	36,057	11
10-15	776	7	15	0	62	0	59	0	2,547	1
=>15	120	0	0	0	11	0	0	0	877	0
Wealth Index of household										
poorest	24,603	14	3,282	18	9,549	20	19,260	20	63,223	19
poorer	28,153	16	3,278	18	10,090	21	20,286	21	60,060	18
middle	34,120	19	3,377	19	9,846	21	20,338	21	61,740	19
richer	41,579	23	3,500	20	9,460	20	19,120	20	66,598	20
richest	52,877	29	4,427	25	8,729	18	17,214	18	76,693	23
Locality										
Rural	105,419	58	11,724	66	21,989	46	46,308	48	203,427	62
Urban	75,913	42	6,140	34	25,685	54	49,910	52	124,887	38
Dependent Variable Women Empowerment (Mean)	3.15		4.34		4.18		3.95		2.98	
Total Observations	153,885		17,725		42,786		88,813		217,359	

Previous Literature proves that education is the most important determinant of women's empowerment. Previous studies proved that education has a strong association with women empowerment in various countries, for Sri Lanka(Malhotra & Mather, 1997), for Zimbabwe(Hindin, 2006), for India(Jejeebhoy, 2000; Roy & Niranjan, 2004), for India and Pakistan(Jejeebhoy & Sathar, 2001b). All these empirical studies presented that education as a strong correlate of women's empowerment.

In South and Southeast Asia, the age of respondent showed that the majority of women (40%) belongs to the age group of 15-25 years. Only 6% of women are above 45 years old. The same distribution has shown in Central Asia, Latin America and Caribbean and Sub Saharan Africa 43%, 43%, and 44% of women belong to the age group of 15-25 years old. Meanwhile, in West Asia, only 24% of women belong to the age group of 15-25 years old. As compared to other regions in West Asia, the majority of women, 36% belong to the age group of 25-35 years old. These results are similar in the findings of Makama (2013).

Concerning the health of women in South and South East Asia, only 73% women have their body mass index more than or equal to 18.5 kg/m2 and other women have their body mass index less than 18.5 kg/m2 as compared to all other regions where body mass index is much better. In Central Asia, 92% women have their body mass index more than or equal to 18.5 kg/m2 and in West Asia Europe 98% women have their body mass index more than or equal to 18.5 kg/m2 which seems to be higher as compared to all other regions. While in the Latin America and Caribbean and Sub-Saharan 96% and 89% of women have their body mass index more than or equal to 18.5 kg/m2.

At her first birth, the age of women is a significant factor for women's health and the health of her children. In South and Southeast Asia, most of women 35% belong to the group of 15-20 years age at her first birth while 31% women are more than 45 years old at her first birth and 6% women are in the age of 10-15 at her first birth which is very alarming for the health of women. The same situation is seen in Sub Saharan Africa, where 33% of women are above 45 years old, and 10 % of women are the age 10-15 years early at their first birth. At the same time, 38% of women are in the age of 15-25 years old at their first birth. The situation is much better in West Asia, where only 17% of women are above 45 years old, and 2 % of women are the age 10-15 years old at their first birth. Women who were above than 45 years old at their first birth, 34% and 32% in Central Asia and Latin America and Caribbean countries.

7.1.2   Women's Husband Characteristics

Women's husband characteristics are distributed by age, and education has presented in Table 6.1. In South and Southeast Asia, most of the husbands 36% and 32% belong to the age group of 25-35 years and 36-45 years. Distribution of age reveals the same results in all the other regions likewise in Central Asia 37% and 32%, in West Asia 33% and 34%, in and Latin America and Caribbean 33% and 31% and in Sub Saharan Africa 32% and 31 % husbands belong to the age group of 26-35 years and 36-45 years.

The education of husbands plays a very positive role in supporting their households' social and wealth status. At the same time, educated husbands always understand their wives' needs and rights. According to the data in South and Southeast Asia, 23% of husbands are uneducated, 45% have secondary, and only 14% have higher education. In Central Asia,

0% of husbands are uneducated, 60% have secondary, and only 39% have higher education. Meanwhile, in West Asia, 9% of husbands are uneducated, 59% have secondary, and only 21% have higher education. In Latin America and Caribbean, 9% of husbands are illiterate, 38% have secondary, and only 9 % have higher education. In Sub Saharan Africa, 34% of husbands are uneducated, 3 % have secondary, and only 8 % have higher education. Current data reveals that the percentage of illiterate husbands is higher in Latin America and the Caribbean and South and Southeast Asia. While the percentage of higher education is more considerable in Central Asia and Africa and West Asia.

7.1.3 Head of Household Characteristics

Head of household characteristics is distributed by the gender of head of household and the age of head of household. These characteristics are crucial explanatory factors to determine women's empowerment. The head of the household has a significant influence on the environment, decision making, culture, and traditions of a household. In the South and Southeast Asia, most households (85%) have males as head of households. The same situation has found in all the regions males are the head of households. Data reveal as 78%, 88%,69%, and 72% head of households found as a male in Central Asia, Africa, and West Asia, Latin America and the Caribbean, and Sub-Sahara Africa.

In Latin America and the Caribbean and Sub Saharan Africa, the percentage of males as head of households seems to be minimal compared to other regions.

In South and Southeast Asia, most heads of households 29% and 23% belong to 35-45 years and 45-55 years old. The distribution of heads of households by their age seems to be almost same in the entire region. In Central Asia, many households, 26% and 32% belong to the age group of 35-45 years and 45-55 years old. In West Asia, the head of households' common age is 30%, and 26% belong to the age group of 35-45 years and 45-55 years old. In Latin America and Caribbean majority of the head of households, 29% and 24% belong to the age group of 35-45 years and 45-55 years old. In Sub Saharan Africa, most of the heads of households 28% and 21% belong to the age group of 35-45 years and 45-55 years old. In Sub-Saharan Africa percentage (24%) of younger heads of households between the ages of 25-35 years is more significant than all other regions.

7.1.4   Women's Children Related Factors

Total ever born children indicated the fertility rate of women. According to data in South and Southeast Asia, 43% women have the number of ever born children between the ranges 0-3, 33% women have a number of ever born children between the range of 3-6, and 24% women have their ever-born children more than six. According to this data, the fertility rate is very high in this region. While in the Central Asia 46% women have a number of ever born children between the range 0-3, 38% women have a number of ever born children between the range of 3-6 and 32% women have their ever-born children more than six. In the West Asia, 36% women have several ever-born children between the ranges 0-3; 38 % women have a number of ever born children between the range of 3-6, and 32 % women have their ever-born children more than six. In Latin America and Caribbean's 50%, women have several ever-born children between the range 0-3, 29% women have a number of ever born children between the range of 3-6 and 21% women have their ever-born children more than six. According to this data, the fertility rate is very high in this region. In

Latin America and Caribbean's 40%, women have the number of ever born children between the ranges 0-3; 38 % of women have the number of ever-born children between the range of 3-6, and 22% of women have their ever-born children more than six. This data analysis reveals that in Latin America, Caribbean, and Sub Saharan Africa, women having their ever-born children in the range of more than six is smaller than the entire regions.

7.1.5   Household's Characteristics

Household's characteristics are distributed by the total members of the household, household wealth index, Locality.

In South and Southeast Asia, most of the households (92%) have total household members equal to or less than five. The same percentage seems to be in all the regions as in Central Asia 91%, West Asia 98%, Latin America and Caribbean's 96% and in Sub Saharan Africa 88% households have the number of households members equal or less than five.

The wealth index of a household presents the socio-economic status of the members of that house. The wealth index was categorized into four groups. In South and South East Asia, only 29% and 23% of households have the richest and richer wealth index. On the other hand, 14%, 16%, and 19% of households have poorest, and middle wealth index. Overall results indicate that only 52% of households enjoy the excellent status of wealth in South and Southeast Asia. Meanwhile, in Central Asia, 20% and 25% of households have richest and richer wealth functional. On the other hand, 18%, 18%, and 19% of households have poorer and middle wealth indexes. In West Asia, 20% and 18% of households have richest and richer wealth index. On the other hand, 20%, 21%, and 21% of households have poorest, poorer and middle wealth index. In Latin America and Caribbean's 20% and 18% of households have richest and richer wealth index. On the other hand, 20%, 21%, and 18% of households have poorest, poorer, and middle wealth index. In Sub Saharan Africa 20% and 23% of households have richest and richer wealth index. On the other hand, 19%, 18%, and 19% of households have poorest, poorer, and middle wealth index. Overall results indicate that in South and Southeast Asia 52%, Central Asia 45%, West Asia 38%, Latin America and Caribbean's 38%, and in Sub Saharan Africa 43% households enjoy the excellent wealth status. In southeast and South East Asia and Latin America, and Caribbean's inequality in wealth seems to be more than other regions.

Locality of households is categorized into rural and urban areas. According to data in South and Southeast Asia 58% of households are placed in the rural area, and only 42% of households are placed in urban areas. In Central Asia, 66%, West Asia 46%, Latin America and Caribbean's 48% and in Sub Saharan Africa 62% households has placed in the rural area while 34%, 54%, 52%, and 38% households are placed in the urban area.

7.2   Extent of Women Empowerment in different Regions

According to the composite women empowerment index score, women got different extent of women empowerment in different regions.

Across the regions, Central Asia (with CWEI score 4.3399; top scorer) stands first, showing the highest empowerment status of women, while Sub-Saharan Africa (with CWEI score 2.986; least scorer) stands 5th showing the lowest empowerment status of women.

With CWEI scores 4.176, 3.953, and 3.152, the regions of West Asia, Latin America and

Caribbean, South, and South Asia are respectively ranked 2nd, 3rd, and 4th for women's

empowerment status.

Table 7.2: Regions' Ranking with respect to Women Empowerment Status (Quantitative)

Regions	Less Empowered (%)	Rank	Regions	Moderately Empowered (%)	Rank	Regions	Highly Empowered (%)	Rank	Regions	CWEI Mean Score	Rank
Central Asia	15.8	1	South and South Asia	79	1	Central Asia	36.7	1	Central Asia	4.339	1
West Asia	13.7	2	West Asia	76.7	2	West Asia	18.7	2	West Asia	4.176	2
Sub-Saharan Africa	11.8	3	Sub-Saharan Africa	72.2	3	Latin America and the Caribbean	16	3	Latin America and the Caribbean	3.953	3
South and South Asia	2.3	4	Central Asia	69.1	4	South and South Asia	15.1	4	South and South Asia	3.152	4
Latin America and the Caribbean	0.8	5	Latin America and the Caribbean	62.5	5	Sub-Saharan Africa	9.6	5	Sub-Saharan Africa	2.986	5

Source: Demographic and Health Surveys(DHS-V   2003 – 2008, DHS-VI 2008 – 2013, DHS-7   2013 – 2018)

7.3　Econometric Analyses of Women Empowerment and its Determinants

7.3.1　Determinants of Women Empowerment in South and Southeast Asia

The determinants of women empowerment in South and South-East Asia has estimated in column one of the Table 7.3. Women's empowerment has positively associated with the age of women. Women's empowerment has intensifications with increasing age of women. An older woman seems to have more power than younger women (Noreen 2011). Women's education classified into four groups, no education, primary education, secondary education and higher education. In the model, no education is considered a reference category.

Women's empowerment was negatively associated with primary education and is positively associated with secondary and higher education. Compared to all education groups, women's empowerment is strongly associated with higher education. Women with higher education seem to have more power than women with less education (Jeckoniah et al., 2012). The age of women in their first birth is negatively associated with women's empowerment. Older women appear to have less power than women who are younger at their first birth.

Table 7.3: Determinants of Women Empowerment in Different Regions

Independent Variables	Women Empowerment Index (WEI)				
	South and South-east Asia	West Asia	Central Asia	Latin America and the Caribbean	Sub-Saharan Africa
(Constant)	3.67***	-.3919	1.23***	1.266***	2.828 ***
	(0.028)	(0.074))	(0.211)	(0.047)	(0.045)
Women Characteristics					
Women's Age	0.032***	0.023***	.007***	.008***	.0134***
	(0.006)	(0.001)	(.002)	(.0011)	(0.0013)
Women Education (No education is reference Category)					
Primary Education	-.049***	0.041**	.266**	.191***	-.485***
	(0.009)	(0.024)	(0.271)	(0.014)	(0.035)
Secondary Education	0.051***	0.104***	0.812***	0.305***	0.648***
	(0.009)	(0.019)	(0.110)	(0.018)	(0.036)
Higher Education	0.271***	0.742***	1.42***	.348***	.357***
	(0.017)	(0.024)	(0.117)	(0.027)	(0.019)
Women's Age at First Birth	-.020***	0.008***	-.011***	-.016***	0.003*
	(0.007)	(0.002)	(.0334)	(.0014)	(.001)
Women Body Mass Index (Less than 18.5 kg/m2 is reference category)					
Body Mass Index	-.0202***	0.126***	.0889**	.2004***	.225***
	(0.007)	(0.055)	(.0412)	(.028)	(.019)
Husband's Age	-.002***	-.004***	-.002	-.005***	-.001
	(.0006)	(0.001)	(.002)	(.0007)	(.0007)
Husband's Education (No education is reference Category)					
Primary Education	.0572***	-.0253	.025	.128***	.138***
	(0.010)	(0.024)	(.0258)	(.0155)	(.016)
	.1211***	.002	.0052	.153***	.052**

Secondary Education	(0.009)	(.021)	(.183)	(.018)	(.018)
Higher Education	0.214***	.0117	.156	.139***	.081***
	(0.14)	(.025)	(.1842)	(.018)	(.027)

Household Head's Characteristics

Age of Head of household	.0008***	.0027***	.0005	-.0006	.0001
	(0.0003)	(.0005)	(.0007)	(.0004)	(.0006)

Gender of Head of Household (Female is reference category)

Male	.1349***	-.027	-.0477	-.082***	.053***
	(0.010)	(.022)	(.0261)	(.011)	(.015)

Women's Children

Total number of children ever born	-.0327***	.0123	-.0197**	-.042***	-.027***
	(0.0004)	(.009)	(.008)	(.003)	(.0037)

Household Wealth Index (Poorest is reference category)

Poorer	-.0526***	-.017	-.042	.690***	.137***
	(0.011)	(.016)	(.029)	(.013)	(.017)
Middle	-.0885***	.011	.0332	1.01***	.192***
	(0.011)	(.017)	(.029)	(.014)	(.017)
richer	-.0307***	.077***	.0619**	1.174***	.377***
	(0.012)	(.018)	(.030)	(.016)	(.019)
Richest	0.126	.087***	.089**	1.253***	. 603***
	(0.014)	(.020)	(.036)	(.019)	(.022)

Locality(Rural is reference category)

Urban	0.132***	-.0138	.007	.163***	.105***
	(0.007)	(.013)	(.027)	(.011)	(.015)

Total number of household members

	0.005***	-.023**	-.0208***	.011***	-.0203***
	(0.014)	(.0026)	(.004)	(.002)	(.002)

R^2	0.036	0.129	0.146	0.387	0.063
Observations	96531	32473	10461	31075	95628

Notes: Significance level <0.01=***,Significant level <0.005=** and Significance level <0.10=*, Standard Error is in ()

Body mass index(equal or higher than 18.5kg/m2) showing negative association with women empowerment as compared to the reference category(less than 18.5kg/m2). This result indicates that women having body mass index higher than 18.5kg/m2 may cause obesity in women which affect the health of women. In Asia, obesity rate increases, in South and Southeast Asia, it is at highest 78%(Ramachandran & Snehalatha, 2010). Women were having husbands with older age showing negative association with women empowerment. As husbands with older age usually taking all decisions related to their wives by themselves. Education of husbands has a positive association with women's empowerment. Husbands with higher education understand all necessary rights and needs of women, and they empowered their wives happily (Noreen, 2011).

The age of the head of the household has a positive association with women empowerment. Households where the head of households are older, women seem to be more empowered than those households where the head of households are at a younger age. Gender of the head of households also shows a vital role in determining the women's empowerment inside the families. The male heads of households positively associate with women empowerment (Ayevbuomwan et al., 2016). Total children ever born both have a negative association with women empowerment.

Women with more children were less empowered as compared to those women who have fewer children. Women belong to households with the richest wealth index seem to be more empowered as compared to households with poor wealth index (Gupta & Yesudian, 2006). Women belong to an urban locality and have more empowerment than those who belong to rural areas (Musonera & Heshmati, 2017).

7.3.2 Determinants of Women Empowerment in West Asia

The determinants of women's empowerment in West Asia were estimated in the second column of Table 7.3. The age of women is negatively associated with women's empowerment. Women's empowerment increased with the increasing age of women. An older woman seems to have more empowered than younger women. Women's education is positively associated with women's empowerment.

An educated woman seems to be more autonomous than uneducated women. Education is a source of power for women. With the acquisition of education, women become more powerful and improve women's efficiency inside and outside of the home. The age of women at the first birth is positively associated with women's empowerment.

Women with a better body mass index show a positive association with women's empowerment compared to the reference category low body mass index. Healthy women seem to have more empowerment than unhealthy women. In West Asia increase in age of husband decreased women empowerment. On the other hand, education of women's husband has favorably link with women's empowerment.

The increase in age of the head of household positively associated with the empowerment of women. The senior head of the household increased the empowerment of women. Sex of the head of the household appeared to become essential for determining the empowerment of women. The male heads of household women have a negative association with women's empowerment. The total number of children ever born was negatively related to women's empowerment.

Women with more children have less power than women with fewer children. Women who belong to families with the richest wealth index seem to be more autonomous than families with a low wealth index.

7.3.3   Determinants of Women Empowerment in Central Asia

The determinants of women's empowerment in the Central Asia have estimated in the third column of Table 7.3. The age of women is positively associated with women's empowerment. An older woman seems to have more power than the younger women of Central Asia.

Women's education is positively associated with women's empowerment. An educated woman seems to have more power than women without education. The age of women at first birth is negatively associated with women's empowerment. Older women seem to have less power than women who are younger at first birth. Women with normal body mass index has shown positive association with women's empowerment compared to the reference category low body mass index.

Women seem to become more empowered with the increase in their age. In this region, the oldest husband's wife seems to have more power than the wives of the younger husbands. Furthermore, women empowerment has adversely affected by the male head of household.

The total number of ever born children also has a negative connotation with women empowerment. Women with more children have less power than women with fewer children. Women belong to families with a richer wealth index that seems to be more powerful than families with a poor wealth index.

7.3.4   Determinants of Women Empowerment in Latin America and the Caribbean

The determinants of women empowerment in Latin America and the Caribbean region have estimated in column four of Table 7.2. The age of women is positively associated with women's empowerment. An older woman seems to have more empowered than younger women in Latin America and the Caribbean's countries. Women's education is positively associated with women's empowerment. An educated woman appeared to stay more empowered as compared to uneducated women. Education is a source of confidence and knowledge of their capabilities for women. The age of women at their first birth is negatively associated with women's empowerment. Older women appeared to stay less empowered as compared to the women who are younger at their first birth. Women with better body mass index showing a positive association with women empowerment as compared low body mass index.

Healthy women seem to be more empowered as compared to unhealthy women. The age of the husband has a negative association with women's empowerment. The education of husbands has a positive association with women's empowerment. The age of the head of household has a negative association with women empowerment. The age of head of household proved a crucial determinant of women empowerment.

The gender of head of households is essential to determine women's empowerment. The male heads of households have a negative association with women empowerment. The total number of children under five years and the number of children ever born has a negative association with the women's empowerment. Women having more number of children are less empowered as than those women who have fewer children.

Women belong to households with the richest wealth index seem to be more empowered than households with poor wealth index. Women residing in urban areas seem to be more empowered as compared to those women who were living in rural areas.

7.3.5   Determinants of Women Empowerment in Sub-Saharan Africa

The determinants of women empowerment in the Sub-Saharan Africa region estimated in column five of Table 7.3. The age of women is positively associated with women's empowerment. An older woman seems to have more empowered than younger women in Sub-Saharan Africa. Women's education is positively associated with women's empowerment. An educated woman appears to be more empowered as compared to uneducated women. Education is a source of confidence and knowledge of their capabilities for women. The age of women at their first birth is positively associated with women's empowerment. Older women appeared to remain more empowered than those women who were younger at their first birth.

Women with other than low body mass index showing a positive association with empowerment. Healthy women seem to remain empowered than those women who were unhealthy women. Women empowerment adversely affected by the age of the husband has a negative association with women's empowerment. Education of husbands has a positive association with women's empowerment. Women empowerment has influenced by the increasing age of head of household. Women empowerment seems to increase with the increase in the age of head of household. The male heads of households have a positive association with women empowerment. The total number of children under five years and the number of children ever born has a negative association with the women's empowerment.

Women having a higher number of children are less empowered than those who have fewer children. Women belong to households with the richest wealth index seem to be more empowered than households with poor wealth index. Women residing in urban areas seem to be more empowered than those living in rural areas.

CHAPTER 8: WOMEN EMPOWERMENT AND CHILD HEALTH

In this chapter, the relationship between child health and women empowerment has developed. Child health is measured by stunting (height for age), wasting (weight for height), underweight (weight for age), and Composite Index of Anthropometric Failure (constructed by stunting, wasting, and underweight). Correlates of child health have been assessed in this chapter by following Anderson and Newman and Grossman Model for child health. The main focus is on women empowerment, and all the characteristics (mother personal characteristics, his husband, children, and household) related to women empowerment included as control variables. All these factors cover the four factors[7] of Anderson and Newman model. The Pearson Chi-Square test has predicted the association between child health and women empowerment, and then econometric analysis has been applied by using Binary Logistic Regression.

8.1 Presence of Malnutrition among the Children of Developing Countries

Malnutrition is considered a severe health burden in developing countries and comes in debates as a risk factor of illness and deaths on the national and international levels. Height for age, weight for height, and weight for age have used as indicators of malnutrition, and then a composite index of anthropometric failure has been formulated to combine all the indicators in an index. Malnutrition indicates poor child health and this malnutrition cause

---

[7] Predisposing Factors, Enabling Factors, Need-Based Factors and Environment factors

many diseases and slow down the physical and mental growth of children under the age of years. A composite index of anthropometric failure is classified into seven groups, one of which is no failure, and another six are having with failure. Classification of Composite Index of Anthropometric Failure has given in Table 8.1.

Table 8.1: Classification of children with Anthropometric failure (CIAF)

Group Name	CIAF	Stunting	Wasting	Underweight	Frequency	%
A	No Failure	No	No	No	164158	61.1
B	Stunting	Yes	No	No	45452	16.9
C	Wasting	No	Yes	No	2342	1.9
D	Underweight	No	No	Yes	8816	3.3
E	Stunting and Wasting	Yes	Yes	No	30658	11.4
F	Wasting and Underweight	No	Yes	Yes	6337	2.4
Y	Stunting, Wasting and Underweight	Yes	Yes	Yes	7685	2.9
	Total				265448	100

*Classification following Nandy et al., 2005.

Regarding incidence of child stunting Timor Leste, Guatemala, and Congo Democratic are amongst the topmost prevalent while Domonique Republic, Jorden, and Armenia are amongst the lowermost prevalent economies.

As regards the prevalence of child wasting Timor Leste, Chad, and Nepal are amongst the topmost prevalent while, Armenia, Jorden, and Kyrgyz economies Republic are at the bottom in the panel of developing.

Table 8.2: Countries' Ranking with Respect to Child Health Status

Country	Stunting (%)	Rank	Country	Wasting (%)	Rank	Country	Under-weight (%)	Rank	Country	CIAF (%)	Rank
Jordan	8.7		Armenia	2.7	1	Peru	0.7	1	Jordan	11	1
Armenia	10.4	2	Jordan	3	2	Guatemala	0.7	2	Armenia	15.8	2
Kyrgyz republic	17.8	3	Kyrgyz republic	3.5	3	Honduras	1.4	3	Kyrgyz republic	20.4	3
Peru	20.2		Peru	4.2	4	Jordan	2.2	4	Peru	20.9	4
Haiti	22.3	5	Azerbaijan	7.3	5	Kyrgyz republic	2.9	5	Gabon	26.7	5
Gabon	22.9	6	Honduras	7.9	6	Malawi	3.1	6	Haiti	26.9	6
Namibia	23.2	7	Gabon	8.3	7	Zimbabwe	3.3	7	Honduras	26.9	7
Tajikistan	23.7	8	Zimbabwe	9.7	8	Gabon	4.1	8	Azerbaijan	29.7	8
Azerbaijan	24.4	9	Tajikistan	11.5	9	Armenia	4.7	9	Namibia	30.7	9
Honduras	25.5	10	Malawi	11.5	10	Tanzania	4.8	10	Kenya	32	10
Gambia	25.8	11	Haiti	11.8	11	Haiti	5	11	Tajikistan	32.7	11
Kenya	27.1	12	Guatemala	12.5	12	Mozambique	5.2	12	Zimbabwe	33.8	12
Comoros	27.7	13	Mozambique	13.1	13	Uganda	5.3	13	Tonga	34.3	13
Tonga	28.3	14	Kenya	13.2	14	Kenya	5.5	14	India	34.9	14
India	29.4	15	Tanzania	13.6	15	Azerbaijan	5.7	15	Cameroon	35.7	15
Cote d' Ivoire	29.8	16	Cameroon	13.7	16	Cameroon	5.7	16	Gambia	36.3	16
Zimbabwe	30.7	17	Namibia	13.8	17	Cote d' Ivoire	7.1	17	Cote d' Ivoire	36.3	17
Cameroon	31.6	18	Uganda	13.8	18	Tonga	7.3	18	Uganda	36.3	18
Uganda	31.8	19			19	Congo Democratic	7.9	19	Malawi	37.8	19
Cambodia	32.5	20	Comoros	14.5	20	Namibia	8	20	Tanzania	38	20
Tanzania	33.4	21	Cote d 'Ivoire	14.6	21	Pakistan	8.7	21	Comoros	38.4	21
Burkina Faso	34.2	22	Sierra Leon	16	22	Sierra Leon	9.4	22	Cambodia	41.6	22
Malawi	35.2	23	Tonga	16.8	23	Tajikistan	9.6	23	Mozambique	43.6	23

Country	Value	#	Country	Value	#	Country	Value	#	Country	Value	#
Ethiopia	35.9	24	Gambia	17.9	24	Cambodia	9.7	24	Sierra Leon	44.9	24
Nigeria	36.1	25	Pakistan	22.3	25	Nepal	10.7	25	Ethiopia	46.3	25
Pakistan	37.7	26	Congo Democratic	23.2	26	Comoros	11.6	26	Burkina Faso	46.5	26
Sierra Leon	37.7	27	Cambodia	23.4	27	Gambia	11.7	27	Guatemala	47	27
Mozambique	39.3	28	Burkina Faso	24.9	28	Ethiopia	11.9	28	Nigeria	49.2	28
Nepal	42.1	29	Ethiopia	25.3	29	India	13.8	29	Nepal	50.2	29
Chad	42.9		Nigeria	26.9	30	Chad	14.2	30	Congo Democratic	50.3	30
Congo Democratic	44.1	31	India	29.4	31	Burkina Faso	15.3	31	Pakistan	52.2	31
Guatemala	46.3	32	Nepal	29.5	32	Nigeria	16.6	32	Chad	52.9	32
Timor Lestee	57.2	33	Chad	32.5	33	Timor Lestee	19.5	33	Timor Lestee	71.6	33

Source: Demographic and Health Surveys(DHS-V   2003 – 2008, DHS-VI 2008 – 2013, DHS-7   2013 – 2018

In contrast with Peru, Guatemala, and Honduras where the occurrence of underweight is at minimum, the prevalence is at maximum in Timor Leste, Nigeria, and Burkina Faso.

In terms of CIAF Timor Leste, Chad, and Pakistan are at the top, whereas Domonique Republic, Jorden, and Armenia are at the bottom.

8.2   Bivariate Analysis and Binary Logistic Regression Analysis

Child Health has very important for the human capital formation of any economy; healthy generation makes the countries developed economically as well as socially. Here in this study, the indicators of malnutrition have used to evaluate child health because malnutrition among children is a sign of ill health. Bivariate analysis has formulated using the Pearson Chi-Square test to determine the association between child health (stunting, wasting, underweight and CIAF) and women/mother empowerment. The Pearson Chi-Square test has also checked the association between child health and other control variables like mother characteristics, father characteristics, household characteristics, and siblings. Binary logistic Regression analysis was applied to find out the effects of women empowerment on child health, and at the same effect of other control, variables have analyzed. Results of bivariate analysis and Binary Logistic Regression models have given in Table 8.3 and Table 7.4.

8.3   Women Empowerment and Child Health

Binary Logistics models were employed to detect the impact of mother/women empowerment on child health as well as control variables, i.e. characteristics of the mother; father, households, and children used to find out their influence on child health. Five dimensions of women empowerment and a composite women empowerment index have constructed to detect all dimensions' combined impact on child health.

Table 8.3: Levels and Dimensions of Women Empowerment and Child Health Measures: Bivariate Analyses

Characteristics	CIAF	Stunting	Wasting	Underweight
Women Empowerment				
Work status Index				
Low	36.20%	29.90%	21.10%	11.10%
Medium	42.90%	35.40%	23.00%	11.10%
Higher	39.60%	33.00%	22.50%	19.90%
Awareness Index				
Low	43.50%	36.00%	24.60%	12.10%
Medium	33.60%	27.80%	17.90%	9.30%
Higher	30.20%	24.90%	14.70%	8.20%
Decision Making				
Low	40.70%	33.20%	28.30%	17.00%
Medium	37.20%	31.40%	22.40%	11.40%
Higher	35.20%	28.30%	19.80%	9.50%
Self Esteem				
Low	44.60%	35.90%	25.90%	13.10%
Medium	40.70%	33.30%	23.80%	11.90%
Higher	37.40%	31.30%	19.90%	10.00%
Self Confidence				
Low	32.90%	28.40%	28.10%	14.60%
Medium	41.40%	34.30%	22.70%	11.10%
Higher	38.60%	31.50%	18.40%	9.50%
Composite Women Empowerment Index				
Low	45.30%	36.20%	28.80%	15.20%
Medium	39.20%	32.50%	22.00%	11.10%
Higher	34.80%	29.60%	14.60%	6.70%
Women Characteristics				
Mother's Body Mass Index				
Less than 18.5 kg/m2	45.90%	38.20%	31.70%	16.30%
More than 18.5 kg/m2	37.00%	30.50%	16.90%	8.60%
Mother's Education				
No Education	46.40%	37.70%	27.20%	13.70%
Primary	38.60%	33.00%	16.70%	7.20%

Secondary	34.50%	28.30%	15.70%	8.40%
Higher	27.50%	21.90%	10.50%	6.70%
Mother's Age				
Below 25	39.40%	32.70%	19.60%	9.70%
25-35	37.50%	31.00%	19.20%	9.60%
35-45	37.10%	30.60%	16.10%	8.20%
Above than 45	36.00%	29.40%	15.30%	7.80%
Mother's Age at First Birth				
Below than 20	37.90%	31.30%	19.50%	9.90%
20-30	31.60%	25.10%	14.70%	8.80%
Above than 30	39.90%	33.10%	17.00%	8.00%
Father's Characteristic				
Father Education				
No Education	47.20%	38.20%	27.40%	14.00%
Primary	38.70%	33.10%	17.60%	7.80%
Secondary	34.10%	28.10%	17.10%	9.20%
Higher	30.20%	23.50%	13.70%	8.70%
Father's Age				
Below 25	39.50%	33.10%	21.70%	10.90%
25-35	37.20%	30.60%	21.00%	11.10%
35-45	38.10%	31.40%	18.70%	9.60%
45-55	37.90%	30.80%	16.70%	8.90%
Above than 55	41.60%	33.10%	19.80%	10.70%
Father's employment status				
Father did not work	41.30%	33.80%	20.00%	10.40%
Father did work	38.70%	31.80%	19.20%	9.40%
Household's Characteristics				
Household's Wealth status				
Poorest	40.80%	33.80%	21.50%	10.50%
Poorer	40.20%	33.40%	20.30%	9.90%
Middle	38.10%	31.90%	18.40%	8.90%
Richer	36.80%	30.50%	17.20%	8.70%
Richest	35.70%	28.90%	15.90%	8.60%
Total household's members				
<=5	37.70%	31.20%	18.10%	9.10%
>5	42.90%	34.70%	22.50%	11.60%
Locality				
Rural Area	40.60%	33.60%	20.70%	10.20%
Urban Area	34.80%	28.80%	15.40%	8.00%
Children at Household				

Total number of Children Alive

<=4	36.60%	30.40%	16.70%	8.30%
>4	41.10%	33.70%	22.00%	11.20%

Total number of Children Ever Born

<=4	37.70%	31.20%	17.30%	17.30%
>4	38.40%	31.80%	19.30%	19.30%

Notes: All chi-square ($\chi2$) test showed a statistically significant association with p < 0.05 at 95% CI;

Table 8.4: Dimensions of Women Empowerment and Child Health: Logit Regression Analyses

Independent Variables	Coefficient (SE., P-value)			
	CIAF <-2SD	Stunting <-2SD	Wasting <-2SD	Underweight <-2SD
Mother/Women Empowerment				
Work Status	.051(.008,.000)	.068(.008,.000)	.040(.009,.000)	-.007(.012,.543)
Awareness	-.139(.010,.000)	-.127(.010,.000)	-.125(.012,.000)	-.095(.016,.000)
Decision Making	-.013(.008,.095)	-.001(.008,.862)	-.039(.009,.000)	-.062(.012,.000)
Self Esteem	-.052(.007,.000)	-.031(.007,.000	-.028(.008,.001)	.022(.010,.037)
Self Confidence	.228(.009,.000)	.214(.009,.000)	.144(.010,.000)	.098(.013,.000)
Mother's Characteristics				
Mother Body Mass Index (less than 18.5 kg/m2 is reference category)				
More than 18.5 kg/m2	-.243(.020,.000)	-.285(.021,.000)	-.367(.022,.000)	-.320(.028,.000)
Mother's Education (No Education is reference category)				
Primary	-.188(.021,.000)	-.168(.022,.000)	-.241(.025,.000)	-.218(.033,.000)
Secondary	-.270(.024,.000)	-.283(.025,.000)	-.305(.028,.000)	-.196(.037,.000)
Higher Education	-.333(.040,.000)	-.404(.043,.000)	-.591(.053,.000)	-.189(.063,.001)
Mother's age (Equal or below than 19 years old is reference category)				
20-25	-.013(.018,.584)	-.012(.021,.787)	-.048(.029,.000)	-.041(.037,.260)
26-35	-.054(.027,.266)	-.031(.030,.422)	-.051(.031,.000)	-.047(.041,.243)
Above than 35	.060(.029,.970)	.001(.028,.999)	-.052(.032,.000)	-.054(.041,.190)
Mother's age on her first birth (Equal or below than 19 years old is reference category)				
20-25	-.007(018, .690)	-.012(.019,.470)	.006(.022,.785)	-.001(.028,.998)
26-35	-.054(.029,.060)	-.044(. 030..039)	-.039(.034,.253)	-.089(045,.048)
Above than 35	-.017(.021,.438)	-.013(.022,549)	-.023(.025, .373)	-.054(.033,.114)
Father's Characteristic				
Father Education (No Education is reference category)				
Primary	-.163(.022,.000)	-.127(.023,.000)	-.149(.026,.000)	-.171(.034,.000)
Secondary	-.211(.023,.000)	-.167(.024,.000)	-.173(.027,.000)	-.137(.034,.000)
Higher Education	-.188(.033,.000)	-.200(.035,.000)	-.164(.040,.000)	-.067(.050,.000)
Father's Age (Below than 25 is reference category)				
25-35	-.066(.025,.009)	-.059(.027,.026)	-.034(.030,.254)	-.048(.039,.218)

35-45	-.031(.028,.276)	-.013(.029,.654)	-.035(.033,.297)	-.085(.043,.047)
45-55	-.081(.032,.011)	-.072(.033,.031)	-.106(.038,.006)	-.105(.049,.033)
Above than 55	-.123(.039,.002)	-.131(.040,.001)	-.168(.046,.000)	-.101(.059,.085)
Father's employment status (Father did not work is reference category)				
Father did work	-.065(.045,.050)	-.036(.047,.043)	-.087(.058,.133)	-.110(.077,.154)
Household's Characteristics				
Household's Wealth Status (Poorest is reference category)				
Poorer	.010(.022,.649)	-.005(.023,.857)	.003(.025,.914)	.006(.033,.862)
Middle	-.086(.023,.000)	-.087(.024,.000)	-.138(.027,.000)	-.076(.035,.031)
Richer	-.096(.025,.000)	-.123(.026,.000)	-.199(.030,.000)	-.064(.039,.101)
Richest	-.063(.030,.037)	-.125(.032,.000)	-.244(.037,.000)	-.080(.045,.094)
Locality (Rural Areas are reference category)				
Urban Areas	-.009(.018,.639)	-.036(.019,.062)	-.038(.022,.088)	-.002(.028,.986)
Sibling's Characteristics				
Total Children Ever Born (More than 4 is reference category)				
<=4	-.083(.019,.000)	-.077(.020,.000)	-.122(.023,.000)	-.093(.029,.001)
Regions (Sub Saharan Africa is reference Category)				
South and South East Asia	.361(.026,.000)	.308(.027,.000)	1.177(.032,.000)	.913 (.045,.000)
West Asia	-1.428(.059,.000)	-1.326(.065,.000)	-1.584(.104,.000)	-1.081(.109,.000)
Central Asia	-.391(.041,.000)	-.314(.044,.000)	-.487(.062,.000)	-.168 (.073,.037)
Latin America and Caribbean	-.381(.035,.000)	.225(.036,.000)	-.426(.053,.000)	-1.002 (.090,.000)
Secular States	.040(.025,.113)	-.034(.026,.194)	.382(.032,.000)	.384 (.046,.000)
Net Imports	.319(.020,.000)	.131(.021,.000)	.337(.025,.000)	.529 (.031,.000)
Constant	-.427(.041,.000)	-.831(.087,.000)	-1.171(.061,.000)	1.806(.096,.000)
Cox & Snell R Square	.063	.047	.084	.035
Nagelkerke R Square	.086	.067	.130	.070

Table 8.5: Levels of Women Empowerment and Child Health Measures: Logit Regression Analyses

Independent Variables	Coefficient (SE., P-value)			
	CIAF <-2SD	**Stunting** **<-2SD**	**Wasting** **<-2SD**	**Underweight** **<-2SD**
Mother/Women Empowerment (Low Empowerment is reference category)				
Medium	-.040 (.030,.176)	-.137(.031,.000)	-.011(.025,.652)	-.048(.031,.122)
High	-.062 (.022,.006)	-.117(.023,.000)	-.005(.036,.891)	-.141(.047,.003)
Mother's Characteristics				
Mother Body Mass Index (less than 18.5 kg/m2 is reference category)				

More than 18.5 kg/m2	-.285(.020,.000)	-.286(.021,.000)	-.370(.022,.000)	-.327(.028,.000)
Mother's Education (No Education is reference category)				
Primary	-.214(.021,.000)	-.192(.021,.000)	-.270(.024,.000)	-.248(.032,.000)
Secondary	-.373 (.023,.000)	-.382(.024,.000)	-.401(.027,.000)	-.268(.035,.000)
Higher Education	-.519 (.038,.000)	-.557(.042,.000)	-.763(.051,.000)	-.317(.061,.000)
Mother's age (Below than 19 years old is reference category)				
20-25	-.009(.024,.697)	-.009(.025,.720)	-.045(.029,.115)	-.041(.037,.264)
26-35	-.019(.026,.462)	-.021(.028,.436)	-.044(.031,.164)	-.044(.041,.278)
Above than 35	.009(.027,.731)	.008(.028,.782)	-.047(.032,.141)	-.053(.041,.196)
Mother's age on her first birth (Below than 19 years old is reference category)				
20-25	-.007(.018,.708)	-.012(.019,.530)	.006(.022,.784)	-.001(.028,.968)
26-35	-.047(.028,.095)	-.038(.030,.197)	-.034(.034,.313)	-.088(.045,.049)
Above than 35	-.008(.021,.710)	-.005(.022,.818)	-.016(.025,.540)	-.048(.033,.141)
Father's Characteristic				
Father Education (No Education is reference category)				
Primary	-.157(.022,.000)	-.120(.023,.000)	-.147(.025,.000)	-.177(.033,.000)
Secondary	-.230 (.023,.000)	-.185(.024,.000)	-.189(.026,.000)	-.173(.034,.000)
Higher Education	-.229 (.033,.000)	-.240 (.034,.000)	-.197(.040,.000)	-.084(.049,.090)
Father's Age (Below than 25 is reference category)				
25-35	-.086 (.026,.006)	-.074(.026,.005)	-.054(.030,.069)	-.071(.039,.066)
36-45	-.025 (.031,.537)	-.003(.029,.908)	-.038(.033,.251)	-.106(.043,.013)
46-55	-.058 (.038,.060)	-.046(.033,.166)	-.095(.038,.012)	-.120(.049,.014)
Above than 55	-.120 (.045,.003)	-.122(.040,.002)	-.170(.046,.000)	-.122(.058,.036)
Father's employment status (Father did not work is reference category)				
Father did work	-.067 (.045,.135)	-.042(.047,.378)	-.090(.058,.120)	-.108(.077,.162)
Household's Characteristics				
Household's Wealth Status (Poorest is reference category)				
Poorer	.014(.022,.513)	-.001(.023,.980)	.003(.025,.891)	.007(.033,.838)
Middle	-.090(.023,.000)	-.094(.024,.000)	-.150(.027,.000)	-.083(.035,.018)
Richer	-.135(.025,.000)	-.165(.026,.000)	-.243(.030,.000)	-.088(.039,.024)
Richest	-.153(.029,.000)	-.217(.031,.000)	-.333(.036,.000)	-.129(.047,.006)
Locality (Rural areas are reference category)				
Urban Areas	.026(. 018,.156)	-.001(.020,.940)	-.005(.022,.817)	.015(.028,.593)
Sibling's Characteristics				
Total Children Ever Born (More than 4 is reference category)				
<=4	-.087 (.019,.000)	-.083(.020,.000)	-.125(.023,.000)	-.088(.029,.002)
Regions				
South and South East Asia	.079 (.023,.000)	.053(.024,.028)	1.208(.030,.000)	.788(.042,.000)
West Asia	-1.468(.057,.000)	-1.385(.063,.000)	-1.659(.102,.000)	-1.111(.108,.000)
Central Asia	-.410(.040,.000)	-.352(.043,.000)	-.536(.061,.000)	-.165(.072,.022)

Latin America and Caribbean	-.492(.034,.000)	-.339(.035,.000)	-.518(.052,.000)	-1.047(.089,.000)
Secular States	.034 (.025,.180)	-.045(.026,.057)	.375(.033,.000)	. .388(.046,.000)
Net Imports	.381(.020,.000)	.190(.021,.000)	.395(.024,.000)	. .573(.031,.000)
Constant	.291 (.053,.000)	-.352(.043,.000)	-.898(.061,.000)	-1.850(.080,.000)
Cox & Snell R Square	.055	.041	.081	.034
Nagelkerke R Square	.075	.057	.126	.068

Work status and self-confidence have a positive effect on stunting, wasting and on a composite index of anthropometric failure of children as the odds ratio is greater than one. These two dimensions of women empowerment increased malnutrition in children while self-esteem and self-confidence have a positive impact on underweight — women with the highest level of work status and self-confidence, showing a chance of malnourished children.

Women with higher self-esteem, awareness, and decision making have less chance of their children to be stunting wasting and underweight. (Table 8.3). These results also proved by previous literature, Siddhanta and Chattopadhyay (2017); Quamruzzaman and Lange (2016); Desai and Johnson (2005); Chipili et al. (2018). The other two dimensions of women empowerment work status and self-confidence are increasing stunting and wasting in the children. Working women have less time to look after their children as compared to the mother stay at home and spend the whole day with their children at home.

Work status showing a gradual increase in the stunting and wasting women with the increase in the level of work status and self-confidence also showing the positive association with stunting, wasting but negative with underweight and women with a higher level of self-confidence showing the more prevalence of stunting and wasting among their children (Table 8.3).

The working women spent most of their time outside of the house, due to which she cannot give the proper time to her house and children. At the same time, working women did not take care of themselves during their pregnancy, due to which children were weak at the time of their birth. Previously it was proved in the study Ibrahim and Pandey (2014) that work status of women cause malnutrition among their children. Goode and Mavromaras (2014) also found working women, causing malnutrition among their children.

All dimensions of women empowerment except the self-esteem and self-confidence were reducing underweight among the children. Composite Women Empowerment Index has been reducing the composite index of anthropometric failure, stunting, wasting, and under-weight among the children as they got the medium and higher empowerment as compared to the level of empowerment, the odds ratio is less than one (Table 8.4).

8.3.1   Mother's Characteristics and Child Health

The mother has a significant role in determining child health through many means. Child health and mother's characteristics are strongly associated with each other. Mother's health, education, age, age at first birth taken as mother's characteristics. All indicators of child health found to be strongly associated with the mother's health. Mother's good health, measured by the mother's body mass index, more than 18.5 kg/m2 has a negative impact on CIAF, stunting, underweight, and wasting (malnutrition/undernourishment) follows by odd ratio is less than one (Table 8.3 and 8.4).

Healthy mothers take better care of their children as compared to unhealthy mothers. Good body mass index makes mothers healthy, and a healthy mother gives birth to a healthy baby. Mother's and child health always linked with each other. These results followed by previous studies by Khan and Raza (2014); (Khan & Raza, 2016a)for Bangladesh and India. Mother with better health having a body mass index greater than 18.5Kg/m2 showing the decline in composite anthropometric failure. Stunting, wasting and underweight among children (Table 8.3,8.4).

A mother's education plays a vital role in determining child health. Mother's education has a negative impact on malnutrition (CIAF, stunting, underweight and wasting) as the odds ratio is less than one. Mother's with primary, secondary, and higher education showing the low level of composite anthropometric failure, stunting, wasting, and underweight among their children as compared to the mothers with no education as the reference category. (Table 8.3 and 8.4).

Education has more contribution in improving the child's health as followed by Keats (2018); Siddhanta and Chattopadhyay (2017); Roy et al. (2018); Endris et al. (2017). Mother's age categorized in four groups, and results expressed that mothers above than 19 years age have, the less tendency to be their children having CIAF, stunting, wasting and underweight. Sujarwoto and Tampubolon (2013); Goode and Mavromaras (2014) found in their study that older mothers have the probability of their children to be in good health as compared to the children of the younger mothers. The mother's age at her first birth categorized into four groups, and each age group is showing different impacts on different indicators of malnutrition. Mothers with age more than 19 years at their first birth have a negative impact the on CIAF, stunting, wasting, and underweight), which shows that younger age at first birth increases the chance of malnutrition in children. The mother with age less than 19 years at their first birth has the probability of giving the birth to stunting, wasting and underweight children. Mother's age at first birth was determined as the most important factor for children's weight at the time of birth in the study of Delajara and Juárez (2013). Mother's age at first birth in the age of 20-25 have very less probability to be the deaths of their children (Akinyemi et al., 2017).

8.3.2 Father's Characteristics and Child Health

Like mothers, fathers have a significant contribution to developing child health and have a direct influence on childcare. Father education has positive involvement in the understanding of how much proper nutrition intake required for their children. With the increase in the education of father, there was a decline in composite anthropometric failure, stunting, wasting and underweight. The role of the father in child health and child growth never neglected because father and mother both have a significant role in nurturing their children. Father characteristics, including father education, age, and employment status, have a significant impact on child health.

The gradual increase in education is showing the decline in the composite index of anthropometric failure among the children as compared to those children whose fathers are uneducated. Father education levels, primary, secondary, and higher showing a negative impact on stunting, wasting and underweight as compared to no education as odd ratios are less than one. The age of the father has a significant impact on child health. Gradually, the age of father shows the decline in the composite index of anthropometric failure, stunting,

194

wasting and underweight. Father age below than 55 years old contributes a substantial and adverse effect on anthropometric failure and stunting compared to fathers with age above 55 years.

Ibrahim et al. (2015) and Goode and Mavromaras (2014) explained the strong relationship between father's age below 35 and education with child health measured by height for age. Father employment status, father, did work negatively and significantly impacted composite anthropometric failure, stunting, wasting, and underweight. Working fathers have the probability of being reducing malnutrition among their children (Goode & Mavromaras, 2014).

8.3.3   Household's Characteristics and Child Health

Household's wealth status, household's locality and the total number of household members have a greater influence on child health. Children living in households with the richest wealth have less probability of being in poor health. The wealth status of the household has a critical and significant role in the nutritional intake of children. Wealth and child health are parallel with each other's, a household with richest wealth status reducing the malnutrition in children of under five years presented by Burroway (2017); Ibrahim et al. (2015); Ibrahim and Pandey (2014).

The type of residence of households has a significant impact on child health. Children living in urban areas have a less probability of having a composite index of anthropometric failure while showing the insignificant effect on stunting, wasting and underweight. In urban areas, all facilities relating to child health were well provided and health of children in urban areas was better than rural areas children (Ibrahim & Pandey, 2014).

8.3.4   Child Health and Number of Children at Households

Child health is also influenced by their siblings, as the total number of children ever born. The total number of children ever born in the family more than four showing the more presence of composite anthropometric failure, stunting, wasting and underweight among the children.   The total number of children ever born has a significant impact on child health.

8.3.5   Impact of macro-level indicators on Child Health

Macro-level indicators, net imports of food and secular states have been used in the model to find out their impact on child health. Net imports of food have a positive impact on stunting, wasting, underweight, and CIAF. Courtiers where imports of food are more than their exports facing malnutrition. Countries that are declared as secular states have a positive impact on stunting, underweight and CIAF while having a negative impact on the underweight. In previous studies macro-level indicators, GDP per Capita, Price Index, Economic Efficiency and Democracy along with micro-level indicators were used to found their impact on child health(Augsburg & Rodríguez-Lesmes, 2018; Burroway, 2017; Ekbrand & Halleröd, 2018).

8.3.6   Impact of Regions on Child Health

When regions are included in the model as independent variables, then regions showed a significant impact on child health. West Asia, Central Asia, and Latin America and Caribbean countries negatively affect the stunting, wasting, and underweight while South and South East Asia have a positive impact on stunting, wasting, and underweight.

CHAPTER 9: WOMEN EMPOWERMENT AND CHILD HEALTH: REGION WISE COMPARISON

In this chapter region-wise comparison of developing countries has been presented. Five regions South and South East Asia, Central Asia, West Asia, Latin America, and the Caribbean, and Sub-Saharan Africa have selected for comparison. The impact of women empowerment on child health has applied through the four Binary Logistic models.

9.1 Child Health Status in Regions

Child health status in different regions has described in Table 9.1. Across the regions, South and Southeast Asia and Sub-Saharan Africa portray the worst statistics, while the region of West Asia (except for under-weight) depicts the least adversities on all child health measures.

Table 9.1: Regions' Ranking with Respect to Child Health Status

Regions	Stunting (%)	Rank	Regions	Wasting (%)	Rank	Regions	Underweight (%)	Rank	Regions	CIAF (%)	Rank
West Asia	15.5	1	West Asia	4.9	1	Latin America and Caribbean	1.5	1	West Asia	22.3	1
Central Asia	21	2	Central Asia	7.8	2	Central Asia	6.5	2	Central Asia	27.1	2
Latin America and Caribbean	28.8	3	Latin America and Caribbean	8.5	3	West Asia	7	3	Latin America and Caribbean	30.2	3
Sub-Saharan Africa	34.5	4	Sub-Saharan Africa	19	4	Sub-Saharan Africa	9.2	4	Sub-Saharan Africa	42.1	4
South and Southeast Asia	39.8	5	South and Southeast Asia	29.8	5	South and Southeast Asia	12.5	5	South and Southeast Asia	50.1	5

Source: Demographic and Health Surveys(DHS-V   2003 – 2008, DHS-VI 2008 – 2013, DHS-7   2013 – 2018)

9.2 Women Empowerment and Child Health in South and South Asia Region

In South and Southeast Asia, Child health was measured by stunting, wasting, underweight, CIAF has taken as a dependent variable, and in the meanwhile, women empowerment, mother characteristics, father characteristics, household characteristics, and the number of children were taken as independent variables in the Table 9.2. Binary logistic regression has used to find out the effect of women empowerment and other attributes along their direction of impact on child health.

Table 9.2: Women Empowerment as Determinants of Child: The Case of South and Southeast Asia

	CIAF <-2SD		Stunting <-2SD		Wasting <-2SD		Underweight <-2SD	
Independent Variables	**Odd Ratio**	**Std. Err.**	**Odd Ratio**	**Std. Err.**	**Odd Ratio**	**Std. Err.**	**Odd Ratio**	**Std. Err.**
Mother/Women Empowerment								
CWEI	.782 ***	0 .010	.933***	0.011	1.003	0.011	1.02**	0.014
Mother's Characteristics								
Mother Body Mass Index (less than 18.5 kg/m2 is reference category)								
More than 18.5 kg/m2	0 .921***	0.030	0.666***	0.017	0.603***	0.015	0.631***	0.018
Mother's Education (No Education is reference category)								
Primary	1.48***	0.060	0.945	0.033	0.863***	0.029	0.885***	0.036
Secondary	1.09 ***	0 .047	0.791***	0.028	0.806***	0.027	0.881***	0.035
Higher	0 .716 ***	0 .067	0.498***	0.039	0.554***	0.039	0.867*	0.070
Mother's age								
Age	1.06***	0 .004	1.03***	0.004	1.01**	0.04	.965***	0.005

Mother's age on her first birth

MAFB	.991	0 .005	0.965***	0.004	.977***	0.004	1.03***	0.006

Father's Characteristic

Father Education (No Education is reference category)

Primary	1.19***	0 .051	1.01	0.038	0.963	0.035	0.906**	0.039
Secondary	0.782 ***	0 .033	0.872***	0.031	0.906***	0.030	0.925*	0.037
Higher	0 .598***	0 .043	0.681***	0.041	0.778***	0.043	0.860**	0.057

Father's Age

Age	1.001**	0 .002	.999**	0.002	0.998	0.002	0.999	0.002

Head of Household's Characteristics

Gender of Head of Household (Female as Reference Category)

Male	.984	.048	.885***	.037	.873***	.034	1.003	.046

Age of Head of Household

Age	.994***	.001	.997**	.001	.998	.009	1.001	.0011

Household's Characteristics

Household's Wealth status   (Poorest is reference category)

Poorer	0.903***	0 .041	0.845***	0.033	0.809***	0.030	0.826***	0.036
Middle	0.787 ***	0 .037	0.685***	0.027	0.671***	0.025	0.771***	0.035
Richer	0.790 ***	0 .041	0.603***	0.027	0.579***	0.024	0.690***	0.035
Richest	0.869 ***	0 .054	0.501***	0.027	0.441***	0.022	0.604***	0.037

Total household's members (Less than 5 is reference category)

<=5	1.02 ***	0.006	1.01*	0.005	1.01	0.005	.998	0.006

Type of Residence (Rural areas are reference category)

Urban Areas	0.850 ***	0.030	0.991	0.030	1.05*	0.030	1.06*	0.088

Sibling's Characteristics

Total number of Children Ever Born (Less than 4 is reference category)

<=4	1.02 **	0.012	1.01	0.011	1.02**	0.011	1.09***	0.015
Constant	.144 ***	0.018	1.46***	0.163	2.002***	0.212	0.472***	0.059
Pseudo R^2	.081		.065		.055		.023	
Observations	33574		.32666		35262		35268	

Notes: Significance level <0.01=***, Significant level <0.005=** and Significance level <0.10=*

Standard Error ()

9.1 .1 Women Empowerment and Child Health

Women empowerment has measured by the composite women empowerment index and its effect on child health. In South and Southeast Asia region, the results of binary logistic regression have found a significant impact of women empowerment on child health measured by CIAF, stunting, wasting and underweight. An increase in women's empowerment reduces the stunting and underweight problems in their children(Bhandari & Chhetri, 2013; Burroway, 2017; Ibrahim & Pandey, 2014; Jamal, 2018a; Malapit et al., 2015).

9 .1.2 Mother Characteristics and Child Health

Women characteristics measured by four different characteristics of maternal body mass index, mother education, mother age and mother age on her first birth and each characteristic have its different effect on child health as stunning, wasting, underweight, and CIAF. According to the results of Table 9.2. The binary logistic regression results proved that mother characteristics of body mass index below 18.5 kg/m2(Jones et al., 2019), all categories of education(Sujarwoto & Tampubolon, 2013), and increase in mother's age at first birth(Pongou et al., 2006) have negative and significant effect on child health as stunning, wasting, underweight and CIAF. While the increase in mother age(Goode & Mavromaras,

2014) has a positive and significant effect on stunting, wasting and underweight. So, the results of binary logistic regression are in favour of Mother characteristics on child health as stunning, wasting, underweight and CIAF, as supposed in model.

9.1.3 Father Characteristics and Child Health

Father's characteristics measured by two different characteristics of father education and father's age; each character has its different effect on child health as stunning, wasting, underweight and CIAF. According to the results of Table 9.2. The binary logistic regression results proved that father characteristics of education(Ahsan & Maharaj, 2018) and increase in age(Ibrahim & Pandey, 2014) have a negative and significant effect on child health as stunning, wasting, underweight except CIAF. In contrast. So, the results of binary logistic regression are in favor of father's characteristics on child health as stunning, wasting, underweight and CIAF, as supposed in model.

9.1.4 Household Characteristics and Child Health

Household characteristics have measured by three different characteristics of household gender of the head, age of head, wealth status, total household members, type of residence, and each character has its different effect on child health as stunning, wasting, underweight, and CIAF. According to the results of Table 9.2. The binary logistic regression results proved that increasing age of head of household, increase in wealth status(Khan & Raza, 2014, 2016b; Vonaesch et al., 2017), and urban areas(Tong, 2009) have negative and significant effect on child health as stunning, wasting, underweight and CIAF while household member(Siddhanta & Chattopadhyay, 2017) more than five increase the chances of the stunting, wasting and underweight among children. So, the results of binary logistic regression are in favor of Household characteristics on child health as stunning, wasting, underweight and CIAF, as supposed in model. Household member less than five or equal than five has negative and significant impact on stunting, wasting, underweight and CIAF.

9.1.5 Total number of children and Child Health

The number of children was measured by two different attributes of a total number of children alive, the total number of children ever born(Arif & Arif, 2012), and each attribute has its different effect on child health as stunning, wasting, underweight, and CIAF. According to the results of Table 9.2. The binary logistic regression results proved that the total number of children alive and total number of children ever born more than four have a positive and significant impact on stunting, wasting, underweight, and CIAF. So, the results of binary logistic regression are in favor number of children on child health as stunning, wasting, underweight and CIAF, as supposed in the model.

9.2   Women Empowerment and Child Health in Central Asia

In Central Asia Child health was measured by stunting, wasting, underweight, CIAF were taking as the dependent variable, and at the meanwhile, women empowerment, mother characteristics, father characteristics, household characteristics, and siblings characteristics were taken as independent variables in Table 9.2. Binary logistic regression used to find out the association between women empowerment and other characteristics along their direction of impact on child health.

Table 9.3: Women Empowerment as Determinants of Child: The Case of Central Asia

Independent Variables	CIAF <-2SD		Stunting <-2SD		Wasting <-2SD		Underweight <-2SD	
	Odd Ratio	Std. Err.	Odd Ratio	Std. Err.	Odd Ratio	Std. Err.	Odd Ratio	Std. Err.
Mother/Women Empowerment								
CWEI	1.07	0 .053	1.02	0.037	.944	0.052	0.979	0.058
Mother's Characteristics								
Mother Body Mass Index (less than 18.5 kg/m2 is reference category)								
More than 18.5 kg/m2	1.39***	0 .349	0.963	0.158	0.862	0.215	0.850	0.224
Mother's Education (No Education is reference category)								
Primary	Omit		0.690	0.392	0.923	0.787	1.59	1.79
Secondary	.356	4.56e	0.586	0.90	0.728	0.552	1.30	1.35
Higher	0 .526	.686	0.559	0.80	0.452	0.348	0.976	1.02
Mother's age								
Age	0 .965 **	0 .014	0.97**	0.010	.985	0.017	1.02	0.019
Mother's age on her first birth								
MAFB	1.02	0 .017	1.03**	0.013	1.001	0.021	.986	0.022
Father's Characteristic								
Father Education (No Education is reference category)								
Primary	0.064*	0 .099	0.782	0.702	598	7.08e	0.177	0.194
Secondary	0 .285	0 .325	0.974	0.791	110	1.31e	0.245*	0.203
Higher	0 .246	0 .281	0.963	0.783	113	1.34e	0.266	.221
Father's Age								
Age	1.02**	0 .012	1.01*	0.009	1.004	0.014	0.986	0.022
Head of Household's Characteristics								
Gender of Head of Household (Female as Reference Category)								
Male	1.26*	.169	1.04	.101	1.08	.59	1.25	.188
Age of Head of Household								
Age	.995	.003	.997	.002	1.01 *	.004	1.01	.004

Household's Characteristics

Household's Wealth status   (Poorest is reference category)

Poorer	0.823	0 .106	0.886	0.101	0.896	0.171	1.03	0.221
Middle	0.685 ***	0 .089	0.988	0.108	0.828	0.156	.823	0.179
Richer	0.506 ***	0 .076	0.923	0.108	1.35*	0.248	1.76***	0.352
Richest	0.114 ***	0 .027	1.03	0.137	1.81***	0.373	2.25***	0.500

Total household's members (Less than 5 is reference category)

<=5	0.884 ***	0.024	1.02	0.017	1.02	0.026	1.04	0.028

Type of Residence (Rural areas are reference category)

Urban Areas	0.885	0.129	0.966	0.097	0.905	0.138	.867	0.138

Sibling's Characteristics

Total number of Children Ever Born (Less than 4 is reference category)

<=4	1.037	0.047	1.04	0.034	1.13***	0.055	1.03	0.054
Constant	1.69e	0.002	.290	0.284	5.74e	0.000	0.114	0.159
Pseudo R^2	.075		.0024		.023		.024	
Observations	5287		5355		5355		5355	

Notes: Significance level <0.01=***,Significant level <0.005=** and Significance level <0.10=*

Standard Error ()

9.2.1   Women Empowerment and Child Health

Women empowerment was measured by the composite women empowerment index and its effect on child health. In the Central Asia region, the results of binary logistic regression have found an insignificant impact of women empowerment on child health measured by CIAF, stunting, wasting and underweight. Women's empowerment does not have any impact on the stunting and underweight problems in their children.

9.2.2   Mother Characteristics and Child Health

Mother characteristics were measured by four different aspects; mother body mass index, mother education, maternal age, and maternal age on her first birth, and each character have its different effects on child health as stunning, wasting, underweight, and CIAF. According to the results of Table 9.2. The binary logistic regression results proved that mother characteristics of body mass index below 18.5 kg/m2(Siddhanta & Chattopadhyay, 2017), all categories of education(Tracey & Polachek, 2018), and increase in mother's age at first birth(Arif & Arif, 2012) have insignificant influence on child health as stunning, wasting, underweight. Mother body mass index more than 18.5 kg/m^2 has a significant effect on CIAF. An increase in the age at first birth has a positive and significant impact on wasting. While growth in mother age has a negative and significant impact on stunting(Siddhanta & Chattopadhyay, 2017), wasting and underweight. So, the results of binary logistic regression are in favor of Mother characteristics on child health as stunning, wasting, underweight, and CIAF, as supposed in the model.

9.2.3   Father Characteristics and Child Health

Father's characteristics measured by two different characteristics of father education and father's age; each character has different consequences on child health as stunning, wasting, underweight and CIAF. According to the results of Table 9.2. The binary logistic regression results proved that father characteristics of education was insignificant and increased in age have a positive and significant association with child health as stunning(Batool et al., 2012), wasting, underweight except CIAF. In contrast. So, the results of binary logistic regression are in favor of Father's characteristics on child health as stunning, wasting, underweight and CIAF, as supposed in the model.

9.2.4   Household Characteristics and Child Health

Household characteristics have measured by three different characteristics of household gender of the head, age of head, wealth status, total household members, type of residence and each characteristic has its different effect on child health as stunning, wasting, underweight and CIAF. According to the results of Table 9.2. The results of binary logistic regression proved that increasing age of head of household has insignificant, and gender of head of household as a male have negative and significant. On the other hand, urban areas have an insignificant effect on child health as stunning, wasting, underweight and CIAF while household member more than five reduce the chances of the stunting, wasting and underweight among children. So, the results of binary logistic regression are in favor of Household characteristics on child health as stunning, wasting, underweight and CIAF, as supposed in the model

9.2.5   Total Number of children and Child Health

The total number of the children measured by two different characteristics of the total number of children alive, the total number of children ever born and each characteristic has its different effect on child health as stunning, wasting, underweight and CIAF. According to the results of Table 9.2. The binary logistic regression results proved that the total number of children alive and the total number of children ever born more than four have a positive and insignificant effect on child health as stunning, wasting, underweight and CIAF. So, the results of binary logistic regression are showing that the number of children ever born on child health as stunning, wasting, underweight and CIAF, as supposed in the model.

9.3   Women Empowerment and Child Health in West Asia

In West Asia Child health was measured by stunting, wasting, underweight, CIAF were taking as the dependent variable, and at the meanwhile women empowerment, mother characteristics, father characteristics, household characteristics, and the number of children were taken as independent variables in the Table 9.3. Binary logistic regression has used to find out the effect of women empowerment and other characteristics along their direction of effect on child health.

Table 9.4: Women Empowerment as Determinants of Child: The Case of West Asia

	CIAF <-2SD		Stunting <-2SD		Wasting <-2SD		Underweight <-2SD	
Independent Variables	Odd Ratio	Std. Err.	Odd Ratio	Std. Err.	Odd Ratio	Std. Err.	Odd Ratio	Std. Err.
Mother/Women Empowerment								
CWEI	.959	0 .104	.989	0.021	1.001	0.036	1.024	0.030
Mother's Characteristics								
Mother Body Mass Index (less than 18.5 kg/m2 is reference category)								
More than 18.5 kg/m2	Omitt		1.87	0.743	0.793	0.369	1.34	0.696
Mother's Education (No Education is reference category)								
Primary	1.29	0.581	1.07	0.096	1.03	0.154	0.811*	0.101
Secondary	1.46	0 .522	1.03	0.072	1.01	0.119	0.751***	0.071
Higher	0 .793	0 .380	0.942	0.088	.802	0.127	0.626***	0.081
Mother's age								
Age	0 .989	0 .029	0.997	0.006	.989	0.010	1.001	0.008

Mother's age on her first birth

MAFB	1.01	0 .032	0.994	0.06	.994	0.011	.998	0.009

Father's Characteristic

Father Education (No Education is reference category)

Primary	0.871	0 .343	0.874	0.073	0.733**	0.101	0.818*	0.096
Secondary	0 .738	0 .256	0.871*	0.064	0.692***	0.082	0.941	0.096
Higher	0 .792	0 .342	0.819**	0.076	0.709**	0.107	0.863	.111

Father's Age

Age	0 .987	0 .022	1.01**	0.004	1.00	0.007	0.996	0.006

Head of Household's Characteristics

Gender of Head of Household (Female as Reference Category)

Male	1.47	.651	1.01	.114	.843	.165	.719*	.127

Age of Head of Household

Age	1.01	.012	1.001	.002	.999	.004	.999	.004

Household's Characteristics

Household's Wealth status   (Poorest is reference category)

Poorer	2.009 **	0 .730	0.917	0.068	1.01	.126	0.891	0.091
Middle	0.763	0 .326	1.10	0.080	0.936	.118	0.695***	0.075
Richer	1.41	0 .553	1.28 ***	0.098	1.12	.145	1.11	0.119
Richest	1.81	0 .750	1.38***	0.119	1.51***	.210	1.79***	0.029

Total household's members(Less than 5 is reference category)

<=5	0.942	0.072	1.001	0.015	1.05**	0.024	1.01	0.021

Type of Residence (Rural areas are reference category)

Urban Areas	1.12	0.299	0.681***	0.037	1.04	0.097	0.857*	0.069

Sibling's Characteristics

Total number of Children Ever Born (Less than 4 is reference category)

<=4	1.011	0.112	0.912***	0.020	0.941*	0.034	0.977	0.029
Constant	.038 ***	0.037	.125***	0.056	1.40***	0.082	0.135***	0.081

Pseudo R^2	.017	.0007	.0085	.0124
Observations	18118	18201	18208	18201

Notes: Significance level <0.01=***,Significant level <0.005=** and Significance level <0.10=*

Standard Error ()

9.3.1   Women Empowerment and Child Health

Women empowerment measured by the composite women empowerment index and its effect on child health. In West Asia region, the results of binary logistic regression have found insignificant effects of women empowerment on child health measured by CIAF, stunting, wasting and underweight. It means women's empowerment does not have any effects on the stunting and underweight problems in their children.

9.3.2   Mother Characteristics and Child Health

Mother characteristics were measured by four different aspects of maternal body mass index, mother education, mother age, and mother age on her first birth, and each characteristic have its different effect on child health as stunning, wasting, underweight and CIAF. According to the results of table 9.3. The binary logistic regression results proved that mother characteristics of body mass index below 18.5 kg/m2, all categories of education(Keats, 2018; Murshid, 2016b), and increase in mother's age at first birth have an insignificant effect on child health as stunning, wasting, underweight and CIAF. So, the results of binary logistic regression are in favour of Mother characteristics on child health as stunning, wasting, underweight and CIAF, as supposed in the model.

9.3.3   Father Characteristics and Child Health

Father's characteristics were measured by two different characteristics of father education and father's age; each characteristic has its different effect on child health as stunning, wasting, underweight and CIAF. According to the results of table 9.3. The binary logistic regression results proved that father characteristics of education(Roy et al., 2018) and increase in age have a negative and significant effect on child health as stunning, wasting, underweight except CIAF. In contrast,the results of binary logistic regression are in favor of Father's characteristics on child health as stunning, wasting, underweight and CIAF, as supposed in the model(Meshram et al., 2012).

9.3.4   Household Characteristics and Child Health

Household characteristics measured by three different characteristics of household gender of the head, age of head, wealth status, total household members, type of residence, and each characteristic has its different effect on child health as stunning, wasting, underweight, and CIAF. According to the results of Table 9.3, results of binary logistic regression proved that gender of the head as male, increasing age of head of household have an insignificant effect on stunting, wasting and underweight. An increase in wealth status has a positive and significant effect on stunting, wasting and negative on underweight(Endris et al., 2017). Moreover, urban areas have negative and significant on stunting and underweight while household members more than five increase the chances of wasting among children. So, the results of binary logistic regression are in favor of household characteristics on child health as stunning, wasting, underweight and CIAF.

9.3.5 Number of Children and Child Health

The number of children has measured by two different attributes of total number of children alive, total number of children ever born, and each aspect has its different effect on child health as stunning, wasting, underweight, and CIAF. According to the results of Table 9.3. The binary logistic regression results proved that the total number of children alive and total number of children ever born more than four have positive and insignificant effect on underweight and CIAF. While negative and significant relationship with stunting and wasting.

9.4 Women Empowerment and Child Health in Latin America and the Caribbean

In Latin America and the Caribbean, child health was measured by stunting, wasting, underweight, CIAF taken as the dependent variable, and women empowerment, mother characteristics, father characteristics, household characteristics, and the number of children taken as independent variables in the Table 9.4. Binary logistic regression has used to find out the effect of women empowerment and other characteristics along their direction of effect on child health.

Table 9.5: Women Empowerment as Determinants of Child: The Case of Latin America and Caribbean

Independent Variables	CIAF <-2SD			Stunting <-2SD			Wasting <-2SD			Underweight <-2SD		
	Odd Ratio		Std. Err.	Odd Ratio		Std. Err.	Odd Ratio		Std. Err.	Odd Ratio		Std. Err.

Mother/Women Empowerment								
CWEI	1.01	0 .027	1.07***	0.029	.968	0.039	0.731***	0.068
Mother's Characteristics								
Mother Body Mass Index (less than 18.5 kg/m2 is reference category)								
More than 18.5 kg/m2	0 .908	.122	0.972	0.132	0.732*	0.138	0.521*	0.186
Mother's Education (No Education is reference category)								
Primary	0 .738***	0.049	0.781***	0.052	0.743***	0.073	0.700	0.158
Secondary	0 .577 ***	0 .047	0.671***	0.054	0.689***	0.084	0.691	0.197
Higher	0 .417 ***	0 .050	0.591***	0.069	0.520***	0.098	0.483	0.225
Mother's age								
Age	0 .989 **	0 .004	0.994	0.004	.998	0.007	.983	0.017
Mother's age on her first birth								
MAFB	1.02***	0 .006	1.01**	0.006	1.006	0.009	1.05**	0.023
Father's Characteristic								
Father Education (No Education is reference category)								
Primary	0.836**	0 .061	0.857**	0.063	0.936	0.105	0.819	0.206
Secondary	0 .654***	0 .055	0.783***	0.066	0.875	0.114	0.899	0.266
Higher	0 .690***	0 .081	0.769**	0.089	1.01	0.184	0.899	.390
Father's Age								
Age	0 .996	0 .003	0.996	0.003	1.00	0.005	1.03***	0.011
Head of Household's Characteristics								
Gender of Head of Household (Female as Reference Category)								
Male	1.04	.054	.962	.050	1.01	.082	1.63***	.279
Age of Head of Household								
Age	.997	.002	.998	.002	.995	.003	.985*	.007
Household's Characteristics								
Household's Wealth status (Poorest is reference category)								
Poorer	1.34***	0 .097	1.19**	0.086	1.13	0.124	1.22	0.311

Middle	1.67 ***	0 .129	1.40***	0.106	1.20	0.140	1.21	0.337
Richer	2.02 ***	0 .169	1.52***	0.125	1.32**	0.168	1.65*	0.495
Richest	2.52 ***	0 .238	1.66***	0.154	1.26	0.184	1.09	0.390
Total household's members(Less than 5 is reference category)								
<=5	1.03 ***	0.011	1.02**	0.011	1.03*	0.018	1.08**	0.043
Type of Residence (Rural areas are reference category)								
Urban Areas	0.817***	0.038	0.915**	0.043	0.868**	0.063	0.927	0.168
Sibling's Characteristics								
Total number of Children Ever Born (Less than 4 is reference category)								
<=4	1.009	0.016	1.00	0.016	0.965	0.024	0.908	0.056
Constant	.583 **	0.130	.563**	0.126	.209***	0..069	0.013***	0.010
Pseudo R^2	.015		.006		.004		.027	
Observations	12658		12658		12658		12658	

Notes: Significance level <0.01=***, Significant level <0.005=** and Significance level <0.10=*
Standard Error ()

9.4.1 Women Empowerment and Child Health

Women empowerment has measured by the composite women empowerment index and its effect on child health. In Latin America and Caribbean region, the results of binary logistic regression have significantly impacted women's empowerment on child health measured by wasting and underweight. While insignificant on CIAF, positive and significant impact on stunting. It means women's empowerment reduces the stunting and underweight problems in their children(Ibrahim et al., 2015; Jones et al., 2019; Kar et al., 1999)

9.4.2 Mother Characteristics and Child Health

Mother characteristics have measured by four different characteristics; maternal body mass index, mother education, maternal age, and mother age on her first birth, and each characteristic have its different effect on child health as stunning, wasting, underweight, and CIAF. According to the results of Table 9.4. The binary logistic regression results proved that mother characteristics of body mass index below 18.5 kg/m2(Huicho et al., 2016), all categories of education(Khan & Raza, 2016a), increase in mother's age and age at first birth have negative and significant effect on child health as stunning, wasting, underweight and CIAF. So, the results of binary logistic regression are in favor of Mother characteristics on child health as stunning, wasting, underweight and CIAF, as supposed in model.

9.4.3 Father Characteristics and Child Health

Father's characteristics have measured by two different characteristics of father; education and father's age; each characteristic has its different effect on child health as stunning, wasting, underweight and CIAF. According to the results of table 9.4. The binary logistic regression results proved that father characteristics of education and increase in age have negative and significant effect on child health as stunning, wasting, underweight except CIAF. In contrast. So, the results of binary logistic regression are in favor of Father's characteristics on child health as stunning, wasting, underweight and CIAF, as supposed in model.

9.4.4   Household Characteristics and Child Health

Three different characteristics of household measured; gender of the head, age of head, wealth status, total household members, type of residence. Each characteristic has its different effect on child health as stunning, wasting, underweight, and CIAF. According to the results of table 9.4. The binary logistic regression results proved that gender and increasing age of head of household have an insignificant effect on CIAF, stunting, wasting and underweight. Increase in wealth status showing a positive and significant effect on CIAF, stunting, wasting and underweight. Urban areas have negative and significant effect on child health as stunning, wasting, underweight and CIAF while household members more than five(Khan & Raza, 2014) increase the chances of the stunting, wasting and underweight among children. So, the results of binary logistic regression are in favor of Household characteristics on child health as stunning, wasting, underweight and CIAF, as supposed in the model.

9.4.5   Number of Children and Child Health

The number of children has measured by two different attributes; the total number of children alive, the total number of children ever born, and each characteristic has its different effect on child health as stunning, wasting, underweight, and CIAF. According to the results of Table 9.4. The binary logistic regression results proved that Sibling's characteristics of total number of children alive have negative, and the total number of children ever born more than four have a positive and significant effect on child health as stunning, wasting, underweight, and CIAF. So, the results of binary logistic regression are in favor of

Sibling's characteristics on child health as stunning, wasting, underweight and CIAF, as supposed in model. Increase in

9.5   Women Empowerment and Child Health in Sub Saharan Africa

In Sub Saharan Africa Child health was measured by stunting, wasting, underweight, CIAF was taking as a dependent variable, and at the meanwhile, women empowerment, mother characteristics, father characteristics, household characteristics, and total number of children were taken as independent variables in the table 9.5. Binary logistic regression was used to find out the effect of women empowerment and other characteristics along their direction of effect on child health.

Table 9.6: Women Empowerment as Determinants of Child: The Case of Sub Saharan Africa

Independent Variables	CIAF <-2SD Odd Ratio	Std. Err.	Stunting <-2SD Odd Ratio	Std. Err.	Wasting <-2SD Odd Ratio	Std. Err.	Underweight <-2SD Odd Ratio	Std. Err.
Mother/Women Empowerment								
CWEI	.974 **	0 .013	1.002	0.005	.975***	0.006	0.977***	0.007
Mother's Characteristics								
Mother Body Mass Index (less than 18.5 kg/m2 is reference category)								
More than 18.5 kg/m2	0 .862*	0 .068	0.969	0.031	0.937*	0.035	0.974	0.047
Mother's Education (No Education is reference category)								
Primary	1.23	0.222	1.18***	0.074	1.06	0.082	0.878	0.084
Secondary	0.580***	0 .106	0.714***	0.046	0.679***	0.053	0.789**	0.078
Higher	0 .651***	0 .062	0.761***	0.026	0.721***	0.030	0.743***	0.040
Mother's age								
Age	0 .984 **	0 .006	0.993***	0.002	.986***	0.002	.985***	0.035

Mother's age on her first birth

MAFB	.994	0 .008	0.996	0.003	.998	0.003	1.00	0.004

Father's Characteristic

Father Education (No Education is reference category)

Primary	0.745***	0 .052	0.893***	0.024	0.728***	0.023	0.707***	0.029
Secondary	0 .828 **	0 .069	0.952	0.030	0.855***	0.032	0.820***	0.040
Higher	1.14	0 .136	0.970	0.045	1.04***	0.057	1.15**	0.080

Father's Age

Age	1.004	0 .008	1.001	0.001	1.004***	0.001	1.006***	0.001

Head of Household's Characteristics

Gender of Head of Household (Female as Reference Category)

Male	.933	.067	.954*	.024	.827***	.026	.806***	.035

Age of Head of Household

Age	.997	.002	.997**	.001	.996***	.001	.999	.001

Household's Characteristics

Household's Wealth status   (Poorest is reference category)

Poorer	1.15**	0 .081	1.07**	0.030	1.13***	.036	1.11**	0.047
Middle	1.07	0 .083	1.01	0.029	1.01	0.035	1.028	0.047
Richer	.961	0 .084	0.916***	0.029	.892***	0.035	0.958	0.049
Richest	1.13	0 .122	0.975	0.038	0.952	0.046	0.971	0.062

Total household's members(Less than 5 is reference category)

<=5	1.001	.010	1.01	0.004	1.006	0.004	1.003	0.006

Type of Residence (Rural areas are reference category)

Urban Areas	0.100	0.070	1.004	0.025	1.01	0.031	1.015	0.041

Sibling's Characteristics

Total number of Children Ever Born (Less than 4 is reference category)

<=4	1.03 **	0.017	1.01**	0.006	1.02***	0.007	1.031***	0.01
Constant	.088 ***	0.018	.880	0.068	.625***	0.058	0.221***	0.026

Pseudo R^2	.0126	.005	.017	.017
Observations	49687	49717	49779	49743

Notes: Significance level <0.01=***, Significant level <0.005=** and Significance level <0.10=*
Standard Error ()

9.5.1 Women Empowerment and Child Health

Women empowerment has measured by the composite women empowerment index and its effect on child health. In Sub-Saharan Africa region, the results of binary logistic regression have found the significant effect of women empowerment on child health measured by CIAF, stunting, wasting and underweight. An increase in women's empowerment reduces the stunting and underweight problems in their children(Deutsch & Silber, 2017).

9.5.2 Mother Characteristics and Child Health

Mother characteristics measured by four different characteristics; maternal body mass index, mother education, maternal age, and maternal age on her first birth, and each characteristic have its different effect on child health as stunning, wasting, underweight, and CIAF. According to the results of Table 9.6. The binary logistic regression results proved that mother characteristics of body mass index below 18.5 kg/m2, all categories of education, and increase in mother's age at first birth have a negative and significant influence on child health as stunning, wasting, underweight and CIAF. While an increase in mother age has a negative and significant effect on stunting, wasting and underweight. So, the results of binary logistic regression are in favor of mother characteristics on child health as stunning, wasting, underweight and CIAF, as supposed in the model.

9.5.3 Father Characteristics and Child Health

Father's characteristics measured by two different characteristics of father education and father's age; each characteristic has its different effect on child health as stunning, wasting, underweight and CIAF. According to the results of Table 9.5. The binary logistic regression results proved that father characteristics of education negative and increase in age have a positive and significant effect on child health as stunning, wasting, underweight except CIAF. In contrast. So, the results of binary logistic regression are in favor of Father's characteristics on child health as stunning, wasting, underweight and CIAF, as supposed in the model.

9.5.4 Household Characteristics and Child Health

Household characteristics measured by three different characteristics; gender of head, age of head, wealth status, total household members, type of residence, and each characteristic has its different effect on child health as stunning, wasting, underweight, and CIAF. According to the results of Table 9.6. The binary logistic regression results proved that gender as male and increasing age of head of household has a negative and significant impact on stunting, wasting and underweight. Increase in wealth status showing positive and significant impact on stunting, wasting and underweight. Urban areas have an insignificant effect on child health as stunning, wasting, underweight and CIAF while household members more than five increase the chances of the stunting, wasting and underweight among children. So, the results of binary logistic regression are in favor of Household characteristics on child health as stunning, wasting, underweight and CIAF, as supposed in the model.

9.5.5   Number of Children and Child Health

The number of children has measured by two different attributes; the total number of children alive, the total number of children ever born, and each attribute has its different effect on child health as stunning, wasting, underweight and CIAF. According to the results of table 9.5. The binary logistic regression results proved that Sibling's characteristics of the total number of children alive and total number of children ever born more than four have a positive and significant effect on child health as stunning, wasting, underweight and CIAF. So, the results of binary logistic regression are in favor of Sibling's characteristics on child health as stunning, wasting, underweight, and CIAF, as supposed in the model.

9.6   Justification of Regional Results

In this study, regional comparative analyses performed separately to analyze the women's empowerment effect on child health. The composite women empowerment index has used to measure its association with child health. In addition, the results of binary logistic regression analysis, have empirically shown the different results in different regions. So, know the difference among regions has arisen the need to do comparative analysis among different regions. The comparative analysis will enable the researchers to recommend different policies for different regions for women empowerment and child health.

In this study, regional comparative analysis among five (South and South East Asia, Central Asia, West Asia, Latin America, and Caribbean Countries, and Sub Saharan Africa) regions of developing countries around the world. The results showed that the composite women empowerment index has insignificant effect in Central Asia and West Asia regions.

It means women's empowerment has no impact on child health in these regions. The reason for these insignificant results is that women are already more empowered in these regions. Women have the freedom to speech, take the decisions regarding their health, self-confident and have respect in society to move freely and do their domestic and professional activities without any restrictions.

On the other hand, the results showed that the composite women empowerment index has a significant effect in South and Southeast Asia, Latin America and Caribbean Countries, and Sub Saharan Africa regions. It means women's empowerment has to affect child health in these regions. In South and Southeast Asia, Latin America and Caribbean Countries, and Sub Saharan Africa regions women are not fully empowered; they need independence, respect, trust, decision making power at their family and professional level. So, the empowerment will give motivation and confidence to women who will balance in the power at home, workplace and social levels, which will boost self-esteem in women to do their work effectively. Besides, women empowerment will reduce the stunning, wasting and underweight problems from their children.

The other main reasons for the difference in regional results are political condition, environmental differences, religious aspect, economic condition, awareness, health facilitating conditions, education level, family system (joint or single), opportunities to grow, use of information communication technologies, laws, and government intervention to empower women and child health. So, all these factors are different from one region to another; that's why the regional results of binary logistics are different in all regions. This comparative analysis will be grounded on different policies to improve child health and women empow-

erment.

CHAPTER 10: CONCLUSION AND POLICY RECOMMEN-DATIONS

10.1 Conclusion

Women empowerment is a complete process to give awareness, freedom, care, respect, confidence, and decision-making power to think about themselves and their families. It will flourish the balance in home, society, and in-country. Women empowerment's ultimate goal is to give women equal power and rights, which are their fundamental human rights(Bhukuth et al., 2019). On the one side of the coin, the male said or thinks that they are considering their women as free, but on the other hand, they are spoiling their human rights. Women do not have full freedom in their homes to eat, wear, treat children, and manage their other activities, as they want to do(UitedNations, 2018).

Women empowerment is beneficial for home, society, and country. Because if women are empowered, they bring diversity and innovation at their home and workplace, which will automatically lead to fruitful results for family, home, and workplace for monetary and nonmonetary economic, political, social, and health-related benefits(Khalid et al., 2020; Samanta, 2020).

But, unfortunately, lack of awareness, self-confidence, self-esteem and decision-making power regarding their family issues make them disappointed. On the other hand, men feel free from domestic responsibilities, and they think all liabilities to run a family and handle the home issues by their females (Lopez-Avila, 2016). Women are not giving full authorities and power to their women to make decisions regarding their homes freely without taking permissions from their husband, and in joint families from their in-laws (Donta et al., 2016; Nasir, Akhtar, & Salim, 2007). Furthermore, in developing countries, the household environment cannot give power and respect to women to take economic initiative for their personal and family status. Also, it is very injustice behavior with women who have family responsibilities, especially those have small children (Bitew & Telake, 2010; Calman, 1992; Grimshaw & Rubery, 2015; Hossain & Hoque, 2015; Sebayang et al., 2019).

Every Child is a national asset with too many capabilities to handle family, society, and country. At the same time, child health is a fundamental human right for every child. It is impossible to be born and bought up a healthy child without a mother's health and proper nutritional food(Demissie & Worku, 2013; Teshome et al., 2009; WHO, 2018). So, a mother's health is directly related to child health, and child health is directly related to the nation's and family's future(Tracey & Polachek, 2018).

In this study, women empowerment measured through work status, awareness, decision making, self-esteem, self-confidence, and composite women empowerment index to explore the effect on child health in terms of stunting, wasting, and underweight. The data was collected from the Demographic and Health Survey, developing countries' annual survey report, conducted in South and Southeast Asia, Central Asia, West Asia, Latin America, and the Caribbean, and Sub-Saharan Africa.

In this study, women empowerment has supported feminism (Liberal feminism, Marxist/Socialist feminisms, and Radical feminism), and the Capability approach "Development as Empowerment" theories provided the conceptual framework for the development of women empowerment. Furthermore, child health and women empowerment have been grounded (Andersen and Newman Framework of Health Services Utilization and Grossman Model of Demand for Health) theories. So, the overall study framework has supported these theories, which will enhance the impact of women empowerment on child health.

In this study, women are getting knowledge about rights by empowering them and how child health can be improved. This study's ultimate goal is to give power to women to improve their health, respect, and freedom, which will lead to a reduction in stunting, wasting, and underweight problems in children. The second benefit was to enhance monetary and non-monetary economic benefits and create a balance of power between men and women, which is beneficial for domestic affairs and official matters.

In this study, the results of women empowerment indicators (work status, awareness, decision making, self-esteem, and self-confidence) has an essential consequence on child health indicators (stunting, wasting, and underweight) in developing countries (Ahmed, Creanga, Gillespie, & Tsui, 2010; Alkire, Roche, & Vaz, 2017; Kabeer, 2011, 2012). These results proved that if women got empowerment, their child would be healthy, happy, and innovative. Furthermore, the literature showed that overall economic growth would be increased through women empowerment (Kabeer, 2012; Musonera & Heshmati, 2017). These results are consistent with previous studies. So, the findings are valid and same phenomenon occurs in developing and under-developing countries.

In this study, the determinants of women empowerment and child health have measured through composite and individual levels. The base of thirteen determinants regarding women empowerment indicators (work status, awareness, decision making, self-esteem, and self-confidence) has found from previous literature (Acharya et al., 2010; Andersen & Newman, 1973, 2005; Desai & Johnson, 2005; Jeckoniah et al., 2012; Khan et al., 2010; Khan & Raza, 2016a; Kritz & Adebusoye, 1999; Kritz & Makinwa-Adebusoye, 1999; Messelu & Trueha, 2016; Rathirani & Semasinghe, 2015; Senarath & Gunawardena, 2009; Siddhanta & Chattopadhyay, 2017; Tadesse et al., 2013; Teshome et al., 2009; Trommlerová et al., 2015; Wiklander, 2010). Besides, fourteen determinants of child health indicators (stunting, wasting and underweight) has found from previous literature (Dasgupta et al., 2014; Dasgupta et al., 2015; Registration, 2018; Roy et al., 2018; Siddhanta & Chattopadhyay, 2017; Solanki, Patel, Shah, & Singh, 2014; Teshome et al., 2009; UNICEF, 2019; Vonaesch et al., 2017). So, both child health and women empowerment determinants are supported and consistent with previous literature.

10.2 Limitations and Future Direction

This study is limited only to women empowerment and child health. In contrast, the other factors related to the medical facility, government spending, women's political participation, religion, and culture have ignored in this study. So, it is recommended to consider these factors in future studies. For child health, only anthropometric indicators were considered for under five years children. In the future, it is also recommended to underline the health problems of children above the five-year pathway through women empowerment. In this study, data from Demographic and Health Surveys have been used to analyze the influence of women's empowerment on child health. In the DHS, some country's data has not been adequately updated. During organizing the data for this study, it was limited to the countries with updated data after 2005 and selected countries with data on the same indicators used for women empowerment and child health. Following this criterion, only thirty-three countries have selected for analysis. So, it is recommended to survey and updated data from the countries which are not considered for this study. In this study, only limited available indicators have used to analyze women empowerment and child health, but other indicators can included after discussing with experts in the future.

10.3 Policy Recommendation

This study has suggested some policy recommendations for the government to enhance women empowerment and child health. Some policy recommendations are given below:

1. There is need to be focused on the formal and informal education of women because education is highly significant determinant of women empowerment and child health. The women who are uneducated can be educated informally through social media. A proper informal education and learning module should be designed by government keeping in mind about the enhancement of empowerment for uneducated women.

2. Health of Women should be the primarily focused by the government to empower the women and to improve the child health. For achieving this goal there should be legalized some necessary health checks for women and make awareness programs for these health checks and increase the medical benefits on the workplace of women, because usually, working women ignored their health. Again, Governments should make it compulsory for women to take regular checkup and proper nutritional diet from pregnancy to the birth of the child.

3. In developing countries trend of early marriages have minimized but not finished. So, it is still needed to set strict punishment rules for early marriages in order to finish this early marriages trends.

4. For the empowerment of women government should increase the employment opportunities for women, with increasing the job vacancies reserves for the women. Because financially empowered women can better care of their children and improve their health.

5. An intervention through focus on education in general, and on women's education in particular can help in achieving women empowerment and child health outcomes.

6. Women's better health status could be an entry point to pursue the goals relating to women empowerment and improved child health in the developing economies.

7. The slogan of "Stop Early Marriages" could catalyze the development initiatives aimed at women empowerment and improved child health.

8. Household's financial empowerment truly translates into the various dimensions of women empowerment as well as into child health outcomes.

REFERENCES

Abbi, R., Christian, P., Gujral, S., & Gopaldas, T. (1991). The impact of maternal work status on the nutrition and health status of children. *Food Nutrition Bulletin, 13*(1), 1-6.

Abekah-Nkrumah, G. (2013). *Women's Empowerment and Household Health in Sub-Saharan Africa: Examining the Importance of Social Norms.* The University of Manchester (United Kingdom),

Abrar-ul-Haq, M., Jali, M. R. M., & Islam, G. M. N. (2017). Empowering rural women in Pakistan: empirical evidence from Southern Punjab. *Quality & Quantity, 51*(4), 1777-1787.

Abrar ul Haq, M., Jali, M. R. M., & Islam, G. M. N. (2018). Household empowerment as the key to eradicate poverty incidence. *Asian Social Work and Policy Review.*

Achakzai, P., & Khan, R. (2016). Nutritional status and associated factors among children less than five years of age in tehsil Zarghoon town, District Quetta, Baluchistan. *Journal of Ayub Medical College Abbottabad 28*(1), 146-151.

Acharya, D. R., Bell, J. S., Simkhada, P., van Teijlingen, E. R., & Regmi, P. R. (2010). Women's autonomy in household decision-making: a demographic study in Nepal. *Reproductive Health, 7*(1), 15. doi:10.1186/1742-4755-7-15

Ahmad, F., & Sultan, M. (2004). *Women's empowerment and mobility in Pakistan: Result from a National Survey.* Paper presented at the Fifth Annual Research conference.

Ahmed, A., & Ahsan, H. (2011). Contribution of services sector in the economy of Pakistan. *Working Papers 2011.*

Ahmed, L. (1992). *Women and gender in Islam: Historical roots of a modern debate*: Yale University Press.

Ahmed, S., Creanga, A. A., Gillespie, D. G., & Tsui, A. O. (2010). Economic status, education and empowerment: implications for maternal health service utilization in developing countries. *PloS one, 5*(6), e11190.

Ahsan, M. N., & Maharaj, R. (2018). Parental human capital and child health at birth in India. *Economics and Human Biology, 30*, 130-149.

Akinyemi, Adedini, & Odimegwu. (2017). Individual v. community-level measures of women's decision-making involvement and child survival in Nigeria. *South African Journal of Child Health, 11*(1), 26-32.

Akram, N. (2018). Women's Empowerment in Pakistan: Its Dimensions and Determinants. *Social indicators research, 140*(2), 755-775.

Akter, S., Rutsaert, P., Luis, J., Htwe, N. M., San, S. S., Raharjo, B., & Pustika, A. (2017). Women's empowerment and gender equity in agriculture: A different perspective from Southeast Asia. *Food Policy, 69*, 270-279.

Al-shami, S. S. A., Razali, R., & Rashid, N. (2018). The effect of microcredit on women empowerment in welfare and decisions making in Malaysia. *Social indicators research, 137*(3), 1073-1090.

Alkire, S., Meinzen-Dick, R., Peterman, A., Quisumbing, A., Seymour, G., & Vaz, A. (2013). The women's empowerment in agriculture index. *World development, 52*, 71-91.

Alkire, S., Roche, J. M., & Vaz, A. (2017). Changes over time in multidimensional poverty: Methodology and results for 34 countries. *World development, 94*, 232-249.

Alkire, S., & Santos, M. E. (2014). Measuring acute poverty in the developing world: Robustness and scope of the multidimensional poverty index. *World development, 59*, 251-274.

Allendorf, K. (2012). Women's agency and the quality of family relationships in India. *Population Research and Policy Review, 31*(2), 187-206.

Alsop, R., & Heinsohn, N. (2005). *Measuring empowerment in practice: Structuring analysis and framing indicators*: The World Bank.

Amartya, S., & Foster, J. E. (1997). *On economic inequality*: Oxford University Press.

Anand, A., & Roy, N. (2016). Transitioning toward sustainable development goals: The role of household environment in influencing child health in Sub-Saharan Africa and South Asia using recent demographic health surveys. *Frontiers in public health, 4*, 87.

Anand, S., & Sen, A. (1994). Human Development Index: Methodology and Measurement.

Anastasopoulos, P. C., & Mannering, F. L. (2009). A note on modeling vehicle accident frequencies with random-parameters count models. *Accident Analysis & Prevention, 41*(1), 153-159.

Andersen, R. (1995). Andersen and Newman Framework of Health Services Utilization. *Journal of Health and Social Behavior, 36*, 1-10.

Andersen, R., & Newman, J. F. (1973). Societal and individual determinants of medical care utilization in the United States. *The Milbank Memorial Fund Quarterly. Health and Society*, 95-124.

Andersen, R., & Newman, J. F. (2005). Societal and individual determinants of medical care utilization in the United States. *The Milbank Quarterly, 83*(4), Online-only-Online-only.

Anderson, S., & Eswaran, M. (2009). What determines female autonomy? Evidence from Bangladesh. *Journal of Development Economics 90*(2), 179-191.

Anselma, M., Chinapaw, M. J. M., & Altenburg, T. M. (2018). Determinants of child health behaviors in a disadvantaged area from a community perspective: a participatory needs assessment. *International Journal of Environmental Research and Public Health, 15*(4), 644.

Antony, G., & Rao, K. V. (2007). A composite index to explain variations in poverty, health, nutritional status and standard of living: Use of multivariate statistical methods. *Public Health, 121*(8), 578-587.

Arif, A., & Arif, G. (2012). Socio-Economic Determinants of Child Health in Pakistan. *Academic Research International, 2*(1), 398-340.

Asaolu, I., Alaofè, H., Gunn, J. K., Adu, A., Monroy, A., Ehiri, J., Hayden, M. H., & Ernst, K. (2018). Measuring Women's empowerment in sub-Saharan Africa: exploratory and confirmatory factor analyses of the demographic and health surveys. *Frontiers in Psychology, 9*, 994-999.

Assaad, R. A., Nazier, H., & Ramadan, R. (2014a). Individual and households determinants of women empowerment: Application to the case of Egypt. *The Economic Research Forum*.

Assaad, R. A., Nazier, H., & Ramadan, R. (2014b). *Individual and households determinants of women empowerment: Application to the case of Egypt.* Paper presented at the Economic Research Forum, Nov.

Augsburg, B., & Rodríguez-Lesmes, P. A. (2018). Sanitation and child health in India. *World development, 107*, 22-39.

Ayevbuomwan, O., Popoola, O., & Adeoti, A. (2016). Analysis of women empowerment in rural Nigeria: A multidimensional approach. *Global Journal of Human-Social Science Research, 16*(6):1-14.

Baig, I. A., Batool, Z., Ali, A., Baig, S. A., Hashim, M., & Zia-ur-Rehman, M. (2018). Impact of women empowerment on rural development in Southern Punjab, Pakistan. *Quality & Quantity, 52*(4), 1861-1872.

Bandura, A. (1982). Self-efficacy mechanism in human agency. *American Psychologist 37*(2), 122-132.

Bartlett, M. S. (1954). A note on the multiplying factors for various χ 2 approximations. *Journal of the Royal Statistical Society. Series B (Methodological)*, 296-298.

Basu, A. M. (1992). In *Culture, the Status of Women, and Demographic Behaviour: Illustrated with the Case of India.* Oxford: Clarendon Press.

Bates, L. M., Schuler, S. R., Islam, F., & Islam, M. K. (2004). Socioeconomic factors and processes associated with domestic violence in rural Bangladesh. *International Family Planning Perspectives*, 190-199.

Batliwala, S. (1993). Empowerment of Women in South Asia: Concepts and Practices. . *New Delhi. FAO. FFHC/AD.*

Batliwala, S. (1994). The meaning of women's empowerment: new concepts from action. In G. Sen, A. Germain, & L. C. Chen (Eds.), *Population Policies Reconsidered: Health, Empowerment, and Rights.* Cambridge, MA: Harvard Centre for Population and Development Studies.

Batliwala, S. (1995). *Defining Women's Empowerment: A Conceptual Framework Education for Women's Empowerment.* Paper presented at the ASPBAE Position Paper for the Fourth World Conference on Women, Beijing, September, New Delhi, Asia-South Pacific Bureau of Adult Education.

Batliwala, S., John, A., Schuler, S., Hashemi, S., Smith, C., McElnay, C., Pyper, C., Schellekens, J., Bartone, C., & Bernstein, J. (1995). The meaning of womens empowerment: new concepts from action. *Family Planning News, 11*(1), 127-138.

Batool, S., Shaheen, A., Rehman, R., Qamar, S., Ahsan Raza, S., Jabeen, R., & Nisa, F. (2012). To assess the nutritional status of primary school children in an Urban school of Faisalabad. *Pakistan Journal of Medical and Health Sciences 4*, 160-170.

Batool, S. A., & Jadoon, A. K. (2018). Women's Empowerment and Associated Age-Related Factors. *Pakistan Journal of Social Clinical Psychology 16*(2), 52-57.

Beal, T., Tumilowicz, A., Sutrisna, A., Izwardy, D., & Neufeld, L. (2018). A review of child stunting determinants in Indonesia. *Maternal Child Nutrition 14*(4), e12617.

Becker, S., Fonseca-Becker, F., & Schenck-Yglesias, C. (2006). Husbands' and wives' reports of women's decision-making power in Western Guatemala and their effects on preventive health behaviours. *Social Science and Medicine, 62.* doi:10.1016/j.socscimed.2005.10.006

Ben-Akiva, M., McFadden, D., Train, K., Walker, J., Bhat, C., Bierlaire, M., Bolduc, D., Boersch-Supan, A., Brownstone, D., & Bunch, D. S. (2002). Hybrid choice models: progress and challenges. *Marketing Letters, 13*(3), 163-175.

Benebo, F. O., Schumann, B., & Vaezghasemi, M. (2018). Intimate partner violence against women in Nigeria: a multilevel study investigating the effect of women's status and community norms. *BMC women's health, 18*(1), 136-144.

Bennett, L. (2002). Using empowerment and social inclusion for pro-poor growth: a theory of social change. *Working Draft of Background Paper for the Social Development Strategy Paper. Washington, DC: World Bank.*

Bhandari, T. R., & Chhetri, M. (2013). Nutritional status of under five year children and factors associated in Kapilvastu District, Nepal. *Journal of Nutritional Health & Food Science, 1*(1), 1-6.

Bhattacharya, J., Currie, J., & Haider, S. (2006). Breakfast of champions? The School Breakfast Program and the nutrition of children and families. *Journal of Human Resources, 41*(3), 445-466.

Bhukuth, A., Terrany, B., & Wulandari, A. (2019). Empowering Women Through Entrepreneurship: A Case Study in East Java, Indonesia. *Gender Studies, 18*(1), 113-128.

Bitew, F. H., & Telake, D. S. (2010). Undernutrition among women in Ethiopia: rural-urban disparity. *Macro Calverton, Maryland: USA ICF Macro*

Black, R. E., Victora, C. G., Walker, S. P., Bhutta, Z. A., Christian, P., De Onis, M., Ezzati, M., Grantham-McGregor, S., Katz, J., & Martorell, R. (2013). Maternal and child undernutrition and overweight in low-income and middle-income countries. *The lancet 382*(9890), 427-451.

Blase, J., & Anderson, G. (1995). *The Micropolitics of Educational Leadership: From Control to Empowerment*: ERIC.

Bloom, S. S., Wypij, D., & Gupta, M. d. (2001). Dimensions of Women's Autonomy and the Influence on Maternal Health Care Utilization in a North Indian City. *Demography, 38*(1), 67-78. doi:10.2307/3088289

Boehm, A., & Staples, L. H. (2004). Empowerment: The point of view of consumers. *Families in Society, 85*(2), 270-280.

Brajesh, & Shekhar, D. C. (2015). Level of Women Empowerment and It's Determinates in Selected South Asian Countries. *Journal Of Humanities And Social Science (IOSR-JHSS), 20*(4), 94.

Browning, T., Bouman, H., Henderson, G., Mather, T., Pyle, D., Schlosser, C., Woodward, E., & Moore, C. (2014). Strong responses of Southern Ocean phytoplankton communities to volcanic ash. *Geophysical Research Letters, 41*(8), 2851-2857.

Burroway, R. (2017). Are all jobs created equal? A cross-national analysis of women's employment and child malnutrition in developing countries. *Social Science Research, 67*, 1-13.

Butler, J. (1986). Sex and gender in Simone de Beauvoir's Second Sex. *Yale French Studies*(72), 35-49.

Calman, L. J. (1992). *Toward empowerment: Women and movement politics in India*: Westview Press Boulder.

Cattell, R. B. (1966). The scree test for the number of factors. *Multivariate Behavioral Research, 1*(2), 245-276.

Chabbott, C. (1998). Constructing educational consensus: International development professionals and the world conference on education for all. *International Journal of Educational Development 18*(3), 207-218.

Chakrabarti, S. (2017). Measuring Women Empowerment in the Household Sector: A Generalized Index and an Application to Indian Households. In *Women's Entrepreneurship and Microfinance* (pp. 17-39): Springer.

Charmes, J., & Wieringa, S. (2003). Measuring women's empowerment: an assessment of the gender-related development index and the gender empowerment measure. *Journal of Human Development, 4*(3), 419-435.

Chaudhuri, S. (2010). Women's empowerment in South Asia and Southeast Asia: A comparative analysis.

Chipili, G., Msuya, J., Pacific, R., & Majili, S. (2018). Women Empowerment and the Nutrition Status of Children Aged Between 6-59 Months. *Journal of Nutrition and Health Sciences, 5*(2), 208.

Chung, B., Kantachote, K., Mallick, A., Polster, R., & Roets, K. (2013). *Indicators of women's empowerment in developing nations.* Paper presented at the Workshop in international public affairs, Spring.

Collard, D. (2006). Research on well-being: Some advice from Jeremy Bentham. *Philosophy of the Social Sciences, 36*(3), 330-354.

Congress, A. N., Organization, W. H., & UNICEF. (1994). *A national health plan for South Africa.*

Cox, D., & Snell, E. (1989). Analysis of binary data. 2nd. *London: Chapman and Hall.*

Crow, B. A. (2000). *Radical feminism: A documentary reader*: NYU Press.

Cueva Beteta, H. (2006). What is missing in measures of women's empowerment? *Journal of Human Development, 7*(2), 221-241.

Daly, M. (2016). *Gyn/ecology: The metaethics of radical feminism*: Beacon Press.

Dasgupta, A., Parthasarathi, R., Biswas, R., & Geethanjali, A. (2014). Assessment of under nutrition with composite index of anthropometric failure (CIAF) among under-five children in a Rural Area of West Bengal. *Indian Journal of Community Health, 26*(2), 132-138.

Dasgupta, A., Sahoo, S. K., Taraphdar, P., Preeti, P., Biswas, D., Kumar, A., & Sarkar, I. (2015). Composite index of anthropometric failure and its important correlates: a study among under-5 children in a slum of Kolkata, West Bengal, India. *International Journal of Medical Science and Public Health, 4*(3), 414-420.

Delajara, M., & Juárez, F. W. C. (2013). Birthweight outcomes in Bolivia: The role of maternal height, ethnicity, and behavior. *Economics and Human Biology, 11*(1), 56-68.

Demissie, S., & Worku, A. (2013). Magnitude and factors associated with malnutrition in children 6-59 months of age in pastoral community of Dollo Ado district, Somali region, Ethiopia. *Science Journal of Public Health 1*(4), 175-183.

Desai, S., & Johnson, K. (2005). Women's Decisionmaking and Child Health: Familial and social hierarchies. In (Vol. 2005, pp. 55-68): ORC Macro Calverton, MD.

Deutsch, J., & Silber, J. (2017). *Does women's empowerment affect the health of children? The case of Mozambique.* Retrieved from

Dhok, R. S., & Thakre, S. B. (2016). Measuring undernutrition by composite index of anthropometric failure (CIAF): a community-based study in a slum of Nagpur city. *International Journal of Medical Science and Public Health* 5(10), 2013-2018.

DHS Program. Retrieved from https://dhsprogram.com/data/Access-Instructions.cfm

Donta, B., Nair, S., Begum, S., & Prakasam, C. (2016). Association of domestic violence from husband and women empowerment in slum community, Mumbai. *Journal of Interpersonal Violence, 31*(12), 2227-2239.

Echols, A. (1989). *Daring to be bad: Radical feminism in America, 1967-1975* (Vol. 3): U of Minnesota Press.

Ekbrand, H., & Halleröd, B. (2018). The more gender equity, the less child poverty? A multilevel analysis of malnutrition and health deprivation in 49 low-and middle-income countries. *World development, 108,* 221-230.

Endris, N., Asefa, H., & Dube, L. (2017). Prevalence of malnutrition and associated factors among children in rural Ethiopia. *BioMed Research International, 2017.*

Farooq, U., Ahmed, M., & Jasra, A. W. (2008). *Natural Resources Conservation for Poverty Alleviation by Making the Farmers Partner with Empowerment.* Paper presented at the 23rd AGM and Conference of PSDE.

Fawole, O. I., & Adeoye, I. A. (2015). Women's status within the household as a determinant of maternal health care use in Nigeria. *African health sciences 15*(1), 217-225.

Ferrant, G., Pesando, L. M., & Nowacka, K. (2014). *Unpaid Care Work: The missing link in the analysis of gender gaps in labour outcomes.* Retrieved from https://www.oecd.org/dev/development-gender/Unpaid_care_work.pdf

Fetterman, D. M., Kaftarian, S. J., & Wandersman, A. (1996). *Empowerment evaluation: Knowledge and tools for self-assessment and accountability*: Sage.

Firestone, S. (2003). *The dialectic of sex: The case for feminist revolution*: Farrar, Straus and Giroux.

Fox, M. (2006). Betty Friedan, who ignited cause in'feminine mystique,'dies at 85. *New York Times, 5.*

Frankenberg, E., & Thomas, D. (2001). *Measuring power*: Citeseer.

Furuta, M., & Salway, S. (2006). Women's position within the household as a determinant of maternal health care use in Nepal. *International Family Planning Perspectives, 32.* doi:10.1363/3201706

Garcia-Moreno Claudia, & Avni, A. (2016). The sustainable development goals, violence and women's and children's health. *Bulletin of the World Health Organization, 94*(5), 396.

García-Moreno Claudia, Zimmerman Claudia , C., Morris-Gehring, A., Heise, L., Amin, A., Abrahams, N., Montoya, O., Bhate-Deosthali, P., Kilonzo, N., & Watts, C. (2015). Addressing violence against women: a call to action. *The lancet, 385*(9978), 1685-1695.

Garikipati, S. (2008). Agricultural wage work, seasonal migration and the widening gender gap: Evidence from a semi-arid region of Andhra Pradesh. *The European Journal of Development Research, 20*(4), 629-648.

Gibson, C. H. (1991). A concept analysis of empowerment. *Journal of advanced nursing, 16*(3), 354-361.

Giele, J. Z. (1977). Introduction: the status of women in comparative perspective. *Women, Roles and Status in Eight Countries. New York: John Wiley.*

Glick, P., & Sahn, D. E. (1998). Maternal labour supply and child nutrition in West Africa. *Oxford Bulletin of Economics Statistics 60*(3), 325-355.

Goldman, M. J., & Little, J. S. (2015). Innovative grassroots NGOS and the complex processes of women's empowerment: An empirical investigation from Northern Tanzania. *World development, 66*, 762-777.

Goode, A., & Mavromaras, K. (2014). Family income and child health in China. *China Economic Review, 29*, 152-165.

Gorey, K. M., Daly, C., Richter, N. L., Gleason, D. R., & McCallum, M. J. A. (2003). The effectiveness of feminist social work methods: An integrative review. *Journal of Social Service Research, 29*(1), 37-55.

Gram, L., Morrison, J., & Skordis-Worrall, J. (2019). Organising concepts of 'women's empowerment'for measurement: a typology. *Social indicators research, 143*(3), 1349-1376.

Greene, W. H. (2000). Econometric analysis (International edition).

Grimshaw, D., & Rubery, J. (2015). The motherhood pay gap: A review of the issues, theory and international evidence. *Conditions of Work and Employment Series.*

Grossman, M. (1972). On the concept of health capital and the demand for health. *Journal of Political Economy, 80*(2), 223-255.

Guinée, N. (2014). Empowering women through education: Experiences from Dalit women in Nepal. *International Journal of Educational Development, 39*, 173-180.

Gujarati, D. N. (2003). Basic Econometrics, McGraw-Hill. *New York.*

Gujarati, D. N., & Porter, D. C. (1999). *Essentials of econometrics* (Vol. 2): Irwin/McGraw-Hill Singapore.

Gupta, K., & Yesudian, P. P. (2006). Evidence of women's empowerment in India: A study of socio-spatial disparities. *Geo Journal, 65*(4), 365-380.

Habibov, N., Barrett, B. J., & Chernyak, E. (2017). *Understanding women's empowerment and its determinants in post-communist countries: Results of Azerbaijan national survey.* Paper presented at the Women's Studies International Forum.

Hadju, V. (2017). Baby Nutritional Status Improvement Through Mother Empowerment in Baby Care in South Sulawesi Indonesia.

Hamad, N., Sarwar, Z., Ranjha, M. K., & Ahmad, I. J. M. C. (2016). Food Utilization As Antil-Stunting Intervention in Pakistan. *Medical Channel 22*(3).

Hanmer, L., & Klugman, J. (2016). Exploring women's agency and empowerment in developing countries: Where do we stand? *Feminist Economics, 22*(1), 237-263.

Haq, A. M., Jali, M. R. M., & Islam, G. M. N. (2017). Empowering rural women in Pakistan: empirical evidence from Southern Punjab. *Quality & Quantity, 51*(4), 1777-1787.

Haraway, D. (1990). A manifesto for cyborgs: Science, technology, and socialist feminism in the 1980s. *Feminism/Postmodernism*, 190-233.

Harwood, R. L., Yalçinkaya, A., Citlak, B., & Leyendecker, B. (2006). Exploring the concept of respect among Turkish and Puerto Rican migrant mothers. *New Directions for Child and Adolescent Development, 2006*(114), 9-24.

Hasan, M. N., & Uddin, M. S. G. (2016). Women empowerment through health seeking behavior in Bangladesh: Evidence from a national survey. *South East Asia Journal of Public Health, 6*(1), 40-45.

Hawkes, C., & Fanzo, J. (2017). Nourishing the SDGs: Global nutrition report 2017.

Heaton, T. B., Huntsman, T. J., & Flake, D. F. (2005). The effects of status on women's autonomy in Bolivia, Peru, and Nicaragua. *Population Research and Policy Review, 24*(3), 283-300.

Hedges, S., Mulder, M. B., James, S., & Lawson, D. W. (2016). Sending children to school: rural livelihoods and parental investment in education in northern Tanzania. *Evolution Human Behavior, 37*(2), 142-151.

Heslehurst, N., Vieira, R., Akhter, Z., Bailey, H., Slack, E., Ngongalah, L., Pemu, A., & Rankin, J. (2019). The association between maternal body mass index and child obesity: A systematic review and meta-analysis. *PLoS medicine 16*(6), e1002817.

Hightower, W. L. (1978). Development of an index of health utilizing factor analysis. *Medical Care*, 245-255.

Hindin, M. J. (2006). Women's input into household decisions and their nutritional status in three resource-constrained settings. *Public Health Nutrition, 9*(4), 485-493.

Hirschmann, N. J., & McClure, K. M. (2010). *Feminist Interpretations of John Locke*: Penn State Press.

Hossain, B., & Hoque, A. A. (2015). Women empowerment and antenatal care utilization in Bangladesh. *The Journal of Developing Areas, 49*(2), 109-124.

Huicho, L., Segura, E. R., Huayanay-Espinoza, C. A., de Guzman, J. N., Restrepo-Méndez, M. C., Tam, Y., Barros, A. J., Victora, C. G., & Group, P. C. C. C. S. W. (2016). Child health and nutrition in Peru within an antipoverty political agenda: a Countdown to 2015 country case study. *The Lancet Global Health, 4*(6), e414-e426.

Ibrahim, A., & Pandey, K. K. (2014). Women's Empowerment and Child Health Outcomes: A Comparative Study between India and Nigeria. *Journal of Medical Science and Clinical Research, 2*(12), 3277-3292.

Ibrahim, A., Tripathi, S., & Kumar, A. (2015). The effect of women's empowerment on child health status: study on two developing nations. *International Journal of Scientific and Research Publications, 5*(4), 1-8.

Ismail, M., Mohd Rasdi, R., & Nadirah Abd. Jamal, A. (2011). Gender empowerment measure in political achievement in selected developed and developing countries. *Gender in Management: An International Journal, 26*(5), 380-392.

Jacobson, A. J. (2010). *Feminist Interpretations of David Hume*: Penn State Press.

Jaggar, A. M. (1983). *Feminist politics and human nature*: Rowman & Littlefield.

Jali, M. R. M., & Islam, G. M. N. (2017). Empowering rural women in Pakistan: empirical evidence from Southern Punjab. *Quality & Quantity, 51*(4), 1777-1787.

Jamal, H. (2017). Explaining Spousal Physical Violence through Dimensions of Women Empowerment: Evidence from Pakistan.

Jamal, H. (2018a). Exploring the relationship between mothers Empowerment and Child Nitritional Status : An Evidence from Pakistan. *Pakistan Journal of Applied Economics, 28*(2), 189-211.

And child nutritional status: An Evidence from Pakistan. *Pakistan Journal of Applied Economics, 28*(2), 189-211.

Janes, R. (2017). On the Reception of Mary Wollstonecraft'sa Vindication of the Rights of Woman. In *Mary Wollstonecraft* (pp. 25-34): Routledge.

Jeckoniah, J., Nombo, C., & Mdoe, N. (2012). Determinants of women empowerment in the onion value chain: a case of Simanjiro district in Tanzania. *Journal of Economics and Sustainable Development, 3*(10), 88-99.

Jejeebhoy, S. (2000). Women's autonomy in rural India: Its dimensions, determinants, and the influence of context. In H. B. Presser & G. Sen (Eds.), *Women's Empowerment and Demographic Processes: Moving Beyond Cairo*. New York: Oxford University Press.

Jejeebhoy, S., & Sathar, Z. A. (2001a). Women's autonomy in India and Pakistan: the influence of religion and region. *Population and Development Review, 27*. doi:10.1111/j.1728-4457.2001.00687.x

Jejeebhoy, S. J., & Sathar, Z. A. (2001b). Women's autonomy in India and Pakistan: the influence of religion and region. *Population and Development Review, 27*(4), 687-712.

Jin, H. (1995). A study of rural women's decision making power on reproduction and fertility. *Chinese Journal of Population Science, 7*.

Jo, H., Schieve, L. A., Sharma, A. J., Hinkle, S. N., Li, R., & Lind, J. N. (2015). Maternal prepregnancy body mass index and child psychosocial development at 6 years of age. *Pediatrics 135*(5), e1198-e1209.

Johnson, D. M., Worell, J., & Chandler, R. K. (2005). Assessing psychological health and empowerment in women: The personal progress scale revised. *Women & health, 41*(1), 109-129.

Jones, R., Haardörfer, R., Ramakrishnan, U., Yount, K. M., Miedema, S., & Girard, A. W. (2019). Women's empowerment and child nutrition: The role of intrinsic agency. *SSM-Population Health, 9*, 100475.

Kabeer, N. (1999). Resources, agency, achievements: Reflections on the measurement of women's empowerment. *Development and Change, 30*(3), 435-464.

Kabeer, N. (2001). Reflections on the measurement of women's empowerment'in 'Discussing women's empowerment: theory and practice'. *Sida Studies, 3*.

Kabeer, N. (2002). Resources, agency, achievements: reflections on the measurement of women's empowerment. *Development and Change, 30*. doi:10.1111/1467-7660.00125

Kabeer, N. (2003). *Gender Mainstreaming in Poverty Eradication and the Millennium Development Goals: A handbook for policy-makers and other stakeholders*: Commonwealth Secretariat.

Kabeer, N. (2005). Gender equality and women's empowerment: A critical analysis of the third millennium development goal 1. *Gender & Development, 13*(1), 13-24.

Kabeer, N. (2011). Contextualising the Economic Pathways of Women's Empowerment: Findings from a Multi-Country Research Programme.

Kabeer, N. (2012). Women's economic empowerment and inclusive growth: labour markets and enterprise development. *International Development Research Centre, 44*(10), 1-70.

Kanamori, M. J., & Pullum, T. W. (2013). *Indicators of Child Deprivation in sub-Saharan Africa: Levels and Trends from the Demographic and Health Surveys*: ICF International.

Kantachote, K., Mallick, A., Polster, R., & Roets, K. (2013). *Indicators of Women's empowerment in developing nations.* Paper presented at the Workshop in International Public Affairs.

Kar, S. B., Pascual, C. A., & Chickering, K. L. (1999). Empowerment of women for health promotion: a meta-analysis. *Social Science and Medicine, 49*(11), 1431-1460.

Keats, A. (2018). Women's schooling, fertility, and child health outcomes: Evidence from Uganda's free primary education program. *Journal of Development Economics, 135*, 142-159.

Khalid, M. W., Samargandi, N., Shah, A. H., & Almandeel, S. (2020). Socio-Economic Factors and Women's Empowerment: Evidence from Punjab, Pakistan. *International Economic Journal 34*(1), 144-168.

Khan. (2010). *Socio-cultural determinants of women's empowerment in Punjab, Pakistan.* UNIVERSITY OF AGRICULTURE FAISALABAD PAKISTAN,

Khan, Mann, Zafar, Hashmi, & Akhtar. (2010). Determinants of women empowerment: a case study from district Rawalpindi, Punjab, Pakistan. *Pakistan Journal of Science, 62*(1).

Khan, R. E. A., & Noreen, S. (2012). Microfinance and women empowerment: A case study of District Bahawalpur (Pakistan). *African Journal of Business Management, 6*(12), 4514-4521.

Khan, R. E. A., & Raza, M. A. (2014). Child malnutrition in developing economies: a case study of Bangladesh. *Quality & Quantity, 48*(3), 1389-1408.

Khan, R. E. A., & Raza, M. A. (2016a). Determinants of malnutrition in Indian children: new evidence from IDHS through CIAF. *Journal of Quality & Quantity, 50*(1), 299-316.

Khan, R. E. A., & Raza, M. A. (2016b). Utilization of prenatal-care in India: an evidence from IDHS. *Journal of Social and Economic Development, 18*(1-2), 175-201.

Khan, R. E. A., Tasnim KHAN, and Shakeela BIBI. (2018). Women Empowerment and Household Wealth: Implication for Child Health-Care. *Pakistan Journal of Applied Economics, Special Issue*(Special Issue), 273-289.

Khan, S. (2016). *Women's empowerment through poverty alleviation: a sociocultural and politico-economic assessment of conditions in Pakistan.* Paper presented at the European Virtual Conference on Management Sciences and Economics.

Khattab, A. S., & Sakr, H. M. (2009). Women's Economic Empowerment in Egypt: challenges and Opportunities. *Social Research Centre, The American University in Cairo.*

Kishor, S. (1995). Autonomy and Egyptian women: findings from the 1988 Egypt Demographic and Health Survey.

Kishor, S. (2000). Empowerment of women in Egypt and links to the survival and health of their infants. *Oxford University Press.*

Kishore, U., & Reid, K. B. (2000). C1q: structure, function, and receptors. *Immunopharmacology, 49*(1-2), 159-170.

Koedt, A., Levine, E., Rapone, A., & Koedt, A. (1973). *Radical feminism*: Quadrangle Books New York.

Krishnan, D. C. (2011). Microfinance for Financial Inclusion and Women Empowerment. *International Journal of Business Economics and Management Research, 2*(9), 135-150.

Krishnan, V. (2010). Constructing an area-based socioeconomic index: A principal components analysis approach. *Edmonton, Alberta: Early Child Development Mapping Project*.

Kritz, M. M., & Adebusoye, P. M. (1999). Determinants of women's decision-making authority in Nigeria: the ethnic dimension. *Sociological Forum, 14*. doi:10.1023/a:1021495418633

Kritz, M. M., & Makinwa-Adebusoye, P. (1999). *Determinants of women's decision-making authority in Nigeria: the ethnic dimension.* Paper presented at the Sociological Forum.

Kumar, D., Mittal, P. C., & Sharma, M. K. (2010). Socio-demographic risk factors of child undernutrition. *Journal of Pediatric Sciences, 2*(1).

Laghari, Z. A., Soomro, A. M., Tunio, S. A., Lashari, K., Baloach, F. G., Baig, N. M., & Bano, S. (2015). Malnutrition among children under five years in district Sanghar, Sindh, Pakistan. *Gomal Journal of Medical Sciences 13*(1).

Lamontagne, J. F., Engle, P. L., & Zeitlin, M. F. (1998). Maternal employment, child care, and nutritional status of 12–18-month-old children in Managua, Nicaragua. *Social Science Medicine 46*(3), 403-414.

Lee-Rife, S. M. (2010). Women's empowerment and reproductive experiences over the lifecourse. *Social Science and Medicine, 71*(3), 634-642.

Long, S. J., Long, J. S., & Freese, J. (2006). *Regression models for categorical dependent variables using Stata*: Stata press.

Lopez-Avila, D. (2016). Measuring Women's Empowerment: lessons to better understand domestic violence.

MacKinnon, C. A. (1983). Feminism, Marxism, method, and the state: Toward feminist jurisprudence. *Journal of Women in Culture and Society, 8*(4), 635-658.

Madjdian, D. S., & Bras, H. A. (2016). Family, gender, and women's nutritional status: a comparison between two Himalayan communities in Nepal. *Economic History of Developing Regions, 31*(1), 198-223.

Mahmud, S., Shah, N. M., & Becker, S. (2012). Measurement of women's empowerment in rural Bangladesh. *World development, 40*(3), 610-619.

Makama, G. A. (2013). Patriarchy and gender inequality in Nigeria: The way forward. *European Scientific Journal, 9*(17).

Malapit, H. J. L., Kadiyala, S., Quisumbing, A. R., Cunningham, K., & Tyagi, P. (2015). Women's empowerment mitigates the negative effects of low production diversity on maternal and child nutrition in Nepal. *The Journal of Development Studies, 51*(8), 1097-1123.

Malapit, H. J. L., & Quisumbing, A. R. (2015). What dimensions of women's empowerment in agriculture matter for nutrition in Ghana? *Food Policy, 52*, 54-63.

Malhotra, A., & Mather, M. (1997). *Do schooling and work empower women in developing countries? Gender and domestic decisions in Sri Lanka.* Paper presented at the Sociological forum.

Malhotra, A., & Schuler, S. R. (2005). Women's empowerment as a variable in international development. *Measuring empowerment: Cross-disciplinary perspectives, 1*(1), 71-88.

Maqsood, F., Ullah, S., & Farooq, F. (2015). Proxy Measures of Women's Empowerment and Use of Contraceptives in South Asian Countries: An Analysis of Seven Sisters. *Pakistan Journal of Social Sciences, 35*(1), 1-10.

Marshall, L. (2006). Aging: A feminist issue. *NWSA Journal, 18*(1), vii-xiii.

Marx, K. (1973). *Karl Marx, Frederick Engels on literature and art: a selection of writings*: International general.

Marx, K. (2000a). *Karl Marx: selected writings*: Oxford University Press, USA.

Marx, K. (2000b). *Marx and Engels collected works*: Lawrence and Wishart Limited.

Marx, K., & Engels, F. (1970). *The german ideology* (Vol. 1): International Publishers Co.

Mary, S. (2018a). How much does economic growth contribute to child stunting reductions? *Economie, 6*(4), 55.

Mary, S. (2018b). How much does economic growth contribute to child stunting reductions? *Economies, 6*(4), 55.

Mason, K. O. (1995). Gender and demographic change: What do we know?

Mason, K. O., & Smith, H. L. (2003). Women's empowerment and social context: Results from five Asian countries. *Gender and Development Group, World Bank, Washington, DC.*

McFadden, D., & Train, K. (2000). Mixed MNL models for discrete response. *Journal of Applied Econometrics, 15*(5), 447-470.

Medel-Anonuevo, C. (1995). *Women, Education and Empowerment: Pathways towards Autonomy. UIE Studies 5*: ERIC.

Mehra, R. (1997). Women, empowerment, and economic development. *The Annals of the American Academy of Political and Social Science, 554*(1), 136-149.

Mei, H., Guo, S., Lu, H., Pan, Y., Mei, W., Zhang, B., & Zhang, J. J. B. o. (2018). Impact of parental weight status on children's body mass index in early life: evidence from a Chinese cohort. *BMJ open 8*(6).

Meshram, I. I., Arlappa, N., Balakrishna, N., Rao, K. M., Laxmaiah, A., & Brahmam, G. N. V. (2012). Trends in the prevalence of undernutrition, nutrient and food intake and predictors of undernutrition among under five year tribal children in India. *Asia Pacific Journal of Clinical Nutrition, 21*(4), 568.

Messelu, Y., & Trueha, K. (2016). Determining Risk Factors of Malnutrition among under–Five Children in Sheka Zone, South West Ethiopia Using Ordinal Logistic Regression Analysis. *Public Health Research, 6*(6), 161-167.

Mill, J. S. (1869). *The subjection of women* (Vol. 1): Transaction Publishers.

Mill, J. S., & Mill, H. T. (1970). *Essays on sex equality*: University of Chicago Press.

Millett, K. (2016). *Sexual politics*: Columbia University Press.

Mishra, A. (2014). Multidimensional measures of female disempowerment. *Social indicators research, 119*(3), 1393-1410.

Mishra, N. K., & Tripathi, T. (2011). Conceptualising women's agency, autonomy and empowerment. *Economic and Political Weekly*, 58-65.

Moghadam, V. M., & Senftova, L. (2005). Measuring women's empowerment: participation and rights in civil, political, social, economic, and cultural domains. *International Social Science Journal, 57*(184), 389-412.

Moonzwe Davis, L., Schensul, S. L., Schensul, J. J., Verma, R. K., Nastasi, B. K., & Singh, R. (2014). Women's empowerment and its differential impact on health in low-income communities in Mumbai, India. *Global public health, 9*(5), 481-494.

Mosedale, S. (2005). Assessing women's empowerment: towards a conceptual framework. *Journal of International Development, 17*(2), 243-257.

Motala, S., Ngandu, S., Mti, S., Arends, F., Winnaar, L., Khalema, E., Makiwane, M., Ndinda, C., Moolman, B., & Maluleke, T. (2015). Millennium development goals: Country report 2015.

Mugo, N., Zwi, A. B., Botfield, J. R., & Steiner, C. (2015). Maternal and child health in South Sudan: priorities for the Post-2015 agenda. *Sage Open, 5*(2), 2158244015581190.

Muhammad, S., Shaheen, G., Naqvi, S., & Zehra, S. (2012). Women empowerment and microfinance: A case study of Pakistan.

Mullany, B. C., Hinde, M. J., & Becker, S. (2005). Can women's autonomy impede male involvement in pregnancy health in Kathmandu, Nepal? *Social Science and Medicine, 61.* doi:10.1016/j.socscimed.2005.04.006

Mumtaz, Z., & Salway, S. M. (2007). Gender, pregnancy and the uptake of antenatal care services in Pakistan. *Sociology of Health and Illness, 29.* doi:10.1111/j.1467-9566.2007.00519.x

Murshid, N. S. (2016a). Mothers' empowerment and father involvement in child health care in Bangladesh. *Children and Youth Services Review, 68*, 17-23.

Murshid, N. S. (2016b). Mothers' empowerment and father involvement in child health care in Bangladesh. *Children Youth Services Review 68*, 17-23.

Musonera, A., & Heshmati, A. (2017). Measuring Women's empowerment in Rwanda. In *Studies on Economic Development and Growth in Selected African Countries* (pp. 11-39): Springer.

Nardo, M., Saisana, M., Saltelli, A., Tarantola, S., Hoffman, A., & Giovannini, E. (2005). Handbook on constructing composite indicators.

Naryan, D. (2002). *Empowerment and poverty reduction: A sourcebook*: The World Bank.

Nasir, J. A., Akhtar, M., & Salim, R. (2007). Measuring and modeling the domestic empowerment of rural women in Pakistan. *Journal of Statistics, 14*, 20-31.

Nayak, P., & Mahanta, B. (2008). Women empowerment in India.

Ndaimani, A. (2018). *The Association Between Women's Empowerment and Uptake of Child Health Services: A Demographic and Health Survey-based Synthesis.*

Njoh, A. J., & Akiwumi, F. A. (2012). The impact of religion on women empowerment as a millennium development goal in Africa. *Social indicators research, 107*(1), 1-18.

Njoh, A. J., & Ananga, E. (2016). The Development Hypothesis of Women Empowerment in the Millennium Development Goals Tested in the Context Women's Access to Land in Africa. *Social indicators research, 128*(1), 89-104.

Noreen, S. (2011). *Role of microfinance in empowerment of female population of Bahawalpur district.* Paper presented at the International Conference on Economics and Finance Research.

Nosheen, F., & Chaudhry, I. S. (2018). Women Empowerment and Micro Finance Programmes in Southern Punjab: An Empirical Study. *Pakistan Journal of History & Culture, 39*(1).

Nussbaum, M. C. (1997). *The feminist critique of liberalism*: University of Kansas, Department of Philosophy.

O'Hara, C., & Clement, F. (2018). Power as agency: A critical reflection on the measurement of women's empowerment in the development sector. *World development, 106,* 111-123.

Odutolu, O., Adedimeji, A., Odutolu, O., Baruwa, O., & Olatidoye, F. (2003). Economic empowerment and reproductive behaviour of young women in Osun state, Nigeria. *African Journal of Reproductive Health,* 92-100.

Okin, S. M. (1989). *Justice, gender, and the family* (Vol. 171): Basic books New York.

Osmond, M. W., & Thorne, B. (2009). Feminist theories. In *Sourcebook of Family Theories and Methods* (pp. 591-625): Springer.

Otekunrina, O. A., Otekunrinb, O. A., Momoh, S., & Ayindea, I. A. (2019). Assessing the Zero Hunger Target Readiness in Africa: Global Hunger Index (GHI) Patterns and its Indicators.

Palamuleni, M. E., & Adebowale, A. S. (2014). Women empowerment and the current use of long acting and permanent contraceptive: Evidence from 2010 Malawi Demographic and Health Survey. *Malawi Medical Journal, 26*(3), 63-70.

Pambe, M. W., Gnoumou, B., & Kaboré, I. (2014). Relationship between women's socioeconomic status and empowerment in Burkina Faso: A focus on participation in decision-making and experience of domestic violence. *African Population Studies, 28,* 1146-1156.

Parveen, S., & Leonhäuser, I. (2005). *Empowerment of rural women in Bangladesh: A household level analysis* (Vol. 72): Margraf Berlin, Germany.

Permanyer, I. (2013). A critical assessment of the UNDP's gender inequality index. *Feminist Economics, 19*(2), 1-32.

Peterman, A. (2015). Women's Economic Empowerment: Indicators and survey design.

Phan, L. (2016a). Measuring women's empowerment at household level using DHS data of four Southeast Asian countries. *Social indicators research, 126*(1), 359-378.

Phan, L. D. (2016b). Women's empowerment and fertility preferences in Southeast Asia.

Pongou, R., Ezzati, M., & Salomon, J. A. (2006). Household and community socioeconomic and environmental determinants of child nutritional status in Cameroon. *BMC public health, 6*(1), 98.

Pratley, P., & Sandberg, J. F. (2018). Refining the Conceptualization and Measurement of Women's Empowerment in Sub-Saharan Africa Using Data from the 2013 Nigerian Demographic and Health Survey. *Social indicators research, 140*(2), 777-793.

Presser, H., & Sen, G. (2000). *Women's empowerment and demographic processes: Moving beyond Cairo*: Oxford University Press.

Quamruzzaman, A., & Lange, M. (2016). Female political representation and child health: Evidence from a multilevel analysis. *Social Science and Medicine, 171,* 48-57.

Ramachandran, A., & Snehalatha, C. (2010). Rising burden of obesity in Asia. *Journal of Obesity, 2010.*

Rappaport, J. (1981). In praise of paradox: A social policy of empowerment over prevention. . *American Journal of Community Psychology 9,* 9-25.

Rappaport, J. (1984). Studies in empoweremnt: Introduction to the Issue. . *Prevention in Human Services, 3,* 1-7.

Rappaport, J. (1985). The Power of empowerment Language *Social Policy, 16,* 215-221.

Rathirani, Y., & Semasinghe, D. (2015). Factors determining the women empowerment through microfinance: An empirical study in Sri Lanka. *International Journal of Social, Behavioural, Educational, Economic, Business and Industrial Engineering, 9*(5), 2328-2185.

Registration, C. C. (2018). Underlying Causes of Malnutrition. Retrieved from https://actionagainsthunger.ca/what-is-acute-malnutrition/underlying-causes-of-malnutrition/

Richardson, R. A. (2018). Measuring women's empowerment: a need for context and caution. *The Lancet Global Health, 6*(1), e30.

Riley, D. (1988). 'The Social','Woman', and Sociological Feminism. In *'Am I That Name?'* (pp. 44-66): Springer.

Rissel, C. (1994). Empowerment: the holy grail of health promotion? *Health promotion international, 9*(1), 39-47.

Rodwell, C. M. (1996). An analysis of the concept of empowerment. *Journal of Advanced Nursing 23*(2), 305-313.

Ross-Suits, H. (2010). Maternal Autonomy as a Protective Factor in Child Nutritional Outcome in Tanzania,(Public Health Theses, Paper 99).

Rowlands, J. (1997). *Questioning empowerment*: Oxford: Oxfam.

Rowlands, J. (1998). A word of the times, but what does it mean? Empowerment in the discourse and practice of development. In *Women and empowerment* (pp. 11-34): Springer.

Roy, & Niranjan, S. (2004). Indicators of women's empowerment in India. *Asia-Pacific Population Journal, 19*(3), 23-38.

Roy, K., Dasgupta, A., Roychoudhury, N., Bandyopadhyay, L., Mandal, S., & Paul, B. (2018). Assessment of under nutrition with composite index of anthropometric failure (CIAF) among under-five children in a rural area of West Bengal, India. *International Journal of Contemporary Pediatrics, 5*(4), 1651-1656.

Sado, L., Spaho, A., & Hotchkiss, D. R. (2014). The influence of women's empowerment on maternal health care utilization: Evidence from Albania. *Social Science and Medicine, 114,* 169-177.

Sakar, E., Keskin, S., & Unver, H. (2011). Using of factor analysis scores in multiple linear regression model for prediction of kernel weight in Ankara walnuts. *Animal and Plant Sciences, 21,* 182-185.

Samanta, T. (2020). Women's empowerment as self-compassion?: Empirical observations from India. *Plos one 15*(5), e0232526.

Samarakoon, S., & Parinduri, R. A. (2015). Does education empower women? Evidence from Indonesia. *World development, 66,* 428-442.

Samari, G. (2017). First birth and the trajectory of women's empowerment in Egypt. *BMC pregnancy childbirth 17*(2), 362.

Sanghamitra, P. (2016). *Empowerment of Rural Women by Participation in Agri-Based Enterprises.*

Sathar, Z. A., & Shahnaz, K. (2000). Women's autonomy in the context of rural Pakistan. *The Pakistan Development Review, 39*, 89-110.

Scantlan, & Previdelli. (2013). Women's empowerment and childhood malnutrition in Timor-Leste: a mixed-methods study. *Oregon: Mercy Corps.*

Sebayang, S., Efendi, F., & Astutik, E. (2017). Womens empowerment and the use of antenatal care services in Southeast Asian countries.

Sebayang, S. K., Efendi, F., & Astutik, E. (2019). Women's empowerment and the use of antenatal care services: analysis of demographic health surveys in five Southeast Asian countries. *Women & health*, 1-17.

Sekaran, U., & Leong, F. T. (1992). *Womanpower: Managing in times of demographic turbulence*: Sage Pubns.

Sekhar, C. C., Indrayan, A., & Gupta, S. (1991). Development of an index of need for health resources for Indian states using factor analysis. *International Journal of Epidemiology, 20*(1), 246-250.

Sen, A. (1993). Capability and well-being73. *The quality of life, 30.*

Sen, G., & Batliwala, S. (2000). Empowering women for reproductive rights.

Senarath, U., & Gunawardena, N. S. (2009). Women's autonomy in decision making for health care in south Asia. *Asia-Pacific Journal of Public Health, 21.* doi:10.1177/1010539509331590

Shah, S. M., Selwyn, B. J., Luby, S., Merchant, A., & Bano, R. (2003). Prevalence and correlates of stunting among children in rural Pakistan. *Pediatrics international, 45*(1), 49-53.

Sharaunga, S., Mudhara, M., & Bogale, A. (2016). Effects of 'women empowerment' on household food security in rural KwaZulu-Natal province. *Development Policy Review, 34*(2), 223-252.

Sharma, B., & Shekhar, C. (2015). Association of Women Empowerment with Inter-Spousal Communication on RCH Matters In Selected South Asian Countries. *International Journal of Social Sciences and Management, 2*(3), 197-213.

Sheikhsoha. (2016). Women Empowerment in Developing Nations. Retrieved from https://mnwomenscenter.wordpress.com/2016/11/18/women-empowerment-in-developing-nations/

Siddhanta, A., & Chattopadhyay, A. (2017). Role of Women's Empowerment in Determining Child Stunting in Eastern India and Bangladesh. *Social Science Spectrum, 3*(1), 38-51.

Smith, B. J., Tang, K. C., & Nutbeam, D. (2006). WHO health promotion glossary: new terms. *Health promotion international, 21*(4), 340-345.

Smith, L. C., & Haddad, L. J. (2000). *Explaining child malnutrition in developing countries: A cross-country analysis* (Vol. 111): Intl Food Policy Res Inst.

Solanki, R., Patel, T., Shah, H., & Singh, U. S. (2014). Measuring undernutrition through z-scores and Composite Index of Anthropometric Failure (CIAF): a study among slum children in Ahmedabad City, Gujarat. *National Journal of Community Medicine, 5*(4), 434-439.

Solomon, A. V., & Adekoya, A. (2006). Women and power transformation in rural households: A case study of Osun State, Nigeria. *The Social Sciences, 1*(3), 231-234.

Spencer, N. (2018). The social determinants of child health. *Paediatrics and Child Health, 28*(3), 138-143.

Sraboni, E., Malapit, H. J., Quisumbing, A. R., & Ahmed, A. U. (2014). Women's empowerment in agriculture: What role for food security in Bangladesh? *World development, 61*, 11-52.

Sridevi, T. O. (2005). Empowerment of Women-A systematic analysis. *India Development Foundation*.

Stone, M., & Brooks, R. (1990). Continuum regression: cross-validated sequentially constructed prediction embracing ordinary least squares, partial least squares and principal components regression. *Journal of the Royal Statistical Society: Series B 52*(2), 237-258.

Subaiya, L., & Vanneman, R. (2016). The Multi-dimensionality of Development and Gender Empowerment: Women's Decision-Making and Mobility in India.

Sujarwoto, S., & Tampubolon, G. (2013). Mother's social capital and child health in Indonesia. *Social Science and Medicine, 91*, 1-9.

Sultana, A. (2010). Patriarchy and Women s Subordination: A Theoretical Analysis. *Arts Faculty Journal* 1-18.

Sundström, A., Paxton, P., Wang, Y.-T., & Lindberg, S. I. (2017). Women's political empowerment: A new global index, 1900–2012. *World development, 94*, 321-335.

Tabachnick, B. G., & Fidell, L. S. (1996). Using multivariate statistics . Northridge. *Cal.: Harper Collins*.

Tadesse, M., Teklie, H., Yazew, G., & Gebreselassie, T. (2013). Women's Empowerment as a Determinant of Contraceptive use in Ethiopia Further Analysis of the 2011 Ethiopia Demographic and Health Survey. *DHS Further Analysis Reports, 82*.

Tareque, M., Haque, M., Mostofa, M., & Islam, T. (2007). Age, age at marriage, age difference between spouses and women empowerment: Bangladesh context. *Middle East Journal of Age & Ageing, 4*(6), 8-14.

Tengland, P.-A. (2008). Empowerment: A conceptual discussion. *Health Care Analysis, 16*(2), 77-96.

Teshome, B., Kogi-Makau, W., Getahun, Z., & Taye, G. (2009). Magnitude and determinants of stunting in children underfive years of age in food surplus region of Ethiopia: the case of west gojam zone. *Ethiopian Journal of Health Development, 23*(2).

Tigga, P. L., & Sen, J. (2016). Maternal body mass index is strongly associated with children-scores for height and BMI. *Journal of Anthropology, 2016*.

Tong, R. (2009). Feminist Thought: A More Comprehensive Introduction Colorado. In: United States: Westview Press.

Torlesse, H., Kiess, L., & Bloem, M. W. (2003). Association of household rice expenditure with child nutritional status indicates a role for macroeconomic food policy in combating malnutrition. *The Journal of nutrition, 133*(5), 1320-1325.

Tracey, M. R., & Polachek, S. W. (2018). If looks could heal: Child health and paternal investment. *Journal of Health Economics, 57*, 179-190.

Trommlerová, S. K., Klasen, S., & Leßmann, O. (2015). Determinants of empowerment in a capability-based poverty approach: Evidence from The Gambia. *World development, 66,* 1-15.

Tsiboe, F., Zereyesus, Y. A., Popp, J. S., & Osei, E. (2018). The effect of women's empowerment in agriculture on household nutrition and food poverty in Northern Ghana. *Social indicators research,* 1-20.

Tzannatos, Z. (1999). Women and labor market changes in the global economy: Growth helps, inequalities hurt and public policy matters. *World development, 27*(3), 551-569.

UitedNations. (2018). Facts and Figures: Economic Empowerment. Retrieved from http://www.unwomen.org/en/what-we-do/economic-empowerment/facts-and-figures

Ukwuani, & Suchindran. (2003a). Implications of women's work for child nutritional status in sub-Saharan Africa: a case study of Nigeria. *Social Sciencem Medicine, 56*(10), 2109-2121.

Ukwuani, F. A., & Suchindran, C. M. (2003b). Implications of women's work for child nutritional status in sub-Saharan Africa: a case study of Nigeria. *J Social Science Medicine 56*(10), 2109-2121.

UNDPI, U. N. D. o. P. I. (2009). *Millennium Development Goals Report 2009 (Includes the 2009 Progress Chart):* United Nations Publications.

UNICEF. (2018). Malnutrition in Children - UNICEF DATA. Retrieved from https://data.unicef.org/topic/nutrition/malnutrition/

UNICEF. (2019). Stunting. Retrieved from http://unicef.in/whatwedo/10/stunting

United Nations Development Fund for, W. (2008). *Progress of the World's Women: UNIFEM Biennial Report:* United Nations Development Fund for Women.

Upadhyay, U. D., Gipson, J. D., Withers, M., Lewis, S., Ciaraldi, E. J., Fraser, A., Huchko, M. J., & Prata, N. (2014). Women's empowerment and fertility: a review of the literature. *Social Science and Medicine, 115,* 111-120.

Upadhyay, U. D., & Karasek, D. (2010). Women· s Empowerment and Achievement of Desired Fertility in Sub-Saharan Africa. *USAID.*

Upadhyay, U. D., & Karasek, D. (2012). Women's empowerment and ideal family size: an examination of DHS empowerment measures in Sub-Saharan Africa. *International Perspectives on Sexual and Reproductive Health,* 78-89.

Vedam, S., Stoll, K., Rubashkin, N., Martin, K., Miller-Vedam, Z., Hayes-Klein, H., & Jolicoeur, G. (2017). The mothers on respect (MOR) index: measuring quality, safety, and human rights in childbirth. *SSM-Population Health, 3,* 201-210.

Voloshinov, V. N., & Bachtin, M. M. (1986). *Marxism and the Philosophy of Language:* Harvard University Press.

Vonaesch, P., Tondeur, L., Breurec, S., Bata, P., Nguyen, L. B. L., Frank, T., Farra, A., Rafaï, C., Giles-Vernick, T., & Gody, J. C. (2017). Factors associated with stunting in healthy children aged 5 years and less living in Bangui (RCA). *PloS one, 12*(8), e0182363.

Wallerstein, N. (1992). Powerlessness, empowerment, and health: implications for health promotion programs. *American journal of health promotion, 6*(3), 197-205.

WHO. (2011). *10 facts about women's health.* Retrieved from Geneva: https://www.who.int/features/factfiles/women/en/

WHO. (2016). What is malnutrition? Retrieved from https://www.who.int/features/qa/mal nutrition/en/

WHO. (2018). Malnutrition. Retrieved from https://www.who.int/news-room/fact-sheets/ detail/malnutrition

Wiklander, J. (2010). Determinants of women's empowerment in rural India: an intra-household study.

Williams, B., Onsman, A., & Brown, T. (2010). Exploratory factor analysis: A five-step guide for novices. *Australasian Journal of Paramedicine, 8*(3).

Williams, R., & Williams, R. H. (1977). *Marxism and literature* (Vol. 392): Oxford Paperbacks.

Winter, C. (1994). *Working Women in Latin America: Participation, Pay and Public Policy*: The World Bank.

Wollstonecraft, M. (1792). *A vindication of the rights of woman: with strictures on political and moral subjects. By Mary Wollstonecraft*: J. Johnson.

Women, U. (1995). Fourth World Conference on Women Beijing Declaration.

Women, Business and the Law 2018. (2018). Retrieved from http://wbl.worldbank.org/

WorldBank. (2019a). Retrieved from https://datahelpdesk.worldbank.org/knowledgebase/ articles/906519-world-bank-country-and-lending-groups

WorldBank. (2019b). World Development Indicators. Retrieved from https://data.worldbank.org/ indicator

Ziba, M., Kalimbira, A. A., & Kalumikiza, Z. (2018). Estimated burden of aggregate anthropometric failure among Malawian children. *South African Journal of Clinical Nutrition, 31*(2), 43-46.

Zimmerman, M. A., & Rappaport, J. (1988). Citizen participation, perceived control, and psychological empowerment. *American Journal of Community Psychology, 16*(5), 725-750.